D0930279

The Perpendicular Style

Frontispiece The Neville Screen in Durham Cathedral, made in London 1372–80. Here attributed to Henry Yeveley

The Perpendicular Style

1330–1485

John Harvey

B. T. BATSFORD LTD., LONDON

BY THE SAME AUTHOR:

Henry Yevele
Gothic England
The Plantagenets
Dublin
Tudor Architecture
The Gothic World
English Mediaeval Architects
A Portrait of English Cathedrals
The Cathedrals of Spain
Catherine Swynford's Chantry
The Master Builders
The Mediaeval Architect
Conservation of Buildings
Early Gardening Catalogues
Man the Builder
Cathedrals of England and Wales
Early Nurserymen
Sources for the History of Houses
Mediaeval Craftsmen
York
The Black Prince and his Age

Bibliographies:

English Cathedrals – A Reader's Guide
Conservation of Old Buildings
Early Horticultural Catalogues – A Checklist

Revised Muirhead's Blue Guides:

Northern Spain
Southern Spain

Edited with translation:

William Worcestre: Itineraries (1478–1480)

First published 1978
Copyright © John Harvey 1978
Filmset by Keyspools Limited, Golborne, Lancs.
Printed in Great Britain by The Anchor Press
Ltd, Tiptree, Essex
for the publishers B. T. Batsford Ltd,
4 Fitzhardinge Street, London W1H 0AH
ISBN 0 7134 1610 6

Contents

Acknowledgments

The author and publishers would like to thank the following for permission to reproduce the photographs included in this book: the Rt. Hon. the Lord Saye and Sele (Broughton Castle); the Trustees of the Great Hospital, Norwich; the Warden and Fellows of Winchester College; the Dean and Canons of St. George's Chapel, Windsor; and the Revd. Canon M. H. Ridgway (for photographs by the late F. H. Crossley); Hallam Ashley for Pl 205; Donovan E. H. Box for 62, 198; J. Allan Cash for 145; Central Press Photos Ltd. for 80; Country Life for 46, 106, 159; the Courtauld Institute of Art for 15, 32, 44, 64, 71, 105, 135, 146, 165, 167, 192, 196; and for 8, 18, 61, 116, 118, 137, 140, 147, 169 by the late F.H. Crossley; the Council for Places of Worship for 97, 102, 133; James Stevens Curl for 129; the Department of the Environment for 53, 162; J. Dixon-Scott for 186; the late Herbert Felton for 21, 33, 34, 98, 158, 175, 193, 204; Fox Photos Ltd. for 3; Leonard and Marjorie Gayton for 23; Humphrey and Vera Joel for 150; A. F. Kersting for 1, 4, 5, 6, 13, 14, 28, 38, 55, 56, 63, 72, 73, 81, 82, 83, 85, 92, 96, 104, 107, 108, 109, 120, 127, 128, 130, 149, 156, 157, 163, 164, 168, 170, 176, 177, 181, 188, 189, 200, 202, 206; W. Leedy for 119; the National Monuments Record for 9, 19, 20, 37, 43, 45, 49, 51, 52, 57, 66, 67, 75, 86, 90, 99, 100, 103, 110, 111, 112, 113, 114, 117, 121, 131, 132, 136, 138, 141, 142, 148, 152, 154, 160, 166, 178, 179, 180, 190, 191, 197, 199; the Royal Commission on Historical Monuments (England) for 24, 87, 124, 153, 172; Messrs. Walter Scott of Bradford for 25, 35; William F. Sherlock for 27 (photo NMR); Society of Antiquaries for 115; E. A. Sollars for 89; the late Will F. Taylor for 2, 26, 36, 50, 54, 79, 84, 101, 161, 183, 187, 194, 195, 207; Thomas-Photos, Oxford for 122, 126, 173; Christopher Wilson for 12, 16, 17, 22, 40, 42, 47, 48, 59, 88, 123, 125; the Warden and Fellows of Winchester College for 79, 80, 89, 144, 145; the Dean and Canons of St. George's Chapel, Windsor for 11, 185. Pls 29, 30, 65 are from photographs by the author; Pls 7, 10, 31, 39, 41, 58, 60, 74, 91, 134, 139, 143, 151, 171, 174, 182, 184, 201, 203 and 208 are from the Publisher's collection; Pls 68, 69, 70, 76, 77, 78, 93, 94, 95 and 155 are from photographs taken specially for the book by Robert Paskin.

List of Illustrations

Photographs

9

Maps

Line Drawings

Preface

The Perpendicular Style is much the most important phenomenon in English art. To it alone among the many schools and periods may the term *unique* be fittingly applied, and without any trace of exaggeration. Within the wider scope of Gothic Perpendicular patterns are instantaneously recognisable, distinct to a degree unmatched elsewhere. Though comparable to other national styles in the mere fact of aesthetic nationalism, the forms taken by English architecture between the middle of the fourteenth century and the close of the fifteenth vary from those of western Europe to an extent without parallel in any other major art at any given period. In national variation itself this architecture was a pioneer: it was not the English version of a general function, *Sondergotik*; on the contrary, there seems no doubt that continental Sondergotik developed because of the creation of Perpendicular, though not in direct imitation of it. By an odd freak, it was the rival Curvilinear that exercised a predominant appeal outside England, and provided a basis for later European exercises in Gothic imagination.

It will have been noted that a limit has been set to Perpendicular towards the end of the fifteenth century. The style has commonly been held to continue until the end of Gothic after 1540, or indeed for another hundred years after that. Certainly there is a continuous thread which links true Perpendicular to its derivative, Tudor Gothic; but in the last quarter of the fifteenth century the English art was invaded by a backwash of Curvilinear pattern from the continent and specifically from Flanders. This tide setting inward across the Channel notably reduced the sharp and distinctive nationalism which had been so characteristic. From the victory of Henry VII at Bosworth, and even earlier, English architecture began to lose its total independence. More probably due to the return of Edward IV from his Flemish exile in 1471 than to the change of dynasty, the new art of around 1500 was moving into the orbit of provincial Flamenco in England as in the Spanish kingdoms. Political motives, bringing about the dynastic marriages between Arthur Tudor and his younger brother Henry (VIII) and the Spanish princess Catherine, set the seal on this movement by introducing Mudéjar planning at Windsor, at Henry VII's Chapel in Westminster, at Thornbury Castle, and in the scheme of Wolsey's great gateway at Cardinal College, Oxford.

This later phase, which turned out to be the last of English Gothic, deserves full study in its own right. It cannot be treated simply as a pendant to the national Perpendicular out of which it grew by a refertilisation. The present study is therefore limited to the period between 1330 and the tragic end of the

Plantagenet dynasty in 1485. There is more than mere accidental convenience in the linking of the style to the dynasty: the starting point can be taken as the accession of Edward III in 1327 after the effective interregnum at the end of his father's reign. The coincidence is even closer, for Edward III did not assume actual power until the autumn of 1330, and the first specific marks of the new style appeared within the next year or so. There may be no trace of cause and effect in this, but the adoption of Perpendicular details in royal work within only a few years from their invention provided the means to success. The accepted or Court style was swiftly revolutionised and henceforth became – we might say, was promulgated as – the official standard of taste for all buildings of quality. The royal taste set a fashion which was soon universal and which had a natural growth under a succession of chief architects, the master masons to the Crown, and their pupils. So far as changes in style were ever dictated, it was by deliberate choice of later sovereigns and of magnates of the realm.

An English Court style was no new thing. From among our regional schools of early Gothic, largely but by no means entirely derived from French models, certain masters under immediate royal patronage had reached the phase of Decorated architecture in the classification of Rickman, more precisely distinguished by Sharpe as Geometrical. Under Henry III three successive chief architects interpreted the personal taste of the art-loving king. For ten years from 1243 it was Henry de Reyns who launched the new epoch with the first work at Westminster Abbey. He had almost certainly been working in Rheims and clearly was imbued with the latest architectural ideas current in northern France. On the other hand the work at Westminster shows so definitely the stamp of English experience and craftsmanship as to suggest that Master Henry was not of foreign origin. He was succeeded by masters respectively from the West and the North: John of Gloucester until 1261 and Robert of Beverley until his death in 1284. Then for more than half a century the charge of the king's works fell to men of Kent, notably Michael of Canterbury and his sons Thomas and Walter. To motives derived from French practice and from the chief provincial schools of England were added highly idiosyncratic types of pattern brought into use at the southern metropolitan see.

This Canterbury or Kentish style incorporated the extensive use of ogee forms: that is, reversed curves of S-shape, with hexagonal patterning and the use of the characteristic split cusps which are the mark of 'Kentish tracery'. The influence of the masters from Canterbury spread far and wide and prepared the way for later acceptance of Perpendicular. Both styles represented an aesthetic revolt against the dead hand of 'classical' French forms and embodied, albeit in two distinct manners, the English love of linear clarity. In the earlier phase, dominated by Canterbury, sharply crystalline shapes were produced by the intersection of compass-arcs, softened by ogee foliations. In Perpendicular the straight line came to rule, after a short transitional period in which it provided a framework for elements derived from the antecedent fashion. As we shall see, there is reason to think that the fundamental ideas underlying both the Kentish and Perpendicular modes were derived from the East, notably from Persia and Egypt. The development of these ideas into a complete architectural style, or rather two successive styles acceptable to the kings of England, was, however, wholly English.

One outcome of these developments was the decisive swing of English architecture away from direct dependence upon France. After the immense achievements of the first Gothic century, French art like French thought came to rest on its laurels. A self-satisfied encyclopaedism based upon the closed circuit of Thomist philosophy steadily pervaded all aspects of French life. In architecture structural experiment gave way to the repetition of formulae, as has been shown by Dr. Jacques Heyman. Clearly this was not enough for the rulers of England, or for inventive English craftsmen. Between the accession of Edward I (1272) and the Black Death (1348) English artists excelled themselves in inventiveness and in the production of new motives and styles in architecture. How far this was due to the personal influence of the first three Edwards cannot be told, but there is evidence of direct contacts with the Near East. Edward I, at the time of his accession, was returning from the Crusade: he had spent eighteen months in Palestine before being almost fatally wounded by an Assassin in June 1272. Among the English Crusaders who then came home, as well probably as among their prisoners, there must have been military engineers and master masons. Twenty years later, after receiving a Persian embassy from the Mongol Ilkhan, Edward was to send out one of his old crusading companions in arms, Sir Geoffrey Langley, at the head of a mission which in 1292 reached Tabriz. One of Langley's suite was Robert the sculptor, evidently an artist.

There were many English pilgrims who, whenever political conditions permitted, undertook the journey to the Holy Land. Some never returned, but among those who got back at least a few must have been artists and architects. We know that the master carpenter of Chichester Cathedral had joined the crusade of 1228–29, and in 1356–57 the leading mason on the works of Westminster Abbey, John Palterton, was away on pilgrimage for a whole year, which implies a visit to Jerusalem. One of the chief freemasons of Exeter Cathedral, John Harry, likewise had leave of absence to go on pilgrimage in 1431. It would be a refinement of scepticism to suppose that these documented cases were the only instances that occurred. Among clerical travellers we know of the Irish Franciscan James who accompanied Oderic of Pordenone on his travels to Persia, India and China between 1319 and 1323; and of two other Irishmen, Simon Simeon and Hugh the Illuminator, who passed through England in 1323 on their outward journey. The artist Hugh died in Cairo but Simon reached Jerusalem and returned to Europe, apparently getting as far as England, where his manuscript survived. Some English Franciscans were in Alexandria in 1332, and there is an account of the Holy Land by an English pilgrim of 1345.

Among the notes made by Friar Simon concerning life in Cairo in 1323 is an account of the Sultan's Christian slaves. These, he says, 'are fairly well off, principally as masons, carpenters, and other craftsmen for whom the Sultan has a special regard. They ... are humanely compensated for their labour by the Sultan with a reasonable amount of bread and money for themselves, and also for their wives and children. In our opinion many of them, at least as regards the necessaries of life, are better off here than they would be in their own native countries.' It is clear from this that these Christian captives were able to converse with pilgrims, who could derive technical and artistic information from them concerning the works on which they laboured. In some few cases, too, it may be that individual captives were ransomed and came home in person. There is, therefore, no reason to doubt that adequate channels of information existed.

The facts speak plainly for themselves. Several successive introductions of new forms into English architecture and its decorative enrichment, between 1290 and 1330, were unparalleled elsewhere. The extensive use, at this period, of the ogee curve was the first of these. Then came the complex geometrical interlaces used notably at Canterbury in the early years of the fourteenth century, and closely related to Persian patterns. In planning there came a sudden concentration of interest upon polygonal and concentric forms: the Eleanor Crosses of 1291–94, the Wells Lady Chapel of c. 1310–19, the octagon at Ely planned in 1322, the hexagonal north porch of St. Mary Redcliffe of c. 1325. Linked with these concentric forms were in some cases attempts at domical roofs. The first was very likely the wooden vault over the octagonal chapter-house at York, originally planned to have a central pillar but converted to an open span about 1286–96. The stone vault of the irregular octagon of the Wells Lady Chapel, the most ambitious of these schemes, was built about 1315–20 and was followed by the timber lantern over the Ely octagon. The Ely vault was erected between 1328 and 1334 and the lantern put up within the next six years. The four-centred arch, never adopted in other parts of Europe (apart from rare and late adaptations mainly in Flanders), suddenly appeared. It was first used, in an ogee form, at the pulpitum of Exeter Cathedral, designed by Thomas Witney and built in 1317–25. Witney had trained at St. Stephen's Chapel in the Palace of Westminster, and was architect to Winchester Cathedral before being called to Exeter. Simple four-centred arches were used for the side windows of the south transept of Gloucester Abbey, work of 1331–35. Both two-centred and four-centred arches were set within square surrounds, at first apparently in the doorways leading from the York chapter-house to the vestibule, probably of the 1290s; later with cusped enrichments in the triangular spandrels at the Exeter pulpitum and in the new choir at Ely Cathedral, c. 1325; and in William Ramsey's cloisters at Old St. Paul's, London, begun in 1332. It was in these same cloisters, and in the associated octagonal chapter-house, that strictly Perpendicular tracery first appeared.

Within a short time a new repertory of art had arrived, at first as disparate motives. Some of these, for example the attempts at domical roofs, were to be discarded. Others, particularly the ogee curve with its offshoots in reticulated and flamboyant tracery, were exploited for a time, then exported to the continent, and finally brought back into English currency after more than a century. What passed into the general tradition of our later mediaeval architecture included the arch within a square surround, the four-centred arch, and the stiffened reticulations which were typical of the earliest Perpendicular.

Of these innovations, the four-centred arch and the arch within a square surround or label were distinctively Persian; the stiff hexagonal reticulations of the tracery as markedly derived from practice in Cairo, going as far back as AD 1211 and continuing until 1319. In some cases the details of Persian origin had also reached Egypt, and were associated with windows of stiff-reticulation as early as 1269–73, the date of the Cairene Mausoleum of Mustafa Pasha. It may be said that English architecture was conditioned by our love of travel.

An adventurous readiness to travel, for reasons of trade, exploration, or religion, undoubtedly had a great deal to do with the sources from which English art was to derive much of its individuality. The motives were not home grown products of sheer creative invention. On the other hand, the English masters of design showed their mastery most clearly in handling these motives from remote sources, to produce within a generation a complete style distinct from what had gone before and also from anything being produced elsewhere. Never have the English qualities of aptitude for organisation and for improvisation showed to better advantage. It was not merely that a set of new motives was put together in a manner aesthetically pleasing to the architects' royal and noble patrons. They were integrated with a whole philosophy of space and light, of unity of structure and composition, to an extent that made Perpendicular an art-form in its own right, almost independent of the Gothic from which it sprang. We need only mention here the tendency towards elimination of the structural vault-rib and also of the flying-buttress, two of the three cardinal factors of Gothic structure. As for the third factor, the pointed arch, it became transformed into the ogee, the four-centred, and even sometimes the three-centred arch, and square-headed windows appeared with increasing frequency.

Before proceeding to serious consideration of the new style we must clear the decks of the lumber of several hoary superstitions. It used to be said that Perpendicular was an economy-style, produced in the aftermath of the Black Death of 1348–49, when labour was dear and simplification of detail was essential. This has long been disproved by the discovery that its essential details already existed in the great south window of Gloucester Abbey not later than c. 1335, and in the fragments of the cloister of Old St. Paul's, begun in 1332. Yet the period 1320–49 was one of lavish expenditure upon the arts. The style was not, then, invented for reasons of economy, however much its later spread may have been facilitated by the cutting of costs. A more recent theory has tried to show that Perpendicular was borrowed from France, where rectilinear patterns in screenwork and blind tracery were used to cover wall surfaces. In France such patterns remained subordinated to the earlier canons of Gothic, and in no case even remotely resembled English work. It was in France above all that resistance to the borrowing of *any* motives from England was carried on longest, and when in the end there was some approximation of styles it was due to the more or less simultaneous acceptance from Flanders of the Flamboyant version of English Curvilinear by France, and the reintroduction of a modified and enriched Curvilinear into England.

There have also been attempts to seek an explanation of Perpendicular tracery in a supposed dominance of the painters of stained glass. Here again economy of work and money has been held to suggest the simplification of all lights, even those in the traceried head of an arched window, into straight-sided vertical lights. Clearly such a simplification did effect economies, and perhaps in ease of design as well as in straightforward construction. But the advent of these vertical lights was not until long after the invention of Perpendicular, and can have had nothing whatever to do with the origins of the style. To sum up: the older theories regarding the *origin* of the new style must be wholly rejected, even though there is a limited truth in each of them. The style as it developed after the Black Death was indeed for a time simple and relatively economical in labour costs. As time went on it was also found possible to simplify the task of the designers and painters of stained glass by eliminating curving lights awkward to set out, both in their masonry form-pieces and in the designs for the glass filling. At the start it is evident that the creators of the style were well informed as to the latest types of detail used in France as well as elsewhere. Their eclecticism did not wholly reject French influences any more than it broke completely with antecedent English tradition. They had the whole of previous Gothic practice to pick from, as well as something else – the oriental ideas brought from Persia both directly and by way of Egypt, where more definitely Cairene window traceries provided the key-motive.

Like all artistic styles, English Perpendicular owed much to precedent, yet remained itself. Mysteriously, a fresh outlook was born, like a new individual. We cannot hope to explain the precise process by which a choice was made among the multiplicity of possible factors, any more than we can explain the genius of Phidias or Wren or Turner. All that we can do is to narrow down to some extent the picture of conditions which controlled the new style. Some can be dismissed out of hand: for instance, the development of the style had nothing to do with building materials. Adapted in detail, Perpendicular was applied to many kinds of stone, to brick, to timber. Though primarily an architecture based upon natural stone masonry, it cannot be said that its forms were shaped by the qualities of any particular kind of stone. Polychrome works exist, but colour had no special part to play in design, except in the glass windows. Even in that respect, colour was subordinated in favour of increased illumination obtained by larger backgrounds of white glass.

The Perpendicular style, as modified by trial and error, became particularly adapted to English needs, both in Court and country. It lent itself to costly enrichment on the one hand, and to an imposing and economical simplicity on the other. Its large windows, glazed in light tones, made the best of our habitually dull climate. Its shapes were mostly straightforward and could be made to appeal to the commonsense strain in the English character. It must have been in response to this practical attitude that in the period of the style the typical steeple lost its pointed spire and became a square tower, bluntly shaking an English fist into the sky. We may regret the loss of a mystical message in this yet recognise its fitness in the scene. Our country is dominated by its parish churches and they in turn by the imprint of the Perpendicular style.

What reasons can be assigned for this almost overwhelming dominance of one style, which even in an extended sense only ruled for two out of the nine centuries since the Conquest? The first and chief reason is obviously that, just as architecture is the dominant art, so Perpendicular was the first and last English national style generally applied to church building. In some towns and cities, where domestic houses predominate, it is our other national style, the Georgian, that similarly exercises predominance. The second reason is geographical: we are on an island, and the greater part of that island: England and Wales, formed a single unit with unified political control. The king's writ ran throughout the land, bearing law and order; and also the fashion of building that had appealed to successive kings, from Edward III downwards. The success or failure of individual sovereigns, politically speaking, was reflected in the vicissitudes of the style.

Perpendicular was an art expressing to the full the national form taken by the aspirations of the ruling dynasty. It was a banner, an aesthetic symbol of the same royal aspirations which led Edward III to declare himself king of France; to take the vow to the Round Table fulfilled in the founding of the Order of the Garter; to promote the national cult of our patron St. George. The king did not himself invent or create Perpendicular: by the time that he had made himself politically independent and held the reins of power, the critical steps had already been taken by the master mason William Ramsey, not yet an official architect. Within five years, however, Ramsey was to receive a royal appointment, and from 1336 until his death in 1349 became the king's chief mason and principal surveyor of the king's works south of Trent. It is to Edward III as patron that credit is due for his deliberate promotion of the creator of a national style.

★   ★   ★

Something must be said of the form and intention of this book. It is an attempt at objective history, based primarily on observation of surviving monuments and on graphic records of those destroyed; in second place on documentary, inscriptional and heraldic records. An attempt has been made to consult all published work of importance, but much local research (e.g. in newspapers or pamphlets) must have been missed. Mr. David Verey's 'The Perpendicular Style in the Cotswolds' (Verey 1976) appeared too late for consultation. Owing to the grave losses suffered by buildings and records, the number of particular builds precisely dated is limited; hence the text is highly selective and deals mostly with material whose date of design is assignable within ten years. For simplicity of expression, a single date of *design* is given when certain; uncertainty is indicated by *circa*, e.g. *c.* 1360. Single dates, unless otherwise qualified, are used throughout in this sense. Double dates imply the existence of evidence both for the start and the completion of a work; dates introduced by, followed by, or placed between dashes, thus: –1360; 1360–; –1360– mean documented knowledge of the year of completion, of the start, or of work in progress.

As far as possible, buildings are assigned to known masters, upon documentary evidence or (when so stated) upon stylistic assessment. The names of the greatest masters of the period, with extremely few exceptions, are already known, with many of those of lesser rank. It is possible to outline the course taken by the style from start to finish, and to give some idea of its principal regional variations. It is not yet feasible to work out in detail the development of each local school of masoncraft or carpentry in the absence of a sufficient number of monographs on given areas and individual architects. Mention must, however, be made here of several specific studies of great importance: those of Professor Ralph H. C. Davis on the Perpendicular of Oxford and the Cotswold region; of Dr. Eric Gee on Oxford Masons and Carpenters of this period; of Mr. Arthur Oswald on the architects and buildings of Cambridge and East Anglia; and of the monographic treatment given by Dr. Eileen Roberts to Hertfordshire and to the work of the Wolvey family, of Robert Stowell, and of the Totternhoe masons.

One serious source of uncertainty has to be mentioned: the extent to which the church restorers of the last century falsified the evidence. In some cases great pains were taken to produce an exact replica of the original, so far as condition permitted; yet in others a mere pastiche was inserted. This is commonly easy to detect; much worse is the unresolved doubt resulting from outstandingly good work done without any full record of the facts. A crucial instance is the church at Adderbury in Oxfordshire **120**, where the chancel is not merely dated precisely to 1408–1418, but by a master of outstanding importance, Richard Winchcombe. It is known that the original tracery of the windows was taken out late in the eighteenth century, and that the present tracery was inserted to the design of John Chessell Buckler in 1831–34. Yet Freeman could say that the east window is 'one of the finest of the examples with depressed arches ... the actual tracery dates only from the last restoration, ... whether it was restored from any record of its original form I know not; if not, nothing can be more creditable to the restorers.'

As far as possible only authentic examples have been used, but it is too much to hope that no deceptively 'correct' details have been included. Their number is, however, likely to be proportionately small, and their effect upon the record of stylistic development minimal. For, insofar as the main changes are concerned, the evidence is mostly that of great and well recorded buildings where no doubt is possible. Sometimes the original masonry still survives; at others, there are adequate graphic records of original forms, generally supported by replica work of high quality and impeccable pedigree.

The material for this book has been gathered over many years and in the process I have been greatly helped by discussion with many other students. It was my father, the late William Harvey, who first encouraged my interest in the later Gothic of England in the course of visits to Westminster Hall and to many other buildings. Next to him my chief debt is owed to my two friends, Professor Ralph H. C. Davis and Mr. Arthur Oswald, both of whom have notably increased my understanding of the style. Professor Davis has also read the draft text; so too has my friend Mr. L. S. Colchester: to both of them I am grateful for valuable corrections and additions.

In past years I derived much assistance from friends and acquaintances now gone from us, and especially from the late Harry Batsford, who with the late Charles Fry was responsible for my researches into the period which resulted in the book *Gothic England* first published in 1947. Others who made important contributions to my knowledge were T. D. Atkinson, Christopher Chitty, Herbert Chitty, Sir Alfred Clapham, Leonard K. Elmhirst, Joseph Fowler, Mrs. Dorothy Gardiner, Dr. Rose Graham, E. A. Greening Lamborn, R. P. Howgrave-Graham, Harold G. Leask, W. Douglas Simpson, and Josep Vives i Miret.

I here tender my warm thanks to all those who have contributed in various ways, particularly Mr. B. J. Ashwell, Dr. Caroline M. Barron, Messrs. A. Clifton-Taylor, N. Drinkwater, R. H. C. Finch, T. W. French, Dr. Eric Gee, Professor Jacques Heyman, Messrs. Christopher Hohler, Kenneth Hopkins, Dr. M. E. Kaines-Thomas (Margaret Wood), Dr. Peter Kidson, Messrs. Dennis King, Michael McGarvie, Richard Morris, Dr. J. N. L. Myres, Mr. M. R. Petch, Dr. Eileen Roberts, Messrs. J. Salmon, L. E. Tanner, Dr. A. J. Taylor, Colonel J. G. O. Whitehead, and Mr. A. B. Whittingham. I am also grateful to many incumbents of churches, owners of buildings, and the staffs of various libraries, record offices, museums and institutes; as well as to the Ancient Monuments Branch of H. M. Office of Works (now Department of the Environment) and the National Monuments Record.

In connection with the preparation of the book my special gratitude goes to the Council of the Marc Fitch Fund for their award of a generous grant in aid of travel and to cover the cost of draughtsmanship of the line illustrations; and also to the Trustees of the Crompton Bequest who have made a grant to my publishers to assist in meeting the now inflated cost of photographic plates. To my publishers, and especially Sam Carr, I am grateful for their acceptance of the book and for the trouble taken over its production, as also to Ian Chilvers for his arduous work in the search for photographs. Messrs. Ray Hollidge and Mike O'Malley of Chartwell Illustrators have likewise placed me in their debt by their meticulous work on the maps, diagrams and line illustrations. My wife, as on many previous occasions, has made the book possible.

John H. Harvey

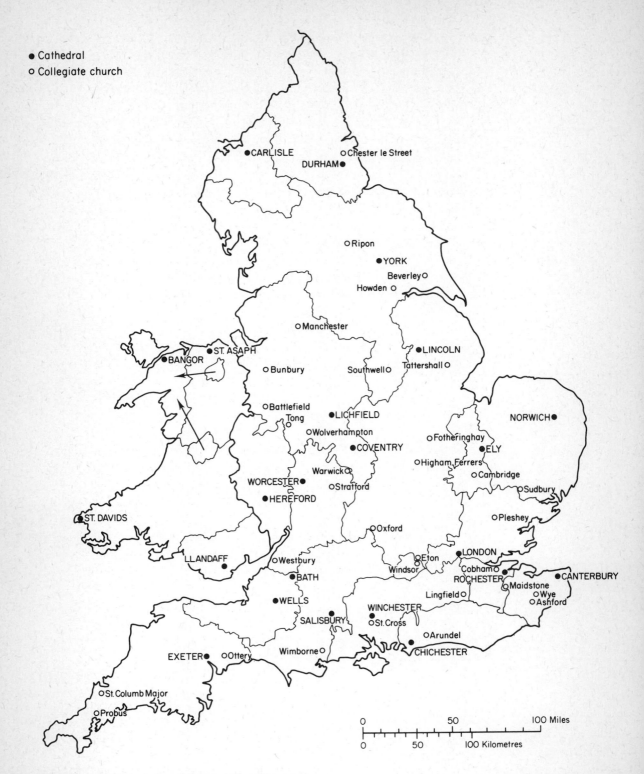

● Cathedral
○ Collegiate church

●CARLISLE
○Chester le Street
DURHAM●

○Ripon
●YORK
Beverley○
Howden ○

○Manchester

●ST. ASAPH
●BANGOR

●LINCOLN
○Bunbury
Southwell○
Tattershall○

○Battlefield
Tong○
●LICHFIELD
○Wolverhampton
●COVENTRY

NORWICH●

○Fotheringhay
●ELY
○Higham Ferrers
Warwick○
WORCESTER●
○Strafford
●HEREFORD

○Cambridge
○Sudbury

●ST. DAVIDS

○Oxford

○Pleshey

LLANDAFF●
○Westbury
●BATH

○Eton
Windsor
●LONDON
○Cobham
ROCHESTER●
○Maidstone
CANTERBURY●
●WELLS
Lingfield○
○Wye
○Ashford

SALISBURY●
WINCHESTER●
○St.Cross

EXETER● ○Ottery
Wimborne○
○Arundel
CHICHESTER●

○St.Columb Major

○Probus

0   50   100 Miles

0   50   100 Kilometres

Map I Cathedrals and Collegiate Churches, facing

Map II Monastic and Parish Churches. The boundaries shown are of the mediaeval dioceses (names of the sees marked in CAPITALS on Map I)

23

■ Castles and fortifications
● Houses and Colleges etc.

BERWICK

Roxburgh
Bamburgh
Alnwick
Dunstanburgh
Warkworth

CARLISLE

Finchale
DURHAM
Brancepeth
Raby

Bolton

Sheriff Hutton
YORK
Beverley
Wressle

Thornton

Manchester
Burtonwood

CHESTER

LINCOLN
South Wingfield
Wainfleet
Tattershall

NOTTINGHAM

Ashby de la Zouch
Kirby Muxloe

NORWICH
Caister

Ludlow
Higham Ferrers
Ely
Wingfield
Kenilworth
Buckden

WARWICK
CAMBRIDGE

Broughton
Swalcliffe

GLOUCESTER
OXFORD
Hatfield
Kings Langley
Rye House
Raglan
Shirburn
St. Albans
Wallingford
Ewelme
LONDON
Cowling
Donnington
Windsor
Croydon
Eltham
Queenborough
Esher
West Wickham
Canterbury
Maidstone
Farnham
Nunney
Saltwood
Dover
Wells
Wardour
WINCHESTER
Norrington
St. Cross
Bodiam
Battle
Southampton
Amberley
Portchester
Arundel
Herstmonceux

EXETER
Corfe

Dartington

0   50   100 Miles

0   50   100 Kilometres

Map III Castles, Fortifications, Houses and Colleges. The boundaries shown are of the ancient counties

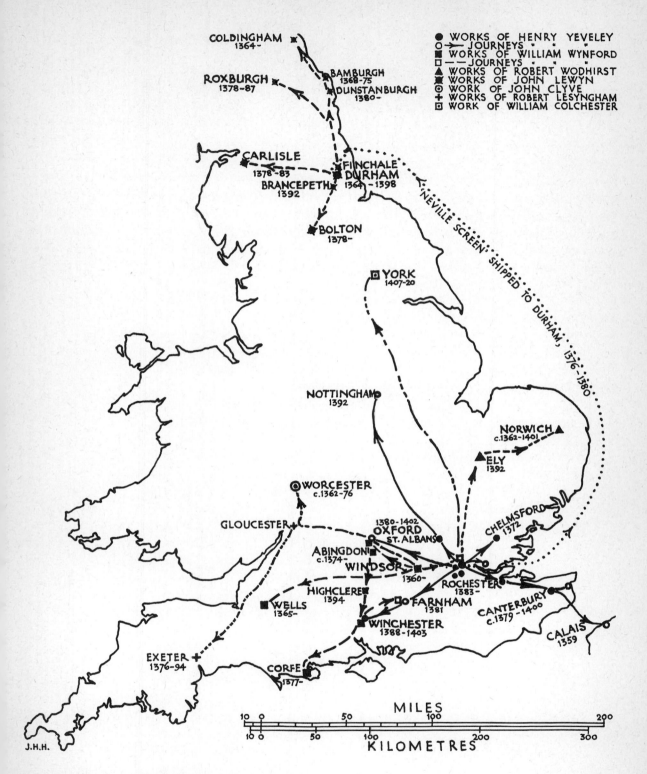

COLDINGHAM
1364-

ROXBURGH
1378-87

BAMBURGH
1368-75

DUNSTANBURGH
1380-

WORKS OF HENRY YEVELEY
JOURNEYS
WORKS OF WILLIAM WYNFORD
JOURNEYS
WORKS OF ROBERT WODHIRST
WORKS OF JOHN LEWYN
WORK OF JOHN CLYVE
WORKS OF ROBERT LESYNGHAM
WORK OF WILLIAM COLCHESTER

CARLISLE
1378-83

FINCHALE
DURHAM
1364-1398

BRANCEPETH
1392

BOLTON
1378-

"NEVILLE SCREEN" SHIPPED TO DURHAM, 1376-1380

YORK
1407-20

NOTTINGHAM
1392

NORWICH
c.1362-1401

ELY
1392

WORCESTER
c.1362-76

GLOUCESTER

OXFORD
ST. ALBANS
1380-1402

CHELMSFORD
1372

ABINGDON
c.1374-

WINDSOR
1360-

HIGHCLERE
1394

FARNHAM
1381

ROCHESTER
1383-

WELLS
1365-

WINCHESTER
1388-1403

CANTERBURY
c.1379-1400

CALAIS
1359

EXETER
1376-94

CORFE
1377-

MILES

10   50   100   200

10   50   100   200   300

KILOMETRES

J.H.H.

Map IV Journeys of Perpendicular Masters

25

Introduction

The first problem to face in discussion of the Perpendicular Style is the reason for its name. Attempts had been made, from John Aubrey's *Chronologia Architectonica* of the 1670s downwards, to produce a typology of the successive divisions of style found in the historical architecture of England. Aubrey's diligent observations remained in manuscript, and it seems to be generally agreed that the first published attempt at analysis of mediaeval style was that included by Thomas Warton (1728–1790) in his *Observations on the Faerie Queene of Spenser* as enlarged in the edition of 1763. There is little to recommend either the choice of dates or of names for the divisions suggested by Warton, but it is of some interest that he regarded 'Absolute Gothic' as reigning from 1300 to 1441 (King's College Chapel), and 'Ornamental Gothic' as then succeeding. Had he realised fully the difference between the ascetic intentions of Henry VI and the style of the Chapel's fulfilment under Henry VII, Warton would presumably have made his division agree better with the end of strict Perpendicular. A more thorough attempt to classify the outstanding English churches was made by James Dallaway in his *Observations on English Architecture* (1806). Dallaway's six divisions came much closer to a true understanding of the phases of insular development: Anglo-Norman, from before 1100 to 1170; Semi or Mixed Norman, 1170–1220; Lancet Arch Gothick, 1220–1300; Pure Gothick, 1300–1400; Ornamented Gothick, 1400–1460; and Florid Gothick, from 1460 to the Close. Dallaway's first two periods correspond well with Norman and Transitional as rightly understood; his 'Ornamented Gothick' setting in after 1400 well expresses the slighter spirit of the age which succeeded to that of Chaucer and Yeveley, and his final phase of the Florid marks the real difference between work before and after the reign of Edward IV, a distinction not adequately grasped by Rickman in his later classification.

With all its faults, it is the *Attempt* of Thomas Rickman (1776–1841) that laid the firm foundations on which all later studies have been based. Coinciding with the onset of the ecclesiological phase of romanticism, and frequently revised in the light of new discoveries, Rickman's deservedly famous work brought vague appreciations into order and offered a scientific organisation. It is in the world of natural history, then in process of classification by scientists like Georges Cuvier (1769–1832), that the work of Rickman finds a parallel. The arts of mankind were, at the same time as the orders of creation, being prepared for the advent of an evolutionary hypothesis. There is, of course, the necessary distinction that, while evolution by natural selection and the survival of the fittest may be construed as a purely mechanistic theory, the arts are inevitably influenced by the discriminatory taste of individuals. The evolution of design is not an internal process, but due to a conscious activity of invention. The touchstone of survival is not one of brute existence, but of competitive qualification for fashionable acceptance.

Rickman's dating as originally promulgated had to be revised, and it would be pointless to discuss the transformation produced by research and controversy between 1817 and 1881, the date of the last revision edited by John Henry Parker (1806–1884). Among the many factors which produced a revolution in knowledge, especially after Rickman's death, the most influential was the contribution of Robert Willis (1800–1875), whose detailed architectural histories provided the model for all subsequent work and set a standard of meticulous accuracy rarely equalled and never surpassed. While it was Rickman himself who laid down that 'the name (Perpendicular) clearly designates the style, for the mullions of the windows, and the ornamental panellings, run in perpendicular lines', it was Willis who refined the sharp distinction between the new style and the antecedent Decorated. At Gloucester Willis pointed out to a meeting of the Archaeological Institute that 'the Perpendicular style . . . must have begun somewhere, in some place the mullion must have been carried up for the first time.' In touring the cathedral Willis 'directed attention to the screen-like design of the east and west walls (of the South Transept); this, he said, generally was considered to be in the Perpendicular style, but it was wanting in its chief characteristic, as the mullions were not carried straight up to the head of the arch; before reaching it they branched off into arches, and the flowing tracery of the windows completely negatived the idea that the style was complete Perpendicular.'

In adopting the terminology of Rickman, we have then to accept the modifications in definition introduced by Willis after Rickman's death. In using 'Rickman' as the name for the standard classification of English architecture, it has to be kept in mind that its authors were in the long run Rickman, Willis and Parker. In this modified sense 'Rickman' became standard usage a century ago, and is accepted here. It is hardly necessary to go into the side issues raised by the coincidence of the Gothic Revival with Victorian ecclesiology. The two movements were indeed intimately connected, but with the artificial canons of taste erected by the notable architects of that day we have nothing to do. Regrettably, those canons of taste approved so strongly only of Early and of Decorated Gothic that much Perpendicular work of high quality and outstanding importance was destroyed in favour of pastiche. Not merely our architectural history, but our artistic heritage, is the poorer as a result.

Carping critics condemned Rickman's names as illogical, objecting to the contrast between the chronological approach implied by Saxon, Norman and Early English on one hand, and the descriptive terms Decorated and Perpendicular English on the other. Perpendicular was regarded as the least permissible of the terms used, and Edmund Sharpe rejected it altogether in favour of Rectilinear, which he regarded as 'more correctly expressive of the character of the tracery'. The Decorated period of Rickman was divided by Sharpe into the Geometrical and the Curvilinear, which have been found conveniently descriptive of the subdivisions of design before and after the introduction of the ogee curve. Strictly speaking, the name of Flowing, in common use before Sharpe's proposals of 1849, was better than Curvilinear, but it is perhaps now too late to turn back the page. None the less, we must approve of Freeman's dictum that 'Curvilinear' is not appropriate, 'the Geometrical being equally Curvilinear'.

Sharpe's illogical approach led him into worse error in his attempt to substitute Rectilinear for Perpendicular, and this at least has never found favour. Notwithstanding its more general use of straight lines, it is precisely the predominance of the vertical over the horizontal that particularly marks the style. Like all the graphic productions typical of England, this is a linear art. Linearity may be shown, as very commonly in the greater churches of England, by extreme length, and in comparison with the contemporary products of France, our buildings are never marked by absolute height. Yet the most may be made of relative height, and the vertical emphasis of Perpendicular was in this respect a major contribution. To quote Freeman again, 'Great length *internally* is not at all opposed to verticality, it is only excess in breadth which has to be guarded against.' Hence the remarkable success, aesthetically, of the naves of Westminster, Canterbury and Winchester; the relative failure of York, where excessive width governed by the Norman foundations of the older nave was a mandatory factor.

As a name, Perpendicular has stood the test of time, more than a century-and-a-half since Rickman's coinage. It does adequately describe the most marked feature of the style and is unmistakeable. Considering the predominant quantity of late mediaeval work in our architecture, it is astonishing that Victorian taste should for so long have prevented proper study. The sheer bulk of the style in surviving monuments, even those built by 1485, is daunting. It is indeed true that anything approaching a complete corpus of Perpendicular details and mouldings is unthinkable except as a vast project in collaboration comparable to the *New English Dictionary*. Yet the architectural vocabulary involved is of no less importance than the linguistic. Inasmuch as the art of building makes a universal appeal, independent of language as music is, its history and its stylistic analysis may even be regarded as transcending the limits imposed upon the spoken and the written word.

History and verbal analysis, however, inevitably fall back upon language, and clear understanding is impossible without an accepted terminology. We have already seen that not only the delimiting dates of stylistic periods have been in dispute, but also their names. Similarly, the vocabulary of architectural detail is largely a sealed book of technical jargon to the ordinary reader. In spite of the enormous architectural literature of the nineteenth century, the general reader has never come to grips with the nomenclature of building to the extent that has been achieved with painting and music. Reference to a glossary (p. 282) is commonly necessary, and diagrams are an essential aid to verbal description. The controversies which have prevented the adoption of recognised standards, and the tendency of armchair critics to break into French rather than learn what English terms are in use, have further clouded the scene.

It was unfortunate that the *Dictionary of Architecture* produced by the Architectural Publication Society, one of the most profound of English works of scholarship, should not have started publication until 1849 nor have been completed until 1892. By the time that a satisfactory work of reference existed, the Gothic Revival was over, and with it the fierce interest of Englishmen in our mediaeval art as a subject for close study. This is not to depreciate the immense body of later work done, especially by Prior, by Francis Bond, and above all by Lethaby, but none of these great authorities attempted monographic treatment of later mediaeval style. Only Bond, in his two standard works *Gothic Architecture in England* (1905) and *English Church Architecture* (1913) gave adequate coverage to Perpendicular/Rectilinear (using both terms), and the one devoted student of the style, F. E. Howard (1889–1934), died at the age of 45 with most of his work undone. The age of official collaboration, led by the massive inventories of the Royal Commission on Historical Monuments, has regrettably failed to give sufficient descriptive detail on style, considering mere chronology (e.g. 'a 14th-century window') as an end in itself.

Substantially greater awareness of the significant change of style has been shown in some recent work, generally of local or otherwise limited scope, notably by the late Dr. Frank J. Allen in his survey of *The Great Church Towers of England* (1932). The national coverage given by the great series on *The Buildings of England* (1951–1974) initiated and edited by Sir Nikolaus Pevsner raises hopes only to disappoint them. The volumes display considerable interest in the change from Dec to Perp, but little attempt is made to document or illustrate the vital period.

Inadequate linkage between surviving structures and records has largely vitiated English architectural history. There are great obstacles to overcome: the widespread destruction both of works and documents, and the difficulty in some instances of establishing a clear relation between the two when both survive. Yet there is for the Perpendicular period a far greater survival of precise records than at earlier dates. Beyond this specific documentation, by accounts, contracts, inscriptions and sometimes heraldry, there is also a great body of looser evidence provided by bequests in wills. In such cases it may be impossible to determine the actual dates of start and finish; but that work was under construction during certain years may be established beyond doubt. Much of this evidence remained unknown when the basic literature, by Rickman, Parker, Willis and others was written. Hence many accepted statements are suspect in that, while typologically sound, they are beyond proof and may give rise to unresolved clashes with evidence from elsewhere.

The relevant typology of later Gothic in this country was worked out, largely on the basis of Rickman's early editions, by Willis in broad outline, but in detail mainly by Edward Augustus Freeman (1823–1892). At the age of 26 Freeman published *A History of Architecture*, unillustrated, but of remarkable penetration. The future historian of the Norman Conquest, even as a young man, had an exceptionally powerful grip on facts. He observed the succession, in mediaeval architecture, of three main attitudes: that of the Romanesque designers, where 'the parts, even to the minutest detail, retain a severe separate existence'; that of Early Gothic, marked by the 'principle of destroying the separate existence of parts only to the construction of the primary parts of the building ... without completely subordinating these to the whole ... they still remain distinct, united by harmonious juxtaposition, but not actually fused into a single existence'; and that of the late or *Continuous* style, both Flowing and Perpendicular, which 'effects the subordination of the secondary parts more completely ... so that the parts sink into nothing of themselves, but exist merely as parts of the whole'. In the later Gothic 'it is the whole alone that is seen and contemplated'.

At the same time that Freeman was writing his *History* he was lecturing to the Oxford Architectural Society on Gothic tracery. His lectures, fully revised and in part completely re-written, formed *An Essay on the Origin and Development of Window Tracery in England* published in 1851. Covering the whole period of the traceried window, and provided with some 400 illustrations, this book is a full and remarkably adequate *typological* history. It has to be stressed that Freeman, though obviously well aware of the simultaneity of different stages of development, was content to avoid chronology. His concern was to trace the intellectual succession of ideas in design as an ideal pattern rather than as strictly consecutive history. In the then state of knowledge his approach was the only one really feasible, and it is a measure of his mastery of the subject that no attempt to supersede his book has been made in 125 years.

Not the least of the benefits conferred by Freeman's book is its extensive and well deployed vocabulary, based on the general usage of his time and particularly on that of the *Manual of Gothic Architecture* (1846) of Frederick Apthorp Paley (1815–1888). Paley, who also produced the standard *Manual of Gothic Moldings* (1845), worked under the same disabilities as Freeman, in that the available sources were inadequate to anchor the observed facts to precise – or even approximately correct – dates. Both men, however, performed yeoman service in putting on record the facts that could then be observed and which were in so many cases to disappear during the subsequent period of drastic restorations. Although the resources of documentary evidence have since been enormously expanded, it has to be remembered that for very much of the accurate record of structures we rely upon the early Victorian and even pre-Victorian architects and antiquaries who noted details meticulously by hand and without benefit of photography.

As we have seen, Freeman regarded Flowing and its derivative Flamboyant on the one hand, and Perpendicular on the other, as equally examples of the Continuous. In Geometrical designs each feature remained separate and tended towards denial of the unity of the whole. After the introduction of the ogee curve there was a new and intensified progress towards continuous flow; and of this continuity the branching Flamboyant and the straight-trunked Perpendicular were alike instances. That Freeman was fundamentally right is demonstrated by the fact that the ultimate exemplifications of Gothic were either Flamboyant – generally on the Continent – or Perpendicular. The latter style had virtually no real extension beyond England and Wales, except for a sprinkle of exported designs at Calais, in the Lowlands of Scotland, or in the

English Pale around Dublin. On the other hand, Perpendicular did assimilate some revived features of an advanced Flowing character into its latest output, as a counter-current to the stark functionalism of much uncusped work of the early sixteenth century.

To Freeman the concept of an internal evolution was implicit, though the Darwinian expression of a scientific evolutionary hypothesis in nature had not yet come. We may accept Freeman's masterly analysis of the steps by which the many possibilities of pattern were explored, leading on by stages from one style of tracery to another, without necessarily excluding the intervention of outside influences. It is indeed probable that all stylistic change is triggered by the application of external stimuli. Lack of foreign contacts, whether due to natural isolation or to self-satisfaction with results already achieved, leads to purely traditional precepts and an art in stagnation. On the other hand given an art in process of continuous change, such as that of England from the twelfth to the sixteenth century, the sources and dates of foreign stimuli assume some importance. It is not enough simply to accept the work itself as sufficient, and decline to seek further. This refusal to see any importance in the date of a work of art is the one dubious feature in the short but noble study of Perpendicular made by John Dando Sedding (1838–1891).

It is fair to point out that Sedding was a practising architect, and more significantly, a diocesan architect for the see of Bath and Wells. Like Freeman at an earlier period, he was deeply impressed by the amazing quality of the late Gothic of Somerset. His lecture, 'The Architecture of the Perpendicular Period', delivered to the St. Paul's Ecclesiological Society on 27 May 1880 and printed in the first volume of their *Transactions*, marks an epoch. Among the first points which had to be made was that 'everybody of consequence, except the great Pugin, Fergusson, and Freeman, has had an ill word for the Perpendicular'. It is highly significant that neither James Fergusson (1808–1886) nor Freeman was an architect, and that Augustus Welby Northmore Pugin (1812–1852), though born in London, was of immediately French extraction and able to take an objective view. Furthermore, Pugin wrote before the full tide of the Gothic Revival had set in and before the fashion of decrying Perpendicular existed. The extreme violence of the objections seems to stem from the new religious convictions of the Tractarian movement. It was an intellectual necessity to construct an ideal 'Perfect Age of Faith' which found expression in a 'Perfect Art'. The dimly apprehended forthcoming theory of Evolution presided over the view of English Gothic as comprising growth, blossom, and decay. The whole of Perpendicular was seen as a falling-off, even a degradation, of the exquisite beauty of the bud and the expanded flower.

Sedding's lecture was a generalised essay to show how false were the arguments advanced against Perpendicular, how nonsensical the artificial idea that it was debased. As he said, 'In the Perpendicular we have not only what is the outcome of national insularity, but that closing phase of Gothic, which has most absorbed the national character'. If you seek 'the full character of national art, you turn to where it is most declared, just as, to find the character of an oak, you go, not to the hide-bound acorn, nor to the struggling sapling, but to the king of the forest in all his pride of ascendant life.' To Sedding it was 'everything . . . that the art is fine of its kind, that the man who gave it birth was a great man. . . . If we would know the whole art-power of mediaeval England . . . we must turn to the art of the Perpendicular period. In brief, the Perpendicular period is the crown and culmination of a long series of effort. It is the harvest-time of all our mediaeval endeavour.'

Sedding died too soon to see much of the results of his preaching, but his enthusiasm was not without its effect upon the tail-end of the Gothic Revival. The style represented by the work of George Frederick Bodley (1827–1907) and his partner Thomas Garner (1839–1906) was essentially a serious attempt to begin again where true Perpendicular had been cut off in its prime. Happily it was in Somerset, on the crown of the Mendips at Downside Abbey, that the finest works of this new Gothic were performed: Garner's presbytery, followed by the nave of Sir Giles Gilbert Scott. These go far towards justification of revival as a means to fine architecture, and are certainly less open to criticism than the spate of designs and restorations that flooded the country after Pugin's work on the Houses of Parliament. Although the revival of forms is irrelevant to the history of the original style, it is at least a speaking witness to the positive feeling which contemplation of that style could generate.

From the historians of the style we revert to Perpendicular itself, beginning with a definition and a sketch of the artistic surroundings in which it took its rise. First, then, for an attempt at defining the phenomenon, in so far as it is a wholly English example of that wider architecture of unity, subordinating the parts to the whole, which Freeman called Continuous Gothic. General features, shared by Perpendicular with all fully developed late Gothic, are emphasis on space produced by the attenuation of supports, the enlargement of windows joined with greater translucency of glazing to let in more light, and an increased rectilinearity produced by intersection of vertical and horizontal members and mouldings. None of these features is found exclusively in Perpendicular, and they merely set the scene for its specific qualities.

In proceeding to enumerate those special features which define Perpendicular, it is necessary to make the proviso that in some cases individual features made their appearance before 1332, the date of the first demonstrably Perpendicular detail at Old St. Paul's. In addition to the unique feature of

> vertical members of tracery rising to cut the curve of the arch without deflection

the following are manifest marks of Perpendicular:

> the four-centred arch and its variants
> the square label, especially surrounding an arch
> the casement, or wide hollow, moulding
> the double-ogee moulding
> the bowtell moulding treated as a shaft
> base-mouldings of double or ogee form.

Rather more generalised are the tendency to use:

> modified curves, produced free-hand rather than by compass regularity of repetition
>
> suppression of variation in like parts (e.g. the traceries of a series of windows) vertical panelling as a common treatment, including the prolongation of mullions beneath sill-level to form blind panels (the 'long Panel' motive) angularity, notably the crystallization of reticulated (Flowing or Curvilinear) forms into polygons with straight, especially vertical, sides unification of mouldings by working them upon the chamfer-plane instead of in recessed orders.

So far as there is a general tendency discernible throughout Perpendicular, it is the formation of linear pattern, seen not only in tracery but in vaults. The angularity, and rectilinearity, of the style are seen in the abandonment of the spire and substitution of the tower with square top and parapet, battlement and pinnacles. This move went hand in hand with the general introduction of roofs of relatively flat pitch, often hidden behind level parapets.

Although, as mentioned above, some distinctive features made their individual appearance rather in advance of the key motive of Perpendicular tracery, we must beware of accepting the loose statements of early writers. As long ago as 1850 Parker had to point out, in the fifth edition of his *Glossary*, that the supposed early examples of the four-centred arch in the doorway of the City School, Bristol, and in the Lady Chapel of Oxford Cathedral, 'appear to be quite accidental, and indeed are often the result of a settlement which has distorted a simple pointed arch . . . by pressing and flattening down the crown, and bending the haunches'. In a footnote of 1905 Francis Bond corrected G. A. Poole's assumption that the pier-arches at Stanwick, Northants., were four-centred from the Early English period, pointing out that 'Inspection suggests that the (Early English) hood-molds at Stanwick have been reset.' The examples in the crypt inserted beneath the western Lady Chapel of Glastonbury Abbey are, of course, not of the twelfth but of the sixteenth century. Bond took the view that the four-centred arch arose accidentally, and some more or less 'four-centred' forms may so have occurred, but its sudden appearance in work of high quality at Exeter and Gloucester between 1317 and 1335, and its wide general adoption later in the fourteenth century, lead to an opposite conclusion. So distinctive a stylistic innovation, linked as it was to other features of Eastern origin such as the square surround, can only have been borrowed.

It is perhaps as well to deal here with the similarly early instances of the ogee curve which have been alleged. Between 1291 and 1294 the ogee was certainly used in England on the Eleanor Crosses, and somewhere about 1296 in the detail of the tomb of Edmund Crouchback in Westminster Abbey. The ogee form also makes an unobtrusive appearance beneath the finial of the 'porch' of the now destroyed shrine of St. Gertrude at Nivelles in Belgium. Only a somewhat vague date can be given to this work, started after 1272 but not completed until 1298, it is said to the design of a Benedictine monk, Maître Jacques. There is general use of the ogee in England soon after 1300, but in

France it is seldom if ever found before the second half of the fourteenth century. On the contrary, by far the earliest curvilinear tracery in Spain was introduced about 1325–30 by a mason, 'Raynardus dez Fonolly', explicitly described as an Englishman. It has been alleged that an ogee arch on a small scale in the wall arcading inside the south porch of St. Urbain at Troyes in Champagne belongs to original work of c. 1266–86, and Pevsner has gone so far as to describe it as 'certainly the earliest of all surviving ogee arches anywhere.' At the same time he remarks that this apparent date was thought so improbable 'that Lasteyrie tried to prove it belonged to the nineteenth century.' Far from this being the case, Lasteyrie in 1927 endorsed the (revised) view of Enlart that the block of stone carved with ogee arches must be a repair of the late fourteenth or fifteenth century. Examination on the spot fully supports Lasteyrie's view that both the carved fleurs-de-lys and the crockets on this block are of far later character than the original work of St. Urbain, stopped in 1286. We are left with the certain fact that ogee forms were in England before 1294, that their use was becoming general within some 15 years, but that outside England the ogee and, a fortiori, all forms of Flowing and Curvilinear tracery belong to a later generation.

The motive of the arch within a square surround seems first to appear in England in the doorways leading from the chapter-house of York Minster. The date may be about 1290, on the ground that the details are very late Geometric without any trace of Curvilinear, but that the building should have been finished before the major transfer of the building staff (evidenced by masons' marks) in 1291 to the new nave. The mere outline pattern of an arch within a square surround might have been derived from arcaded transoms, as in the inner transparencies of some French churches, but the moulded sunk spandrels at York prefigure those of early fourteenth-century date in this country and notably in work of the Court style and the first Perpendicular. The wide shallow casement mould occurs in Prior Crauden's Chapel at Ely in work of c. 1324, rather earlier than the 'first Perpendicular' works at Old St. Paul's, the cloister and chapter-house begun in 1332. A rather similar shallow moulding is also found in the south cloister of Norwich Cathedral, certainly built about 1325; and in the south transept of Gloucester Abbey, designed not earlier than 1331.

One invention, and as far as we know, one only, was brought direct from France: the base with a double-fold. This formed part of the corpus of mouldings used by Pierre des Champs about 1311 for the south transept doorway of Clermont-Ferrand Cathedral. At that time this was one of the most up-to-date works in the French Court Style, and during the early years of the reign of Edward II there were close relations between England and France. For a short time English masons of high standing might be expected to work during their wanderyears at the greater French monuments. Another link with French works in a highly significant area is provided by the political relationship between England and Champagne. This was formed in 1275 when Edmund of Lancaster (1245–1296), the younger brother of Edward I, married the widow of Henri III, count of Champagne. During the infancy of his wife's daughter,

Fig. 1 Moulding profiles at Ely c. 1324 and London 1332

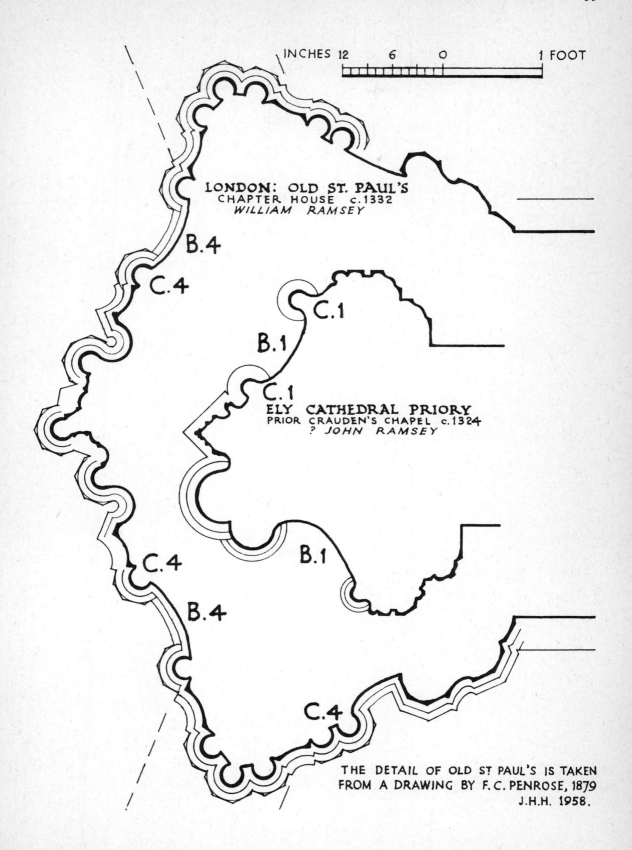

INCHES 12   6   0   1 FOOT

LONDON: OLD ST. PAUL'S
CHAPTER HOUSE c.1332
WILLIAM RAMSEY

B.4

C.4

C.1

B.1

C.1

ELY CATHEDRAL PRIORY
PRIOR CRAUDEN'S CHAPEL c.1324
? JOHN RAMSEY

B.1

C.4

B.4

C.4

THE DETAIL OF OLD ST PAUL'S IS TAKEN
FROM A DRAWING BY F.C. PENROSE, 1879
J.H.H. 1958.

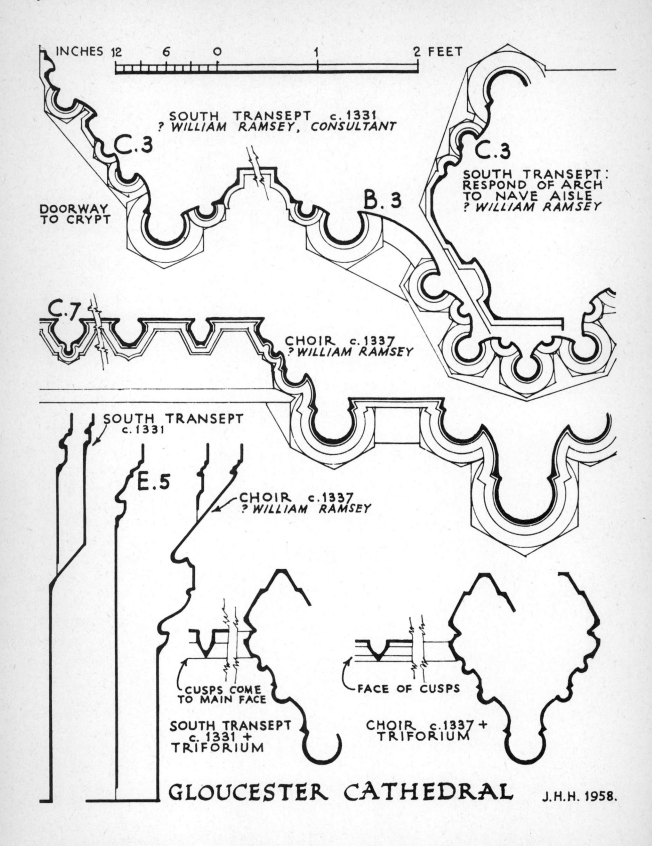

INCHES 12   6   0   1   2 FEET

SOUTH TRANSEPT c. 1331
? WILLIAM RAMSEY, CONSULTANT

C.3

DOORWAY
TO CRYPT

B. 3

C.3

SOUTH TRANSEPT:
RESPOND OF ARCH
TO NAVE AISLE
? WILLIAM RAMSEY

C.7

CHOIR c. 1337
? WILLIAM RAMSEY

SOUTH TRANSEPT
c. 1331

E.5

CHOIR c. 1337
? WILLIAM RAMSEY

CUSPS COME
TO MAIN FACE

FACE OF CUSPS

SOUTH TRANSEPT
c. 1331 +
TRIFORIUM

CHOIR c. 1337 +
TRIFORIUM

GLOUCESTER CATHEDRAL

J.H.H. 1958.

Edmund had the custody of Champagne by right, and in fact was able to exercise control even after his step-daughter came of age in 1284. It must be emphasised that the evidence of dated buildings shows as much influence of English art upon that of Champagne as in the opposite direction.

The relatively harmonious relations between England and France during the reign of Edward I, which had led to his own marriage to a French princess in 1299 and his son's to Philip the Fair's daughter Isabella in 1308, were succeeded by a period of increasing enmity which was to lead to the Hundred Years War. The independent path taken by English art and architecture from the opening of the fourteenth century has to be seen against this background of estrangement from France. Yet it is clear that the germs of our aesthetic particularity were present before the serious worsening of dynastic relations after 1328. There seems to be no French or continental parallel for the Kentish style which by 1300 was emerging in and around Canterbury. Elements of this idiosyncratic fashion were brought by Kentish master masons working for the Crown into the amalgam of the contemporary Court style and thus appear at St. Stephen's Chapel and on monuments such as that of Aymer de Valence (died 1324) in Westminster Abbey. Associated with the 'Kentish' geometrical forms used by the masters Michael of Canterbury and his son Thomas, was another motive, probably of remote oriental origin. This is the quatrefoil formed of four ogee lobes, found in the window tracery of the crypt of St. Stephen's, and known as an ancient Chinese pattern based on the leaves of the water-chestnut (*Trapa natans*). The tracery belongs stylistically after 1300 and is unlikely to be later than 1324 when work was already in progress on the lower stage of the upper chapel.

In the generation preceding the first appearance of Perpendicular, English style is notable for the many distinct schools of design found, in late Geometrical and in Curvilinear. It was a period marked by extraordinary fertility of invention and nothing so sharply marks it off from French work with its strong resistance to innovation. The roots of this insular inventiveness go back to the regional schools of Early English: south-eastern, western, and northern, but there was much cross-fertilisation and movement of masters from one part of the country to another. Not only the immense political prestige of Edward I, but his great architectural works – the Welsh castles as well as St. Stephen's Chapel – and his employment of foreign experts such as James of St. George from Savoy, all tended to promote this diverse activity. We have only to think of the many simultaneous programmes of work, at the cathedrals alone, to realise how rich England was in creative talent. Within the half-century 1290–1340 there were major building programmes at Wells, Exeter, York, Lichfield, Norwich, Bristol and Ely, besides smaller but no less significant works at Canterbury, Carlisle, Chester, Gloucester, Hereford, Lincoln, Southwell, Winchester and Worcester. Within the overall scope of late Decorated, Curvilinear, and the earliest Perpendicular there was displayed a wealth of individual creation in planning, in spatial ideas, and in pattern.

The Decorated style with its Flowing, Curvilinear, and Flamboyant offshoots has, unlike Perpendicular, always attracted a good share of attention.

Fig. 2 Mouldings at Gloucester *c.* 1331 and *c.* 1337

At the same time that Freeman was lecturing on the history of English tracery as a whole, Edmund Sharpe was writing *A Treatise on the Rise and Progress of Decorated Window Tracery in England* (1849), and a half-century later Edward Schroder Prior (1852–1932) stressed Decorated as 'the Summit of Gothic Art' in *A History of Gothic Art in England* (1900). The Gothic built after 1350 was accorded a single chapter amounting to only one-twentieth of the book. It was left to our own time, however, for a monograph on the Decorated Style to be written, by Dr. Henning Bock and in German (*Der Decorated Style*, Heidelberg 1962). Though handicapped by unavoidable reliance on inadequate sources, Dr. Bock has demonstrated the creative adaptation displayed by English artists which, in the first half of the fourteenth century, had placed our Late-Gothic fifty years ahead of that of continental Europe. Frenchmen, notably Camille Enlart, had already admitted the priority of Curvilinear over continental Flamboyant; Germans, including Dr. Bock, have greatly widened the scope of this priority.

The political conditions which allowed insular art this remarkable pre-eminence over that of the other nations of western Europe need only be outlined. The immense reputation of Edward I was certainly a major factor, and it is probable that the English wool trade and the ventures of our merchants abroad were already exercising an influence much greater than might have been expected. The French leadership of Europe, already imperilled by Thomist encyclopaedism and a consequent academicism in art, was cancelled by the dynastic crisis of 1328 and the first phase of the Hundred Years War. Edward III was able to become the close ally of the German Emperor Louis IV, in 1338 his Vicar-General over the parts of the Empire west of the Rhine; and when Louis died in 1347 it was the English king whom the electors wished to have as their next emperor. It is surely not fanciful to see in this political ascendancy the main reason why Europe was ready and eager to accept elements of English art as the latest thing.

It is at least possible that another development in the practice of English architecture had considerable weight. This was the organisation of stonemasons into a corporate body with professional standards of conduct and, in view of their movement from place to place, with courts of their own independent of municipal jurisdiction. In this holding of free courts the masons were paralleled by other bodies such as the Minstrels of Tutbury, the Tinmen of the Stannaries, the Free Miners of the Forest of Dean, the Marblers of Purbeck, and the Weavers of London and other cities. As early as 1275 the German masons' lodge of Strassburg Cathedral assumed the privileges of 'freed masonry after the English fashion', and in the following year obtained official confirmation of their liberties from the Emperor Rudolf I. We thus know that, at the beginning of the reign of Edward I, English masons already had a free jurisdiction, and this is explicitly confirmed by the grant in 1305 of a free court of jurisdiction over the workmen building Caernarvon Castle to Master Walter of Hereford, mason. This external evidence buttresses the masons' own account of their traditions in the Constitutions of Masonry. Though surviving in manuscripts of about 1390–1400, the Constitutions in their English form certainly go back in part to a Latin original of the mid-fourteenth century or earlier.

According to their own claims, the masons both of France and England traced their exemptions back to Charles Martel, who ruled in 715–743, and in England further rules were laid down for their conduct by King Athelstan (924–939). The masons practised the art of Geometry as laid down by the 'worthy clerk' Euclid. Discarding this legendary account of the origins of the masons' craft, we are left with a body of nine rules for the masters and nine points governing the conduct of subordinate masons, and with some valuable information as to their organisation in England. The most notable feature was the holding of an assembly once a year or once in three years, constituting a congregation of all master masons and fellows of the craft, to be held 'from province to province and from country to country'. The word 'country' meant a county or other administrative area, and this might be a municipality, since the Sheriff (of a county) or Mayor or Alderman of a town where the assembly was held might be called upon to support the authority of the Master of the Congregation.

There is some evidence to show that such assemblies were actually held. By the fifteenth century several such meetings are recorded from different parts of Germany, and their written deliberations have been preserved. In England at a much earlier date we know that in 1245 Henry III sent his master mason and master carpenter to York to advise upon the works of the Castle after conference 'with other masters expert in the like skills.' In 1320 Hereford Cathedral proposed to carry out works 'upon the ancient foundation which is thought to be firm and solid in the judgment of masons or architects regarded as skilled in their art.' Although a merely private consultation with advisers is possible in either case, it seems likely that at York and at Hereford advantage was taken of a session of some regular congregation of the kind described by the Constitutions and known from the ample German evidence.

The importance of this country-wide organisation can hardly be exaggerated. It explains the rapidity with which plans, tracery, and types of moulding moved across England, and also accounts for the observed existence of regional or county 'schools' of design. The characteristic appearance of Somerset church towers, in spite of the many individual variations among them, is well known. We shall see too that, within the region approximately covered by the mediaeval diocese of Worcester – Worcestershire, Gloucestershire and the western half of Warwickshire – there was a markedly individual style through the later fourteenth and fifteenth centuries. One of the chief marks of this style was its adherence to trefoiled cusping for main lights of windows, which elsewhere had become almost universally cinquefoiled after 1400. It does not follow that an official county or regional style was actually promulgated and upheld by authority, but it does appear that there was a strong tradition within certain boundaries, while outside them the same details would appear only by the accidental employment of a master at some distant place.

In many cases the counties of England seem to have had fairly distinctive styles, but elsewhere the regions were larger. It may well be that there were assemblies on at least two levels, one by counties and at less frequent intervals another by larger regions. So far there seems to be no positive evidence that masters from the whole of England were ever brought together in one place, yet if this had happened, the distances to be covered by those summoned would have been much less than at the Regensburg Congress of 1459, where masters attended from Strassburg, Basel and Bern in the West, Vienna, Passau and Salzburg in the East, and a substantial number of other places in central Germany. To judge from the architectural evidence it seems likely that the main divisions were those that had persisted from Early English times, Northern, South-Eastern and South-Western. Individual masters called into consultation would generally be found within the region or else be brought from not far outside it: from London to Lichfield, to Rochester, to Bury St. Edmunds; from Winchester or from Gloucester to Exeter; from Durham to Ripon and to Louth in north Lincolnshire. York, though a capital able to call upon talent from a wide area in the North, also brought in masters from the Home Counties, from Norwich, and from Lincoln. Traits of personal style were carried far from the school in which they had been learned; yet diversity of regional tradition persisted and gave a local tone and feeling providing ample variety within the ruling character of Perpendicular.

CHAPTER ONE

The Men and their Art

Before we can form any clear idea of how a great style of architecture came into being, and was propagated, we must become informed as to the men who made it. All periods of art have been products of individual artists exercising their creative talents upon antecedent tradition and upon newly imported ideas from afar. Obvious qualifying factors affect the ability of the artists to follow their bent: the patrons they served, and the extent to which those patrons forced their ideas within a strait-jacket of precisely programmed detail; or, on the contrary, left them free within wide limits. The social relation of the artists, to their employers on the one hand, and on the other to the craftsmen and labourers who carried out their designs, is another factor of importance. Both the general standards of education and of literacy (for the two are not identical), and the standards found among artists, are also relevant. Transport and travel, holidays, the length of the working day and week, are all additional components.

We need the answers to a long series of questions. These questions, posed as they commonly are in respect of the whole Middle Ages, are difficult and at times impossible to answer. In regard to England alone within the Perpendicular epoch the case is quite different. Virtually all the answers are known in general terms if not invariably in precise detail. It is no longer necessary to enter into controversy upon the extent of clerical intervention in the design of architecture: whatever may have been the case at earlier periods, it was now merely that degree of participation usual between any client and any architect. The architects, trained either as stonemasons or as carpenters, were invariably laymen, most of them with worldly burdens and married men with families. Many if not most of them were a good deal more than competent master craftsmen. In general they had some literate education, having attended primary school and then probably a grammar school for two or three years before entering their apprenticeship at the age of 13 or 14. They would know at least a little Latin; many of them a fair amount of French. All of them would have an adequate knowledge of arithmetic and the casting of accounts, as well as an advanced grasp of practical geometry.

In modern times we tend to think of the stonemason and the carpenter as mere operatives translating the architect's design into concrete terms. Since about 1800 a wider and widening distinction grew up between the older type of craftsman-architect and the new 'professional' man of pretensions to gentility and social status. In the course of less than three centuries, since the Reformation, there had been a reversal of positions. In the later Middle Ages, covering rather more than the whole Perpendicular and Tudor Gothic periods, the master artisans of the highest level – masons, carpenters, carvers, painters, smiths – had a comparatively high position in society. They were all, of necessity because of the rules of their crafts, free men by blood and position. More than that, they ranked, even in official tables of Court precedence, above yeomen and equal to or even just above 'gentlemen' of minor degree. Chaucer's group of artisans were 'ech of hem a fair burgeys', and well-to-do financially; their wives could dress richly and exercise their self-esteem: 'It is ful fair to been y-clept "*ma dame*" '.

If those craftsmen who were city burgesses and aldermen could reach this level, how much more might the outstanding artists in the King's service attain giddy heights. The dominant position of a William Ramsey, a Henry Yeveley or a Hugh Herland was comparable, *mutatis mutandis*, to that of a Wren, Vanbrugh or Lutyens in more recent times. It is a cardinal error to suppose that English mediaeval society was barbarous or unsophisticated, still more so to think it parochial. Communications were on the whole better than they were to be again until after 1790, when the canals and stage-coaches provided a false dawn of the railway age. From the Reformation onwards for two hundred years the great increase in wheeled transport caused such deterioration of the roads that the speed of human displacement tended to be reduced rather than accelerated. Yet in the Middle Ages vast numbers of men, skilled craftsmen by the score and labourers by the hundred, could be rapidly assembled for work on jobs a hundred miles or more from their places of origin. The King's writ used for the works of the Crown, and official licences to impress men obtained by courtiers and great churches, produced speedy and effective supplies of manpower.

The greater part of England was, by the opening of Edward III's reign, a highly civilised country. It had a tradition of erecting large buildings going back nearly three centuries to the time of Edward the Confessor. The technological revolution, involving a higher degree of geometrical and mechanical skills, with improved engineering plant, had taken place in the years immediately after 1100. For over two hundred years there had been a developing tradition in the design and construction of churches, castles, monasteries and houses, together with the provision of stone bridges on the main roads, water-borne sanitation and piped supplies of drinking water. Paved streets were taking the place of mud, and at the Court and in the homes of the wealthy there was an extremely high degree of comfort and of artistic elegance. Embroidered hangings, clothes and accoutrements of all kinds, illuminated books, were produced to a standard of exquisite quality hardly ever equalled, and in western Europe never excelled.

The number of men engaged, in the capacity of skilled artisans, in the various trades of artistic character was very large. In York during the reign of Richard II, as shown by the information extracted from the poll taxes, there were over a thousand men of identifiable occupations, some 850 of them working as their own masters in about a hundred different crafts. Of these 14 separate skills were involved in the building and allied trades, and were exercised by 107 masters, not counting assistants, apprentices, and unskilled labourers. That is to say that, of the category of independent skilled men in York, just over one-eighth was concerned with building: churches, houses, shops, wharves, the Castle and Walls. In addition there were other craftsmen employed upon York Minster and its dependencies within the Close, part of St. Peter's Liberty. Like other liberties in London and many mediaeval towns, this was completely independent of the City of York, having its own courts, its own constables, and its own administration. It is an important fact of mediaeval life that artists and craftsmen could often set up in business within a liberty without paying the heavy dues required of the free citizen.

Out of the large numbers of craftsmen, only a few played a significant part in artistic design, and not all of these were concerned with architecture. The men who originated and carried on the Perpendicular style were a small and select minority. With few exceptions they were stonemasons by training, and masonry detail marked the progress of fashion. In a few cases timber-workers achieved equivalent standing as creative artists, but it was the specialised master masons who shaped the course of national art through the fourteenth and fifteenth centuries. The minor arts tended to be auxiliary to building, and the artists took their cue from the masons so far as details of architectural character were concerned. Even the goldsmiths, responsible for much of the small-scale art of highest quality, followed architectural fashion so far as it was applicable to the pieces they produced. Thus articles of plate, or seals, incorporating reduced versions of canopies, niches, tracery and the like, were seldom quite abreast of the latest features of architectural style. .

At this point something must be said of the hypothesis that, before the Renaissance, art was purely traditional. It has repeatedly been alleged that, at a given place and time, buildings were erected in one particular manner because it was the only way the builders knew. Now it is perfectly true that the methods of individual crafts, devoted to making standard objects, remain unchanged for centuries. The influence of changing fashion is eliminated from purely technological processes. It is quite the contrary with architectural style in its higher levels, for not only is there change from one generation to the next, but at one and the same time distinct regional and personal styles co-exist. There may be simultaneous conservative and progressive modes of building, some national and others borrowing extensively from foreign models. Even within the field of motives available in the pre-existing architecture of a country or region, there is likely to be considerable scope for eclecticism. As a general rule the more distinguished the architect, the wider will be the area from which his inspiration is drawn.

It is then not to be expected that the early stages of the Perpendicular style presented a single uniform face to the world. Once the essential details had been brought together, by William Ramsey at Old St. Paul's as far as we know, the resulting fashion lay open to plagiarism and to variation. At a later stage we shall consider some of the different types of design produced within fifty years of the moment of invention in or about 1332. The speed of assimilation to the new vogue varied greatly in different parts of the country. In some places conservative designers adhered to the canons of Curvilinear for forty or fifty years. Elsewhere slight concessions were made to the new style; or the two methods of design were employed side by side. To us the outcome appears incongruous, but it would seem that it was only at the highest levels of the Court that a full and completely mature Perpendicular was required much before 1400. The fact that the style eventually became integrated was due to the forceful stamp of several great individuals: the masons Henry Yeveley and William Wynford, and the carpenter Hugh Herland.

Yeveley was presumably born within the decade 1320–30; Wynford perhaps five to ten years later; Herland seems to have been about the same age as Yeveley, though he survived him for five years, until 1405, which was also the year of Wynford's death. Yeveley had reached London by 1353, when he took up the freedom of the city, and the period of his technical education must have lain mainly in the 1340s. He was just old enough to have learned his trade and the elements of design by the time that the Black Death of 1348–49 cut off most of the great architects of the older generation. If we are to understand how it was that Yeveley and his colleagues in the royal service, between 1360 and 1400 could establish a new national style, we have to go back to these older men. The style, or rather series of individual styles, practised in England in the first half of the fourteenth century, take on a particular retrospective significance. It was among these highly personal and distinct styles that the first Perpendicular arose, and some features of the earlier fashions were perpetuated. In spite of the differences, there was not merely continuity between earlier and later regional styles across the aesthetic break, but some conformity to regional canons of proportion. Thus we see throughout Devon, both in Decorated and in Perpendicular works, the use of the broad arch, only slightly pointed; in Gloucestershire and in the old diocese of Worcester, the perpetuation of trefoil cusping almost to the exclusion of the more common cinquefoil. In both cases it seems likely that the permanent influence was that of a cathedral lodge or a monastic works department, such as those of Exeter and Gloucester.

The background from which Perpendicular sprang was not, however, simply a chequerwork of diversity. There was besides a strand of architectural history which tended towards unity. This was the more or less continuous work, from 1292 until 1348, on the building of the royal chapel of St. Stephen within the Palace of Westminster. Although not to be compared with the larger cathedrals and monastic churches in scale, it was in some ways the most influential building in the country. Its design was created and modified by a succession of masters employed by Edward I, his son and his grandson: Michael of Canterbury, his son Thomas, and William Ramsey. Under them worked a large team of the best masons, and several of them had distinguished careers in their own right. The lodge of St. Stephen's, from 1292 onwards, was the finest training ground in the country for young and ambitious architects. Largely taken down in 1692, mutilated further in 1800, and finally burnt out in 1834, the upper chapel of St. Stephen has disappeared, though its crypt (St. Mary in the Vaults) happily survives. Fortunately enough detail was recorded to enable the chapel's historical significance for English architecture to be assessed.

St. Stephen's was not, as some have asserted, an early or 'pre-Perpendicular' work. With the slight exception of details of its western porch, completed under William Ramsey after 1336, its architectural character was wholly Decorated, and Kentish rather than Curvilinear. None the less, the long and tall chapel, with slim angle turrets and two tiers of large windows, exemplified the same movement towards unification of parts, the same aspiring quality, the same emphasis on illumination. In spite of pauses in the work, the long period of building, going back eight years into the thirteenth century, made St. Stephen's an immediately formative influence upon two generations of men, and half a dozen school generations of trainees. Masons, and other craftsmen, were brought together for the works from much of the country. These men, whether as architects or merely builders, often returned to their own parts, bearing with them the elements of the Court style.

Before discussing the appearance of Perpendicular detail, we must consider the general picture of English architecture as it was in the previous half-century. What were the principal works at greater churches in progress after the return of Edward I from the Crusade in 1274? At Westminster Abbey, after the great campaigns of Henry III, work was more or less quiescent, but at St. Paul's Cathedral in the city of London the magnificent choir and presbytery, begun in 1251, were moving steadily on towards completion by 1312. The west front of Lichfield, another slow work, was already well begun but was not to reach completion, with its spires, until the 1320s. At Exeter the building of the eastern Lady Chapel, from 1275, was a prelude to almost total reconstruction from east to west between 1288 and 1342. The choir of Chester Abbey was being built between 1283 and 1315; the nave of York from 1291 until 1338; the east end of Carlisle between 1293 and 1322. All these were, in various ways, examples of the general English tradition working within its limits of regional variation, and bringing in, as at York, elements from recent French practice. At the Augustinian abbey of Bristol, however, a revolutionary experiment was to take place after 1298: a new choir exemplifying ideas borrowed from the hall-churches of south-western France as well as a form of internal buttressing in the aisles taken from the lower story of the Sainte Chapelle in Paris.

Besides these major works there were eastern Lady Chapels at Chichester, built between 1288 and 1304; at St. Albans Abbey (1308–1326); and at Wells (c. 1310–1319), of unusual plan and vaulted in a way unique in England for its essentially domical form. Polygonal planning was employed for noble chapter-houses at Salisbury, perhaps designed about 1275 and built a few years later (coins of 1279 were found built into the foundations); at York, started earlier, but completed to an altered design c. 1286–96 – with a domical vault of wood; Wells, closely following metropolitan style, c. 1286–1306; and Southwell, another octagon in free span without a central pier, c. 1293–1300. A cloister of exceptional magnificence was begun at Norwich Cathedral in 1297; the upper part of the central tower at Lincoln was added in 1307–11; and a tower was built above the crossing at Wells in 1315–1322.

At Canterbury, though no major part of the church itself was in progress, the richly carved and traceried stone screens of the choir were begun in 1304 and finished by 1320. Diaper work on these screens, as has already been mentioned, approximates in character to geometrical interlaces of Persian origin, and the tracery has foils of rich ogee curves. The mouldings are still those of the late Decorated but include plain chamfers and very simple jambs and mullions formed of chamfers and narrow fillets. In contrast to these plain features were the major moulds: roll-and-fillet of rather bulbous section, scroll mouldings and detached shafts. These were to be transformed in the first Perpendicular into slender bowtells treated as shafts, while the bulbous roll-and-fillet was modified into a graceful pear-shaped section sometimes used for mullions and very commonly for vault-ribs.

What is particularly striking is that, in almost every case where the masters' names are known, connections can be traced between works at remote places. The links may be direct, where the same master is found working in more than one place; or indirect, where the masters had a common grounding in the royal works. At St. Paul's Cathedral it is all but certain that Michael of Canterbury was the architect for the east front with its notable rose window and pinnacles closely resembling those of the royal tombs which he designed. The later parts of the Decorated work at Exeter were by Thomas Witney, who had trained at St. Stephen's and who had had charge at Winchester and also probably at Wells. Richard Lenginour, one of the masters of the King's works, seems to have been in charge of the choir of St. Werburgh's, Chester. The Salisbury chapter-house was manifestly closely based upon that at Westminster Abbey, and indeed the whole tradition of the Salisbury lodge appears to have been formed on the model of Westminster. The architect of Lincoln Cathedral when the cloisters and the central tower were built was Richard of Stow, who also made the Lincoln Eleanor Cross for Edward I in 1291–93. Very strong circumstantial evidence indicates that Ivo de Raghton, who worked for Archbishop Melton at York and must have produced the Curvilinear work of the west window, belonged to the family of Raughton in Cumberland, who held their estate by the serjeanty of keeping the King's hawks. The same highly individual style, approaching the Flamboyant, is found in the east window of Carlisle and in parts of Beverley Minster, Selby Abbey, and Southwell, all under the patronage of Melton.

Different aspects of the Court style were emphasized by the various masters formed by or in some way linked to its influence. Through Thomas Witney a variety of factors including the use of spherical triangles can be traced at Winchester, Wells, Exeter, and very likely also at Merton College, Oxford, where he may well have been the Master Thomas employed on the crossing of the chapel in 1330–32; and at Malmesbury Abbey in Wiltshire. Witney's was clearly the dominant influence in the south-western sector of England from soon after 1300 until about 1340. In the North Ivo de Raghton must be considered the leader of advanced Flowing treatment, a form never fully accepted at Court. To the West a very different style was developed, depending for its effect on the lavish employment of ballflower carved as an enrichment in hollow mouldings. This perhaps began on the west front of Lichfield Cathedral and the Wells chapter-house in the early years of the century, was employed at

Hereford on the central tower of *c.* 1315–18, at Gloucester south nave aisle (1319–29), and at Salisbury, where the great tower was designed soon after 1320.

One major region of England has not been mentioned: East Anglia. Its two ancient cathedrals, Norwich and Ely, both survive, and it was their building works during the first half of the fourteenth century that were especially significant for the development of Perpendicular. At Norwich the church had been built long before, but the grandiose cloister was rebuilt. Within the precinct, too, the Carnary Chapel was erected: of small scale but standing on an undercroft. The great work at Ely was intended to be the new Lady Chapel, north of the choir, begun in 1321; but the project was overtaken by events. The old central tower collapsed a year later, and a vast octagon was set out in its place, with a rebuilt choir of three bays next to it. Within a single generation the Lady Chapel, the Octagon with its wooden lantern, and the new choir were all structurally completed; and during the same period the small but exquisite chapel of Prior Crauden was also built.

In the same region were several other churches of comparable scale: those of the abbeys of Bury St. Edmunds, Ramsey and Peterborough. The last has, of course, survived as a cathedral, and its central tower is of this period (*c.* 1335) though rebuilt in 1883–86. At Bury there is a large gatehouse constructed after a riot of townsmen in 1327; Ramsey has nothing of relevance. This is possibly the worst loss of all, so far as the sources of the Perpendicular style are concerned. For both at Ely and at Norwich there were among the masters in charge in the first half of the fourteenth century masons called 'de Ramsey' who can be traced back to property of Ramsey Abbey; and of the same family was the William Ramsey who worked at St. Paul's and for Edward III and who created – as far as a human artist may be said to create – the new style.

From deeds of Norwich properties it is known that the father of John de Ramsey, master mason of the cathedral by 1304, was named Richard Curteys. It has further appeared from the researches of Mr. A. B. Whittingham that the Curteys or Curteis family held property under the Abbot of Ramsey at Wyke Fen in Well, the parishes of Outwell and Upwell on the borders of Norfolk and Cambridgeshire. The family name is explained by the chronicle and chartularies of Ramsey, which show that William Curteys held the Wyke Fen lands in 1202, that his father Walter Curteys had been on pilgrimage to Jerusalem, and that Walter's father was Alfelin *Facetus*, the courteous, englished as Curteis. The estate descended from William to Simon Curteis who was living in the reign of Henry III, and to a Richard Curteis who may have been father of the Richard Curteys who settled in Norwich. The fact of this long descent is of considerable importance as it confirms, in this particular instance, the contention that mediaeval master masons were free men of good lineage. Beyond this, we learn that the family's male line descent was from a man with the presumably Saxon name Alfelin, and that one of the family undertook the pilgrimage to the Holy Land in the twelfth century.

A great deal is known of members of the Ramsey family who were master masons at Norwich, London and elsewhere in the period from 1294 to 1371.

Their relationships are complex, but they can be divided into a senior and a junior generation, the elder consisting of three brothers, John, Nicholas, and William; the younger of two brothers, another John and another William, the architect at St. Paul's and later King's Master Mason. The earlier William was one of the working masons at St. Stephen's Chapel from 1294, and the younger John (who died in 1371) was warden of the masons there at the completion of the Chapel in 1344–48. His brother, the younger William Ramsey, had himself been a mason working on St. Stephen's in 1325, when he was paid 6*d*. a day in making the cloister or passage (*alura*) from the Chapel to the Painted Chamber. At Norwich the south walk of the cloisters was begun under one John de Ramsey in 1324 and after 1326 continued under a Master William de Ramysseye into the 1330s, when robes were provided for Master William 'and his brother', and 16*s*. 8*d*. paid for their expenses on journeys from Norwich to London and from London to Norwich. The moulds or templates for the work of the cloister had to be brought from London, so that there can be no doubt of the family identity, even if the precise individuals concerned are somewhat uncertain.

From stylistic evidence it is extremely probable that the Master John who was mason at Ely during the first years of the work on the Octagon in 1322–26 was John Ramsey the elder. It is reasonably certain that the John atte Grene who worked there later was identical with a man of this name who took up the freedom of Norwich in 1322–23 (being described as of Tasburgh) and who in 1335–37 was warden of the work on the Norwich cloister under the elder John de Ramsey. From 1339 John atte Grene was named as master at Ely, and he succeeded to the position of master of the masonry and works of the King south of Trent on the death of the great William Ramsey in June 1349. He seems himself to have died of the plague within the next year, and was in turn succeeded by Master John Box, who had worked at Westminster Palace in 1333–34 but by 1350 was in the service of the prior of Christ Church at Canterbury.

There is a possibility of even wider travel on the part of Nicholas Ramsey, brother of the elder William and John. Nicholas was living in London late in 1331, in 1348 supplied plaster for the works at Westminster, and was still alive in the following year when his brother John made his will. But in the long gap in his career might be fitted the fact that in August 1333 the master of the works of the city of Paris was Nicholas de Londres, Nicholas of, or from, London. The employment of English masters and other artists in France was not unusual. At Avignon Hugh Wilfred, Englishman, built the chapel of the Angels in Notre-Dame des Doms in 1315–22, and Master John the Englishman was working on the walls of the Palace in 1336–41. Thomas Daristot the Englishman, a master painter, was employed in the Palace in 1333. The outbreak of war between England and France in 1337 would sufficiently account for the return to London of Nicholas Ramsey, if indeed the Paris master were he.

Even were the Paris Master Nicholas not one of the Ramseys, his English origin and that of the others who worked in France remains. The tomb at Avignon of Pope John XXII, who died in December 1334, is completely in the

Fig. 3 Mouldings at Norwich *c.* 1325 and London 1332

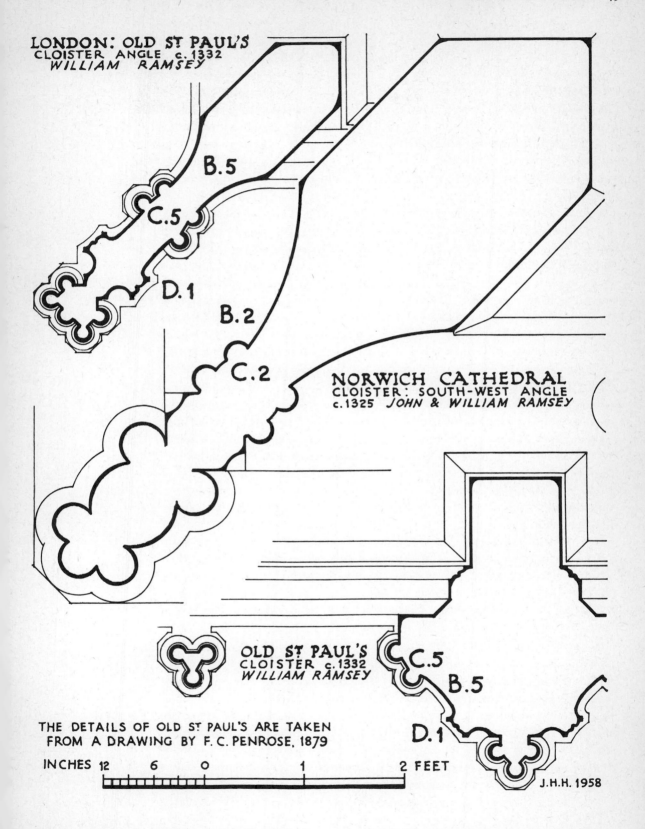

LONDON: OLD ST PAUL'S
CLOISTER ANGLE c. 1332
WILLIAM RAMSEY

B.5

C.5

D.1

B.2

C.2

NORWICH CATHEDRAL
CLOISTER: SOUTH-WEST ANGLE
c.1325 *JOHN & WILLIAM RAMSEY*

OLD ST PAUL'S
CLOISTER c. 1332
WILLIAM RAMSEY

C.5

B.5

D.1

THE DETAILS OF OLD ST PAUL'S ARE TAKEN
FROM A DRAWING BY F. C. PENROSE, 1879

INCHES 12   6   0   1   2 FEET

J.H.H. 1958

English Court style in every detail, and not merely English, but precisely in the manner of the works of Michael and Thomas of Canterbury, and particularly the latter. Here are all the latest English forms of ogee trefoil and cinquefoil cusping, cinquefoil double-cusping, ogee-cinquefoil inscribed in a circle and set on a pair of ogee trefoils, as in the Canterbury screenwork and St. Stephen's Chapel wall panelling, rows of quatrefoil, miniature battlementing, mouldings studded with ranges of the four-petalled flower. In this English monument of a French pope the style of Canterbury and Westminster found its final and highest expression, the last word of the Decorated style. If it was not actually made in England, a complete set of detailed drawings must have been prepared and sent.

Fortunately there is ample evidence for the career of Thomas of Canterbury as an architectural draughtsman. In 1293, during the early stages of planning and building St. Stephen's Chapel, Thomas *fil. Magistri*, i.e. son of the Master, Michael of Canterbury, was being paid 5*d.* a day for *pictura*. The word, besides its basic sense of painting, also meant drawing or portrayal, and it was undoubtedly as a draughtsman that Thomas was employed by his father. Work on St. Stephen's was suspended from 1297 until 1320, when Master Michael was still in charge, but shortly gave place to Thomas of Canterbury, for whom in 1323 a wooden *trassour* or drawing-board was made, for the detailing of pinnacles. Rules and squares, answering to modern tee-squares and set-squares, were also made, and in the accounts of 1331, when the final campaign of work had begun, Master Thomas appears as working upon the drawing of the moulds (templates), and as drawing upon the *trasura*. This word may have been used in a general sense of designs and details, but could literally mean either a wooden drawing-board, or the large plaster tracing-floor made at St. Stephen's in July 1332. From the accounts of 1324 we know that 'false moulds', made of three ells of canvas, were sent to Caen in Normandy for stones to be cut there. This had previously been done in 1292, at the start of work, and patterns were likewise sent in 1345 from Norwich Cathedral to Corfe in Dorset. The making of details from drawings produced at a distance was, therefore, already commonplace. Not only might a splendid tomb such as that of John XXII be made hundreds of miles from its designer, but the spread of the most modern details in all directions is explained.

Thomas of Canterbury is last heard of in 1335, and by the autumn of that year a commission of masons ordered to make an official survey of the Tower of London included William Ramsey. On 1 June 1336 Ramsey was appointed chief mason in the Tower of London and also chief surveyor of the king's works in the Tower and other castles south of Trent, with a fee of 12*d.* a day and a yearly robe. At the same time William Hurley received a similar patent as chief carpenter and surveyor of carpenters' work, and Walter le Fevre became chief smith, though at only 8*d.* a day. This major reorganisation of the royal works marks the definite assumption of control by Edward III over the architectural establishment, and also provided official channels for the dissemination of methods and style. It has to be stressed that Ramsey had been in charge of the revolutionary work of the new chapter-house and cloister at St. Paul's for four years, since June 1332, when he had been said to be especially and assiduously giving his whole attention to the business of the cathedral church. His formulation of the Perpendicular style can thus be assigned to the years 1332–1335.

The significance of these dates is twofold. Ramsey himself, though he had worked in a subordinate capacity at St. Stephen's in 1325, had won his architectural spurs in private practice and not as a civil servant. He was no doubt the most highly regarded designer within the metropolitan area when engaged by the king to be chief architect, filling the gap left by the loss – presumably the death – of Thomas of Canterbury. In spite of the heavy duties of his office, Ramsey was still able to undertake private commissions, and in May 1337 agreed to advise upon the works of Lichfield Cathedral, at a fee of £1 a visit, besides 6s. 8d. for the travelling expenses of himself and his servants. Ramsey's characteristically advanced details show exactly what he designed at Lichfield, but the bombardment in the Civil War has robbed us of his window traceries. For the Crown Ramsey took charge at St. Stephen's and at Windsor Castle, and there was a lawsuit concerning robbery of his goods and assault upon his servants by the retinue of the Abbot of St. Augustine's, Canterbury, at Reculver in east Kent in 1345. Though Edward III may not have realised the stylistic importance of Ramsey's work at St. Paul's, it is evident that his patronage enabled the new fashion to spread over a wide area.

The second inference which can be drawn from the date of 1332–35 for the St. Paul's designs is that they preceded the appearance of any definitely Perpendicular detail at Gloucester Abbey. In spite of the parallel developments in the wall-panelling of the south transept, where work went on for six seasons ending in 1336, we have seen that the four-centred side windows have flowing tracery **8**. Only the great south window, which employs the split cusps of Kentish origin and other features from the Canterbury–Westminster style, has also in an unobtrusive way a minimal employment of the Perpendicular type-detail **9**. The marked change in character between the traceries of the lateral and south windows implies that the design of the latter was not earlier than c. 1335 and that in its Perpendicular detail it followed St. Paul's just as in its Kentish quirks it borrowed from the Canterbury style ruling at Westminster. Official works in progress at Gloucester Castle from 1331 to 1335, and again after 1337, provide the obvious channel for information, while the transformation at the abbey church was being effected with the offerings of pilgrims at the tomb of the murdered King Edward II, a cult with which Edward III was anxious to identify himself.

After completion of the new work in the south transept at Gloucester, before the death of Abbot John Wigmore on 28 February 1336/7, a similar scheme was devised for the choir and presbytery, but with changed details. Not only were the moulds and minor characteristics distinct, but the window traceries were completely Perpendicular in character. The dates within which this whole work was designed and executed cannot be made more precise than the 30 years 1337–1367, but the building of the great vault of the choir, recorded for 1337–50, probably implies that the whole of the general designs had been made

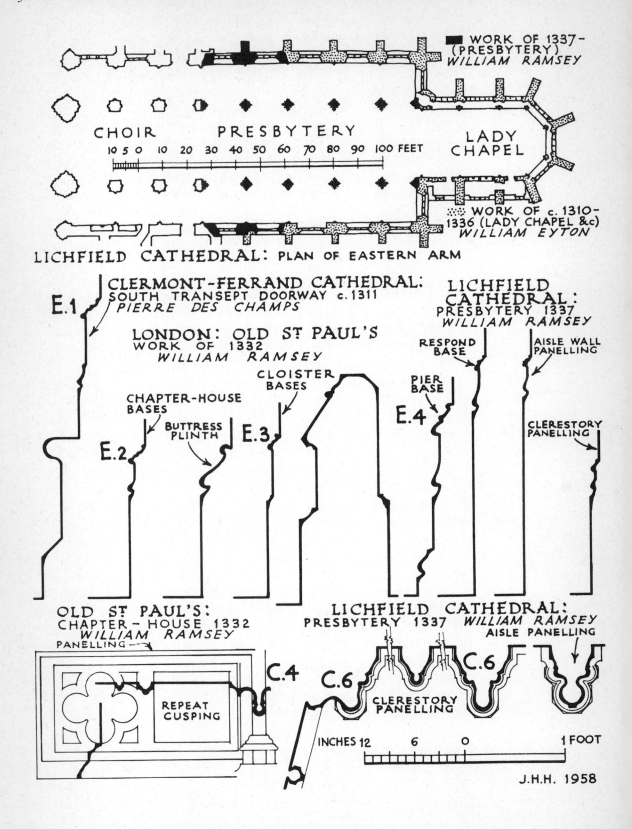

WORK OF 1337–
(PRESBYTERY)
WILLIAM RAMSEY

CHOIR   PRESBYTERY

10 5 0   10 20 30 40 50 60 70 80 90 100 FEET

LADY CHAPEL

WORK OF c. 1310–
1336 (LADY CHAPEL &c)
WILLIAM EYTON

LICHFIELD CATHEDRAL: PLAN OF EASTERN ARM

CLERMONT-FERRAND CATHEDRAL:
SOUTH TRANSEPT DOORWAY c.1311
PIERRE DES CHAMPS

E.1

LONDON: OLD ST PAUL'S
WORK OF 1332
WILLIAM RAMSEY

CLOISTER
BASES

CHAPTER-HOUSE
BASES

E.2

BUTTRESS
PLINTH

E.3

LICHFIELD
CATHEDRAL:
PRESBYTERY 1337
WILLIAM RAMSEY

RESPOND
BASE

AISLE WALL
PANELLING

PIER
BASE

E.4

CLERESTORY
PANELLING

OLD ST PAUL'S:
CHAPTER – HOUSE 1332
WILLIAM RAMSEY

PANELLING

C.4

REPEAT
CUSPING

LICHFIELD CATHEDRAL:
PRESBYTERY 1337 *WILLIAM RAMSEY*
AISLE PANELLING

C.6   C.6   C.6

CLERESTORY
PANELLING

INCHES 12   6   0   1 FOOT

J.H.H. 1958

by then. The work of the high altar and presbytery, however, was not carried out until after 1351. It has often been stated that the glass of the great east window was made by 1350, but this view rests purely upon the heraldic evidence that the window is largely a memorial to those who fought at Crecy in 1346 and at the Siege of Calais in 1347. On the other hand, three of the greatest authorities have regarded its style as certainly later: Westlake and J. A. Knowles put the glass at *c.* 1360, and J. D. LeCouteur considered that on style alone it might well be of 1370, even though he accepted the heraldry as implying an exceptionally advanced date, earlier than that. It would be rash to assume that the stone tracery as erected was designed before the Black Death **203**.

Apart from the surviving fragments of Perpendicular detail from Ramsey's works at St. Paul's **10**, and the views of it by Hollar, the first phase of the new style is represented only by a handful of works. Of these the earliest is the south window at Gloucester, designed about 1335 **9**. Then there are the singular mullioned windows, with cusped heads but no tracery, at Ottery St. Mary, where the relevant work was in progress in 1338–42, and a similar use of blind mullions rising – in this case to a four-centred arch – in the wall-panelling of the south porch of St. Mary Redcliffe by Bristol. Though this porch is not precisely dated, its character closely resembles that of work done under the master William Joy at Wells Cathedral between 1329 and 1345. There may be specific significance in this, since the next example of strictly Perpendicular detail, with straightened reticulations, occurs in the great east window of Wells Cathedral **15**. There is strong cumulative evidence that the glass of this window is of about 1340 (and not 1330, as used to be said), and the combination of Flowing and Perpendicular motives in the tracery is perfectly compatible with design in 1339.

At Winchester Cathedral the design for the new work on the nave, begun by Bishop William Edington, might conceivably have been made at any date after his consecration in May 1346; but all that is certain is that work had been begun before the bishop made his will in 1366, and the old Norman front had to be demolished before the new details attributed to Edington could have been erected. The western porches, which belong to this work, have details closely derived from those of Gloucester and use four-centred arches **19, 21**. The Perpendicular traceries of the aisle windows are hesitant and primitive, but quite sharply distinct from antecedent Decorated and Curvilinear examples. More closely dateable is the south cloister of Westminster Abbey, built from 1349 to 1362, and with tracery of straight-sided reticulations enclosing double-cusped quatrefoils and supported on double-cusped cinquefoil lights **22**. This design is undoubtedly of primitive character and early in the new style, intermediate between Ramsey's cloister at St. Paul's and the Dean's Cloister in Windsor Castle built by John Sponlee in 1353–56 **17**.

One other building of this earliest phase, barely touched by Perpendicular, remains to be mentioned: the parish church of Buckland in Hertfordshire, beside the Old North Road and 36 miles from London. The church was built for Sir Nicholas de Bokeland and finished in 1348, and was apparently designed piecemeal over a period of a few years before that. The east window of the

Fig. 4 Mouldings at Lichfield Cathedral 1337, compared with Clermont-Ferrand *c.* 1311 and London 1332

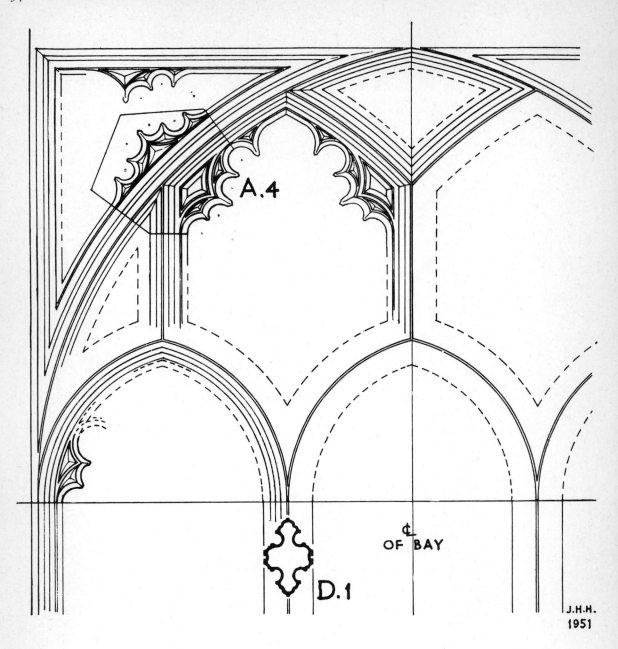

A.4

℄ OF BAY

D.1

J.H.H.
1951

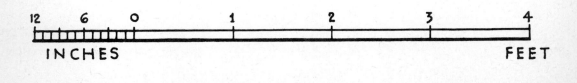

12   6   0   1   2   3   4

INCHES   FEET

chancel is Curvilinear, the side windows two-light with a single reticulation and trefoiled ogee heads. The easternmost window on the north side of the nave presents another version of standard ogee-reticulation; but the next windows, in other respects identical, have changed this to an approximation to the two-light Perpendicular window. The ogee heads have been drawn upwards, giving vertical emphasis, and the sides of the central oculus are so managed as to appear vertical where they are cut by the arch **fig. 6.1**. Nobody could describe Buckland as in any sense a Perpendicular church, yet the transformer's wand had just reached it by the time of its completion.

Fig. 5 Tracery of the cloister at Old St. Paul's 1332–(49), by William Ramsey, reconstructed from the foundations and fragments

CHAPTER TWO

The Grammar of a Style

The successive styles of mediaeval architecture are closely comparable to periods of development within a literary language. Just as a given period produces its typical vocabulary and forms of phrasing, so elements of detail and preferred proportions together make up a fashion of building which can be recognised. The expert may say of a piece of prose or verse that it was composed in the South-West Midlands within the second half of the fourteenth century; and much the same is true of a work of architecture. In both cases the precise conclusion may be upset by the phenomenon of the expatriate, who writes or practises outside his home district; but this does not really invalidate the fundamental truth of the proposition. Again it is true in literature and in architecture that some individual artists have highly personal styles and exercise by force of suggestion and imitation an influence beyond the average. Occasionally a whole epoch may be dominated by one man, in the way that Chaucer controlled and even largely created the English language and Yeveley the English national way of building, in the last generation of the fourteenth century.

Neither Chaucer nor Yeveley started from scratch. Both worked upon pre-existing elements handed down to them; but their treatment of these elements and the resulting synthesis gave a characteristic and highly distinctive form. In the case of Yeveley and the masters associated with him on the royal works between 1360 and 1400, we have a fairly clear idea of the different details normally used and of the ways in which these were assembled to form compositions. In many instances these motives were drawn from a distant past, being parts of the general vocabulary of architecture. In the renewed versions which they assumed in Perpendicular guise the same details might continue on to the very end of Gothic in the sixteenth, seventeenth or even eighteenth century. The four-centred arch, the square label or surround to an arch, the simple clustered pier of four shafts and four hollows, the usual two-light window with a Perpendicular reticulation in the head – these are among the cardinal marks of the style and persisted long after 1485. As individual features all but the last, which is specific to Perpendicular, had a backward extension also. Each had appeared in England before the style itself came into being. They are, in effect, words. Each may be spelt in more than one way, and we get minor variants such as the steeper or flatter forms of the four-centred arch, differing proportions of shaft to hollow, or several forms of cusping to the heads of window-lights.

It has already been emphasized that the guiding principle of the period was unity, or at least the attempt at unification. In every aspect of design there is a kind of single-heartedness, a move together of all the parts, held by an invisible net of exquisite proportions, if not by a real net of panelling. Systems of proportion there had been at all periods, used to generate by geometrical process both plans and elevations, with duly modulated parts and details. Modern architectural education concentrates upon the classical system laid down by Vitruvius and alleged by him to constitute the method of design employed by the Greeks and Romans in the centuries BC. Also in practical use, throughout the Roman Empire and long after its downfall, was the mesh of squares of standard size in feet or multiples of feet such as 25, 50 and 100. Differences in the value of the foot might somewhat enlarge or diminish the actual scale of the resulting building, but the principles of design remained identical.

After 1100, when returning Crusaders brought back direct knowledge of the Near East and of the methods of design used by the Arabs, architectural geometry became considerably more subtle and complex. By means of direct manipulation of a pair of compasses it was learnt how to produce both repetitive patterns, and highly sophisticated proportions. Mathematically these proportions could only be expressed in terms of square and cube roots, but they were attainable in actual practice by a few simple operations performed in the correct order. More than one system, or 'order' of proportion existed, notably those yielded by the equilateral triangle (known as Ad Triangulum) and by the square (Ad Quadratum). The former was extensively used in mediaeval Italy, the latter in northern Europe. Certain episodes in architectural history can be explained as belonging to a battle of systems between different architects. One incident of this kind in England was the sudden appearance around 1300 of the hexagon and other derivatives of the equilateral triangle. In a small way hexagonal planning appeared in some of the Eleanor Crosses of 1291–94, but monumentally not until about 1325, when the outer north porch was added to St. Mary Redcliffe. Later, from the beginning of the new work in the south transept of Gloucester Abbey in 1331, hexagonal (rather than octagonal) bases became a mark of the regional style. There are other hexagonal porches, of the same date or later, at Chipping Norton in Oxfordshire and Ludlow in Shropshire.

The geometry of the hexagon, however, was not limited to the planning of major structures nor even, necessarily, to the use of visible hexagons. Regular hexagons lie concealed in any continuous mesh of equilateral triangles. Likewise, with the radius of any circle, merely stepping around the circumference with a pair of compasses produces a regular hexagon; and this in turn may be divided into six component triangles. Thus there is a close relationship between the use of manifest hexagons at Bristol, Gloucester and elsewhere, and the traceries of spherical triangles – based on an equilateral mesh – used so extensively by Thomas Witney. Witney had made use of this motive in the design of the Bishop's Throne for Exeter in 1312. Witney was at Winchester before he was called to Exeter, and by 1329 had an adult son known as 'de Sparkforde', almost certainly implying birth in the suburb of Sparkford one mile south of Winchester, and site of the famous Hospital of St. Cross. It may be more than a mere coincidence that the new clerestory windows of the nave at St. Cross, inserted soon after 1335, have tracery of hollow-sided hexagons inscribed in circles. This unusual form had occurred at Canterbury and variants were used in the south window at Gloucester.

The significance of this hexagonal detail is not only that in its 'snowflake' form it runs parallel to the crystalline character of early Perpendicular. It was also taken up, as part of the existing Canterbury–Westminster style, into the first phase of Perpendicular itself. As one method of filling the oculus of a two-light window, six-foil cusping was used by Henry Yeveley in the detail of the Neville Screen for Durham Cathedral (1372) **1, 40, 42**, by William Wynford on the south-west tower of Wells Cathedral (*c.* 1385) **20**, and almost at the end of the century in the octagonal lantern of the tower of St. Michael, Coventry, completed in 1395 **3**. At York Minster it appeared in the aisle windows of the Lady Chapel designed in 1361 by William Hoton the younger, but was discarded from the closely imitated choir windows designed about 1390 by Hugh Hedon **6**. The fate of the hexagon is instructive: it formed part of an exotic invasion that could not be fully absorbed because of its geometrical origin in the Ad Triangulum system. Fundamentally the genius of Perpendicular belongs to the North and to the rival system of squares and rectangles, formed in proportions derived from squares.

To become acceptable, the regular hexagon had to be drawn out into an elongated form, set vertically. This was already happening in Ramsey's traceries of 1332 at St. Paul's **fig. 5**, and in the modified versions of 1335 set in the south window at Gloucester **9**. The shape so formed was the basis of one great division of Perpendicular tracery, what Freeman called Alternate; in contradistinction to the Supermullioned, or what is now generally (but imprecisely) called Panelled **fig. 9**. In the latter, vertical lines of mullions not only reach from sill to head, but supermullions rise from the head of each light, splitting the tracery lights into two panels of half-width. We shall return to panelled forms shortly, but must here remark two points concerning the use of the elongated hexagon. It became an integral part of the whole Perpendicular style and indeed survived later, and so is a vital component of the stylistic vocabulary. Secondly, the modification of the regular hexagon to produce this new shape was in progress from the beginning. Apart from the limited number of early survivals of the cusped regular hexagon, the hexagonal form was disguised in one of two ways. Either it was cusped, or as in Ramsey's and other early works, double-cusped at the head only, thus emphasizing the vertical sides; or the opening pierced between the mesh of tracery-bars was a quatrefoil. This again was an earlier element derived from Flowing and Reticulated patterns. Once the hexagon had been substantially pulled upwards, the quatrefoil could be broken apart into an upper and a lower half, each amounting to trefoil cusping: at the lower end, of course inverted. Almost always this lower, inverted, cusping was of ogee form, accommodated to the curve of the arched heads below, and so adding to the impression of verticality in the window.

The surviving fragments of Ramsey's work at St. Paul's, together with the foundations uncovered by Penrose in 1878 and Hollar's views, show that the first known Perpendicular was of Alternate type **fig. 5**. Hollar's large view might be thought to indicate split or panel-tracery in the cloister, but he was certainly mistaken in dividing each bay into only two lights instead of three. In the chapter-house he shows tracery of Perpendicular (i.e. straight-sided) reticulations, possibly meant for regular hexagons, though drawn as at least slightly verticalized. In the background is seen one of the five-light Gothic windows inserted in the Norman nave aisles, and similar windows are shown throughout the south aisle in Hollar's antiquarian plate showing the cathedral as it was before the loss of its spire. These nave windows appear to have been inserted in or about 1300, and if so afford a metropolitan origin for the untraceried mullioned windows of Ottery St. Mary and for the many later examples of this simple type.

The untraceried mullioned window has a long pedigree, being the adaptation to the bar-tracery period of the earlier sets of graduated or stepped lancets. Cusping was generally introduced at the heads of the lights. In such late examples as Ottery the effect given resembles that of a traceried window, and it is not surprising that at an early stage its vertical lines should have been incorporated into emergent Perpendicular. We have to remember, too, the long tradition of vertical shafting and ribs both in France and in England. Setting aside the unique development of Perpendicular tracery and its specific detail, the movement towards unity was producing grilles of upright ribs, either forming free-standing transparencies or blind panelling. This is particularly marked in Ramsey's chapter-house of St. Paul's **10**. Hollar's view shows that the building had an open undercroft: between each pair of buttresses was a four-centred arch within a square frame, the spandrels being filled with narrow vertical panelling. Above this was a horizontal band of quatrefoils framed between vertical ribs. Every second rib was carried up to the springing of the main windows above, forming beneath the sill of the window four blind panels each provided with a bracket and canopy for statuary. In principle this provides the bay-design for the Perpendicular screenwork at Gloucester **2**: four-centred arch at the base, band of quatrefoils two to a panel, four panels to the bay, and alternate tracery.

The adaptation of the supermullioned design to tracery came later. It was foreshadowed in the great east window at Gloucester **203,** where the canted plan demands that the central section be separated from the lateral lights by two grand mullions. Within the central window of six lights, however, these are again grouped into twos by two intermediate mullions. In every separate part of the window the tracery is alternate, but the main reticulations at the heads of the lateral lights are divided by a supermullion carrying a smaller sub-reticulation beneath the subordinate arch. This supermullion with the arcs branching from it is a particular kind of Divergent or Y-tracery, and this in turn was to become one of the most important features of later traceries. At Gloucester the detail is subservient to a reticulation borne upon it, but tracery of the 'supermullion Y' type goes back to a date before the start of Perpendicular.

The main windows of the Carnary Chapel at Norwich, dateable to the ten years 1316–25, and designed by John Ramsey the father or uncle of the St. Paul's master, give so deceptive an impression of being Perpendicular that they are actually described as 'Perp' by Pevsner. They are of three lights, with cinquefoil cusping, and upon the archlets stand two stilted spherical triangles. The central stilt, branching into a Y filled with a double-cusped dagger, is supported by slender supermullion Ys at the base of the spherical triangles, which are cinquefoiled above and ogee-trefoiled below in each Y. Although at a little distance the windows look like Perpendicular work of a century later, their real date is confirmed by their mouldings, which are in recessed orders, and by the fact that the stilts of the spherical triangles are not carried up to cut the main arch. Among the earliest strictly Perpendicular versions of this pattern are the York Minster aisle windows of 1361, already mentioned, but they combine with the Y-tracery true reticulations of alternate type in the head.

The case of the two-light window with a Y in the head instead of a foiled reticulation deserves special study. Though certainly later than the very first, reticulated, Perpendicular tracery, it may not have been so very much later. Blind tracery of analogous form occurs above the west doorway of Edington church, Wiltshire, which may well have been designed by about 1365. By the 1380s the form was widespread and a characteristic of the Court style: used for the hall of Winchester College by William Wynford in 1387 **fig. 6.6**, and probably by him still earlier at Yeovil church in Somerset, under construction in 1382 **5**. In the south aisle of South Benfleet church, Essex, it occurs in what may be work of 1384–86, perhaps detailed by Henry Yeveley for Westminster Abbey. Later it was to become one of the principal standard details for the rest of the period, a hallmark of Perpendicular. There is at least one example that may be a good deal earlier than any of those named. This is at Sandon in Hertfordshire, where the works of the middle of the fourteenth century deserve particular attention **fig. 6.2, 6.3**.

The interest of Sandon derives in part from the fact that church and manor had belonged to the dean and chapter of St. Paul's Cathedral since before the Norman Conquest. They also owned the great tithes, valued in 1291 at 22 marks, while the vicar was supported by small tithes and offerings coming to less than ten marks. What is more, the muniments of St. Paul's preserve a contract made on 11 July 1348 for the complete rebuilding of the chancel. This has been printed twice, by the late Dr. Rose Graham and by the late Dr. L. F. Salzman, each having been able to make out some words illegible to the other. Notwithstanding the badly stained condition of the document, none of the essential matter is lost. Two of the canons, Masters Alan de Hothom and John de Barnet, visited Sandon to seal the agreement, which was with a local mason, Thomas Rikelyng of Barkway, four miles to the east. Buckland, whose church was completed in this year as already mentioned, lies on the main road half way between Sandon and Barkway. It may be that the new work at Buckland at the expense of the local landowner inspired the chapter to rebuild their chancel at Sandon, described as far back as 1297 as very dark and in need of repair. Rikelyng was to take down the old chancel to the foundations and upon them

2 Gloucester Cathedral: presbytery screenwork (1337–67), probably based on designs by William Ramsey

3

4

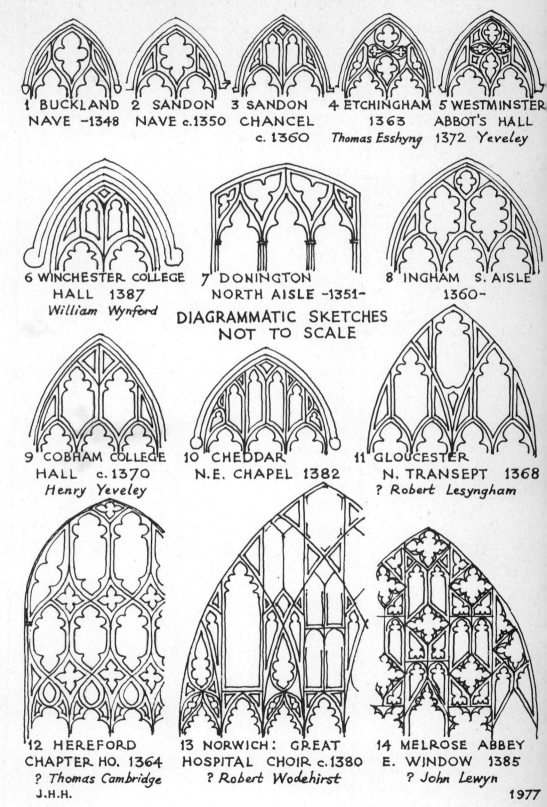

1 BUCKLAND NAVE –1348

2 SANDON NAVE c.1350

3 SANDON CHANCEL c.1360

4 ETCHINGHAM 1363 *Thomas Esshyng*

5 WESTMINSTER ABBOT'S HALL 1372 *Yeveley*

6 WINCHESTER COLLEGE HALL 1387 *William Wynford*

7 DONINGTON NORTH AISLE –1351–

8 INGHAM S. AISLE 1360–

DIAGRAMMATIC SKETCHES NOT TO SCALE

9 COBHAM COLLEGE HALL c.1370 *Henry Yeveley*

10 CHEDDAR N.E. CHAPEL 1382

11 GLOUCESTER N. TRANSEPT 1368 *? Robert Lesyngham*

12 HEREFORD CHAPTER HO. 1364 *? Thomas Cambridge* J.H.H.

13 NORWICH: GREAT HOSPITAL CHOIR c.1380 *? Robert Wodehirst*

14 MELROSE ABBEY E. WINDOW 1385 *? John Lewyn*

1977

3 Coventry: St. Michael's steeple 1373–95, possibly by Robert Skillyngton; spire 1395–1433

4 Rotherham Church, tower 1409–

Fig. 6 Examples of Early Perpendicular tracery

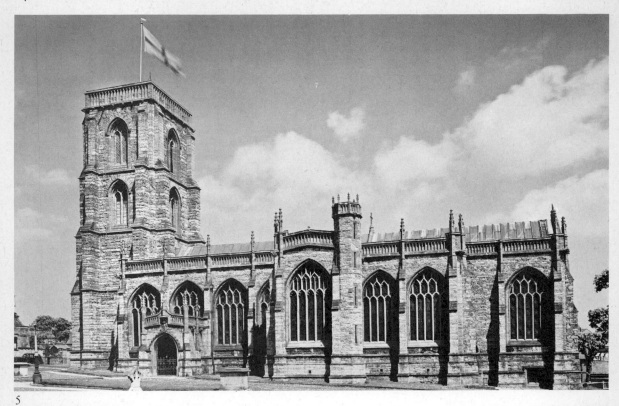

5

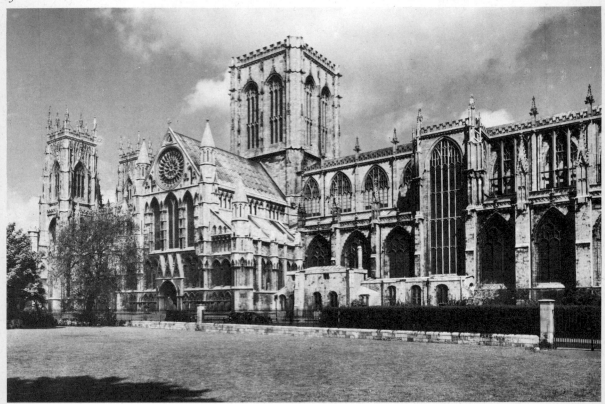

6

build new walls 17 feet high with the east gable of an appropriate height. In this he was to make a window of three lights and in each side wall two windows of similar form but of two lights. There were to be two angle buttresses and a single buttress on each side, with a doorway on the south side. The skews of the buttresses were to be of Barnack stone, and the other masonry 'of good white stone'. On the day before sealing Rikelyng had taken oath before the vicar, Martin de Hoxton, to abide by the contract. He was to have all the material of the old chancel, and 20 marks paid by instalments as the work went ahead, less than one year's yield of tithes.

Several difficulties arise in applying the terms of the record to the actual building. It is to be noticed that the date was only about a month before the Black Death reached England, and less than a year before the heaviest mortality. All the same, there are signs internally that Rikelyng did indeed begin to build. He probably died within the year, and there must have been a period without a chancel. Possibly for this reason the parishioners began work on the nave, which has early Perpendicular two-light windows, with trefoil-headed lights and a hexagonal reticulation; the impression given is of a date not long after 1350 **fig. 6.2**. When work was resumed on the chancel the height of the walls was reduced by some four feet and the south door omitted. The east window is a nineteenth-century restoration, but the four side windows are of two lights and made of good white stone as specified. The buttresses too agree with the plan laid down. While it is impossible to give the windows a precise date, their trefoiled lights look early, and the triangular spandrels in the head are delicately cusped so as to suggest the period of Curvilinear overlap, probably before 1365.

We cannot connect what was actually done at Sandon either with the precise date 1348, or with the new style in which William Ramsey was then working for the chapter of St. Paul's. But both the nave and chancel show by their two distinct forms of early Perpendicular tracery the extension of the style to a rural parish within a generation or so of the start. It is necessary to stress the importance of such individual links as the ownership of Sandon by St. Paul's. All over the country were manors, churches or chantry chapels belonging to the Crown, to members of the courtly nobility, to the greater monasteries, to the bishops or to cathedral chapters. Although the same patron, individual or corporate, might employ many different artists, it is common experience that, far more often, a single architect or painter of distinction is set to carry out many jobs for the same client and for his friends. Personal recommendation counts for a great deal, and still more when the advice comes from those of high rank.

Besides the effect of direct recommendation there is the force of emulation. Work of a special kind, particularly in a new and fashionable style, is productive of imitations. There is, therefore, no difficulty in accounting for the spread of Perpendicular as a general phenomenon. Its regional differentiation is similarly explained, partly as the result of varying local traditions surviving from an earlier period, but also because of the regional congresses of masters and particular consultations of local architects called in to give advice. Variation from the personal norm of design was also conditioned by the amount of

5 Yeovil Church from south, −1382−, probably by William Wynford. Note buttresses and panelled parapets

6 York Minster: Lady Chapel (*right*), aisles 1361–68, by William Hoton junior; clerestory 1369–72, by Robert Patrington; choir (*centre*) 1385–1400, by Hugh Hedon; central tower *c.* 1415–72, by William Colchester and John Porter

delegation at a given job. The growth of great consultative practices during the fourteenth century inevitably implied dependence upon the resource of the subordinate in charge on the site. This might be a personal assistant sent for the purpose, but was usually the warden of the masons. The warden, if at times a mere foreman, was certainly a man of standing: his professional conduct was laid down in the Eighth Point of the Constitutions of Masonry, 'that he be true mean between his master and his fellows and that he be busy in the absence of his master to the honour of his master and profit to the lord that he serveth.'

As with all arts at all periods and places, the quality of Perpendicular buildings as aesthetic designs varies greatly. Any one artist produces works of differing value, and whereas an outstanding architect may create several masterpieces, even a minor practitioner occasionally achieves one in the course of a lifetime of relative mediocrity. The general rule may be that masterpieces are recognised and exert an influence proportionate to their deserts. Yet there is also the case of the flower born to blush unseen, whose special virtues are not perpetuated, and which may go for centuries more or less unrecognised. The unusual and even the freakish have their own values, as well as those notable but more balanced works which take their place in the main stream and form parts of the accepted chain of development. Success does not solely consist in self-perpetuation, but rather in quality of impact.

The impact of a building depends far less on the elements of which it is made up – walls, windows, piers, arches, vaults or roofs – than upon the way they are handled. Scale, in relation to human stature and so to eye-level, is of the utmost importance. Although a very small building may show the most exquisite design and adjustment of parts, it is bound to lack the force and dominance of a great hall or mighty tower. On the other hand, mere size cannot make up for imperfect proportions or crude detail. The exigencies of each particular case, largely economic, exert an outside control upon what the artist is able to do. At worst, his masterpiece may remain for ever unfinished, or wait so long for completion that its later parts are out of harmony with the first. Even at best the personal whims of members of the building committee, or merely shortage of funds, may deny to the architect some of his most cherished dream-children. As spectators we have to accept each work upon its merits and see it as the outcome of an experiment in what is possible.

The limiting factors upon English architecture in the Perpendicular period have had much to do with its dubious reputation. Overshadowed in its opening phase by the inordinate disaster of the Black Death, the style had to survive extraordinary financial inflation, then political unrest at times developing into full-scale civil war, and many resulting changes of patronage due to death or disgrace. The outcome amounts in many cases to fragmentation: either of design or of execution, or both. If completion were indefinitely delayed, the original architect would die, and his drawings and details might or might not be followed later. Delay was so common that even a single build such as a nave or a tower, finished according to the original intentions, is the exception rather than the rule. Time has taken its toll even of what was completed and has discriminated against the more important rather than the less significant. Great size implies costly upkeep, and this factor alone has militated against preservation. Taking all these adverse conditions into account, we have largely to view Perpendicular as a series of small specimens or even fragments.

The better to do this we must pass in review, besides the general system or grammar of Perpendicular, the main items in the vocabulary of the style. In the plan of buildings there was one great advance: the adoption of the organised quadrangle as a multi-purpose system. At earlier periods the design of houses and castles, colleges and hospitals, had been serial and additive. It was the rare exception to produce at the start a thought-out scheme for the finished product. Although the regular and concentric planning of Edward I's great castles in Wales foreshadowed Perpendicular treatment, it was due to a foreign master, James of St. George from Savoy, and was altogether exceptional. Only after 1350 was there a general tendency towards regular and unified plans; and then it rapidly swept the country. From the tiny quadrangle of Yeveley's college at Cobham in Kent to his enormous courtyard of the London Charterhouse, the whole range of planning was affected more or less simultaneously, about 1370. Even this can- be derived from the very earliest of Perpendicular works, Ramsey's cloister at Old St. Paul's and Sponlee's Dean's Cloister at Windsor, together with the regular blocks of royal apartments built there from 1358.

This major change in plan-forms, or rather from non-planning to fully rationalised planning, affected virtually all forms of architecture except churches. No major change in liturgy required an altered plan, though the increased demand for chantry chapels led to the building of double aisles, or rather of an outer range of chapels beyond an aisle. Churches built, or totally rebuilt, on clear sites were rarely provided with a central tower, and western towers became the rule. Often, as at Wells St. Cuthbert, a new western tower was built and, after a shorter or longer interval, an earlier crossing tower was demolished. This was a change in the interests of internal unity, visual and also liturgical. Though the demand for preaching space, tending to reflect that provided in the friars' churches, long preceded the advent of Perpendicular, it was another factor tending in the same direction and adopted in the formulation of the new style.

The desire for greater physical illumination, perhaps vaguely connected with the teachings of Wycliffe and the movement towards open rather than obscurantist religion, tended towards the production of what has been called the glasshouse-church. Windows were enlarged to reach their practical limits, stretching from buttress to buttress and eliminating wall-space. Their verticality of effect was emphasized, not only by Perpendicular detail and other tricks of design, but by actual height, generally made possible by ranges of transoms to lend support and to bind the mullions and jambs together visually. More light was given to the interior of aisled churches by adding clerestories to existing low naves, or incorporating them in new designs. Where the nave notably overtopped the chancel, the opportunity was taken to place an eastern nave window in the gable. The advance in engineering skill and in precision of stonecutting enabled supports to be still more slender than they had been. Not only were the outer walls pared down to a minimum to give window-space, but piers were reduced in cross-section. The appearance of slim verticality was enhanced by shafting carved in the solid pier and often continuous with the arch mouldings. This form of continuity, though a feature of the English western and south-western tradition ever since the later twelfth century, took on a new life.

Not only the tendency towards continuous mouldings, but the demand for vertical emphasis, reduced the importance of the capital. Even when not eliminated it was relatively perfunctory. Ranges of caps as an opportunity for carvings to display the prowess of the sculptor were replaced by smoothly turned concave bells such as those of the early Perpendicular at Gloucester. In windows, whereas small capitals had often been used at springing level, on mullions as well as jambs, continuous moulding or chamfering became universal. On the other hand, the base took on a fresh importance, due very largely to practical reasons. Whereas it had formerly been the universal practice to stand in church, apart from the minority of aged and infirm, the increase of preaching and consequently of longer services necessitated the provision of seating. To show above the general level of seats, instead of above the floor, bases had to be raised and provided with sub-bases or plinths. Aesthetically the taller bases could be made to lead the eye upwards into the shafting and so still more increase the apparent height of the building.

In arches and in vaults variety reigned. There was no longer a restrained choice between simple two-centred arches struck from closer or wider centres. The introduction of the four-centred and ogee arches, together with variants

Fig. 7 Diagram of Arch-forms, two-centred and four-centred

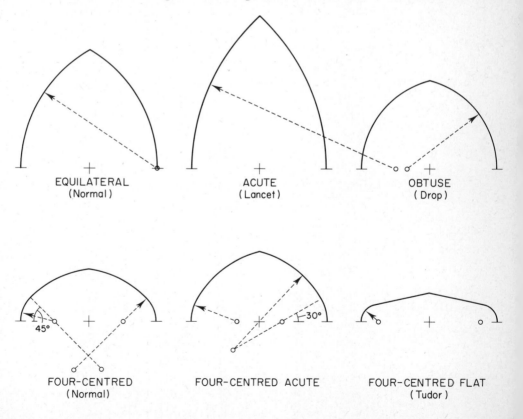

EQUILATERAL
(Normal)

ACUTE
(Lancet)

OBTUSE
(Drop)

45°

FOUR-CENTRED
(Normal)

30°

FOUR-CENTRED ACUTE

FOUR-CENTRED FLAT
(Tudor)

such as the three-centred and the segmental-pointed, greatly widened the scope for effects of fenestration. Besides this there was a wide latitude of proportions even in two-centred arches. Still more, the extensive use of square-headed windows, and of square and other frameworks surrounding windows, offered possibilities which must at the time have seemed unconventional in the extreme. The ranges of windows in aisle and clerestory might be identical, or similar in form but distinct in tracery; or introduce diversity now by placing four-centred clerestory windows above two-centred lighting in the side aisles, or the other way round **70**. Doorways too admitted of great variety, though the ruling form was contained within a square labelled surround and provided with enriched or armorial spandrels. Niches and canopies, designed as points of emphasis on towers, porches, or elsewhere, vary almost infinitely according to the fancy of the designer. Here too there were certain ruling types promulgated from the Court, but adapted to the usage of different regions.

Independently of the shapes of arches, tracery had its own variations, of which something has already been said **fig. 9**. There was first of all the distinction between Alternate tracery and Mullioned (Supermullioned or Panelled); and in the latter there was the refined distinction insisted upon by Freeman: that supermullioned tracery had half-width panels divided by (super)mullions rising from the head of each arched light; whereas in the panelled form the lights were carried at their full width up to the arch, between the main mullions only. Panelled tracery is commonly, as Freeman objected, unsightly; and it was comparatively little used. Its name has in modern times

Fig. 8 Diagram of Arch-forms, segmental, ogee and three-centred

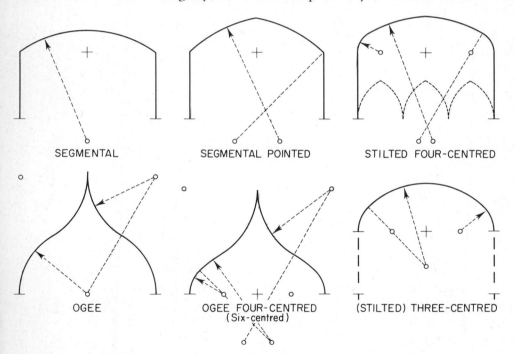

SEGMENTAL   SEGMENTAL POINTED   STILTED FOUR-CENTRED

OGEE   OGEE FOUR-CENTRED (Six-centred)   (STILTED) THREE-CENTRED

been largely applied to the supermullioned category. It should be noted that, whereas the term *mullion* is applied to a vertical dividing member rising from sill to springing, or to the main arch, or to any point between; *supermullion* means primarily a mullion rising from the head of an arched light; but also a diminished mullion continuing, above springing level, in the same vertical line as a principal mullion.

All types of traceried windows have a series of arched heads or *archlets* to the lights in the lower part of the window. Generally, but not always, the springings of these archlets are on one level, and that is normally the same as the springing of the main arch of the window. After the introduction of the four-centred arch, the smaller arcs at the haunches were at first large enough to permit of archlets beneath them, allowing space for tracery above them and below the relatively steep upper part of the arch, of large radius. Later, with the lowering of the upper arcs, no adequate space for tracery was left, and the springing of the archlets was dropped some distance below the main springing. This produced a *stilted* four-centred main arch, and *drop*-tracery. The shallow band of tracery possible between the springing and head of a flattened four-centred arch, a type mostly used at a late date after 1485, has been described by Professor R. H. C. Davis as *squash*-tracery. Other useful terms, used by Dr. Eileen Roberts to differentiate between the two kinds of four-centred drop-tracery commonly found in Hertfordshire and some neighbouring areas, are *strong vertical* and *top-panelled*. The strong vertical window has main mullions carried up at their full width to the arch, whereas in the top-panelled window, narrower supermullions stand on the main mullions between the archlets, continuing the line to the head but not continuing the main division into lights.

Comparatively little variation is possible in the design of simple windows of two lights. As we have already seen, the first Perpendicular type has a single straight-sided reticulation, or *oculus*, and this may be filled with six-foil cusping in some early examples, occasionally with the upper part of a spherical triangle treated as a trefoiled head, commonly with a quatrefoil. A notable alternative, carried on from the Decorated period, is the insertion into the head of a four-petalled foliation containing *daggers*, set either cardinally or ordinally, that is to say with the tracery ribs forming a cross or an X. The type with a cross, that is to say with the daggers set X-wise, was used by the Ramseys in pre-Perpendicular times in the south cloister at Norwich and in the choir triforium at Ely. The other main form of the two-light Perpendicular window was, as we have seen, that with a pair of panels formed by a Y-supermullion in place of the oculus.

The scope for variation in design becomes much greater in windows of three or more lights. The primary, alternate, form consists of straight-sided reticulations filled with cusping or foliation of different kinds. Secondly, the oculus may be split by a supermullion as in the two-light window, and there may be an *eyelet* at the head, usually filled with a simple quatrefoil. The word eyelet is here used to imply a relatively small central piercing, in contradistinction to the *oculus* or larger opening. Instead of this the central Y may carry a reduced oculus, forming a miniature two-light within the major reticulation. Such tracery, having one reticulation within another, is called *subreticulated* **Map VII**. Very rarely the supermullion may be carried up to the apex of the window, splitting it completely into two; such splitting, either of the main arch or a subordinate tracery light, is I-split, and is a less common variant of the usual Y-tracery.

Any alternate window of four or more lights, or any supermullioned of three or more, may be divided by subarcuation, and is described as *subarcuated*. Subordinate arches are formed in the tracery, beneath the main arch but spanning one or more lights (in alternate tracery, two or more), above the archlets of the main lights. The separate subdivisions of the window may then be treated as independent traceries, as if they were windows in their own right; or with greater subtlety, united into a single composition by *through reticulation* **Map VIII**, where supermullions are carried up through the subordinate arches to the head of the window. In this case too there may be a single oculus, open or foliated, or else split panels. In subarcuated windows the subordinate tracery arches may cut one another, as with pre-Perpendicular intersecting tracery, and in this case the window may be defined as *subarcuated intersecting* **Map IX**.

One other important component of Perpendicular tracery remains to be mentioned: the *supertransom* **Map V**. Just as a transom is a horizontal masonry member carried across the window at right-angles to the mullions and below springing level, so is a supertransom a similar horizontal bar across one or more lights, or the whole window, above the springing. Strictly speaking, the term *rectilinear* should be reserved for those Perpendicular windows which have supertransoms and are thus divided horizontally as well as vertically. It is, of course, unusual for tracery to consist merely of a rectangular mesh of such divisions. Supertransoms may be combined with subarcuation, and very often

Fig. 9 Diagram of types of Tracery, with nomenclature

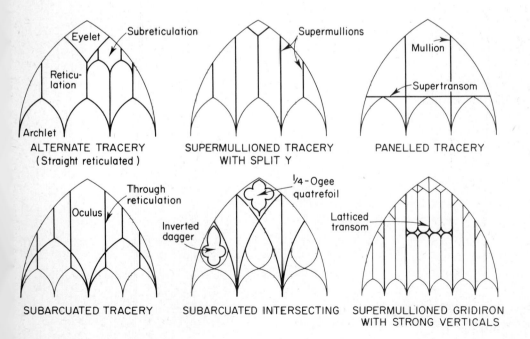

Eyelet Subreticulation

Reticu-lation

Archlet

ALTERNATE TRACERY
(Straight reticulated)

Supermullions

SUPERMULLIONED TRACERY
WITH SPLIT Y

Mullion

Supertransom

PANELLED TRACERY

Oculus Through reticulation

SUBARCUATED TRACERY

¼-Ogee quatrefoil

Inverted dagger

SUBARCUATED INTERSECTING

Latticed transom

SUPERMULLIONED GRIDIRON
WITH STRONG VERTICALS

with the intersecting variety. They are common in traceries of the supermullioned type, but relatively rare in alternate designs. Among strictly dateable examples the proportions are about eight to one in favour of the combination of supertransoms with supermullioned tracery.

Now this statistic is not simply a matter of aesthetics: it is directly connected with geographical distribution. For in most counties of England there is a marked predominance either of alternate or of supermullioned forms. The eastern half of the country, from Kent and Surrey north to Yorkshire, and as far west as Oxford, has a strong leaning to the supermullioned forms; the south-west and west as markedly favour the alternate. This is surprising for two main reasons. The first is that, before the invention of Perpendicular, Decorated reticulation had a wide distribution and was strongly represented in eastern England, the east Midlands and Yorkshire. It might have been expected that the straight-sided (Alternate) version of reticulation would similarly have a general rather than a one-sided distribution. Secondly, the earliest Perpendicular was alternate, with a clear start of a generation over its rival. It seems evident that the sheer effect of verticality, the leading feature of the style, had most appeal in London and Court circles at Westminster, but was unable to overweigh south-western regional conservatism.

The predominance of supertransoms, therefore, is also in the eastern half of England, and subarcuated intersecting tracery is all but exclusively a phenomenon of north of the Thames and east of Oxford and the lower Trent valley. It is commonest in East Anglia, Lincolnshire and east Yorkshire. Another feature which has a somewhat distinctive topographical scatter is the counterpart of the supertransom formed by horizontal bands of crossed ogees linking mullion to mullion. This lattice, or lazytongs, or X-transom is not very common, and again considering only dateable examples, is most strongly represented in Suffolk, Oxford and Oxfordshire, and Gloucestershire, with rare instances elsewhere and mostly to the south **Map VI**. Looking back over regional distribution of special features, there is one marked negative characteristic to put beside the positive ones: very little that is distinctive is peculiar to the north Midland counties. It is as though there were no definite school of Perpendicular within this area, in contradistinction to the notable regional traditions found elsewhere, in Yorkshire, Lincolnshire, East Anglia, the south and south-west Midlands, and the South-West. One main reason for this is undoubtedly the relative lack of good building stone as the north-western edge of the oolite belt is left behind. Similarly the relative lack of distinction in the local buildings of Middlesex, Essex and Surrey can be traced to their lack of outstanding quarries.

Not much need here be said of Perpendicular vaults. They are rather uncommon except for those of small scale over porches and in towers. The one outstanding development of the period was the creation of the fan-vault. Like Perpendicular itself, the fan-vault is a peculiarity of England, though it never achieved a national extension. In its earlier phase, before 1485, it was centred upon a small region in the West around Hereford, Tewkesbury and Gloucester. As a mark of personal style it travelled with individual masters called from this

7 Westminster Hall: interior looking south 1394–1400, by Henry Yeveley; timber roof by Hugh Herland

7

area to work elsewhere, with Robert Lesyngham to Exeter, for instance **32**. A very beautiful counterpart in timber, approximately fanlike, was designed by the King's carpenter Hugh Herland for Winchester College Chapel by 1390 **89**, but it was not until a century later that the form seems to have aroused keen interest outside the district of its birth. It may well be that its tendency towards suppression of the structural rib, though in the interests of unity, was felt to be inimical to the nervous, linear quality inherent in most English art.

There remains the open timber roof, one of the most characteristic of all the achievements of the time. The development of the hammer-beam truss, a technological advance of the first importance, was roughly contemporary with the onset of Perpendicular style. The truly great roofs, constructionally and aesthetically, belong almost exclusively to the period as strictly defined. Mastery of structural purpose was, in fact, beginning to break down before 1485. The building of structural shams such as the 'false hammer-beam truss', and curiously inept versions such as the roof of the great hall at Eltham Palace (1475–80) marked a weakening at the higher levels of the carpenter's craft **189**. This may well have been due to the increasing predominance of the master mason ever since the opening of the fourteenth century. There is no need, however, to apologise for the noble and magnificent works which had gone before. On the brink of or during the extension of the Perpendicular style we can boast of a number of the most remarkable timber constructions of history: the lantern at Ely, the Guildhall roofs of London and York **110**, that of Crosby Hall **188**, and most splendid of all – in England or anywhere else – that over the King's Great Hall at Westminster **7**, Hugh Herland's masterpiece.

CHAPTER THREE

The First Perpendicular

1330–1360

The bare chronological outline of the earliest phase of Perpendicular has already been given. It remains to take stock of English architecture at the opening of the period, and to discuss those major works which had been designed within the first generation, roughly the thirty years from 1330 to 1360. As we shall see, it was in the latter year that Henry Yeveley became disposer of the works of Edward III at Westminster and the Tower of London. The advent of Yeveley as principal architect under the Crown, even though his responsibility was not made nation-wide until 1378, marks the beginning of orthodox consolidation. Before then the new style had begun to formulate its grammatical structure and to re-spell the old vocabulary, but can hardly be said to have had an existence independent of that of the regional varieties of Curvilinear Decorated. In use in London, at Westminster and Windsor, and a hundred miles away to the west at Gloucester, its quality was as yet tentative.

This uncertainty, a vacillation between the character of old and new, is naturally marked in the earliest work of all, William Ramsey's chapter-house and cloister at Old St. Paul's 10. The tracery and some other details, such as the four-centred arches surmounted by vertical panelling, were already what was to become expected in buildings of the future, but the total effect is unusual rather than revolutionary. The two-storeyed cloister was a fresh departure and demanded the marked verticality of the central chapter-house. The eight great buttresses, each with three ranges of pinnacles recessed behind each other, gave the impression of a crown surrounding the casket within. The windows took up the whole of the space between the buttresses and, as has already been described, were an adaptation of pre-existing reticulated and panelled patterns. Above each window was a tall gablet enclosing a five-foiled circle and with patterned spandrels. It can hardly be doubted that the truncation of the fourth and final stage of the buttresses, and omission of any crowning member from these crocketed gablets, was unintentional. Surely this was what remained to be done when Ramsey died on 3 June 1349. The chapter-house was structurally complete and usable, within its double cloister; the pestilence stopped the work and later it can hardly have seemed worthwhile to build new scaffolds.

This unachieved aspect, as seen in Hollar's and Wyck's drawings, probably had an unintended psychological effect. Here was the predecessor of the cut-off towers of Perpendicular England, devoid of the once universal spires that crowned all the steeples of Europe. So, prematurely cut short by the great plague, the square panelled pillars push bluntly skywards, symbols of human effort. Thus far and no farther were they permitted to go. Ten or twenty years

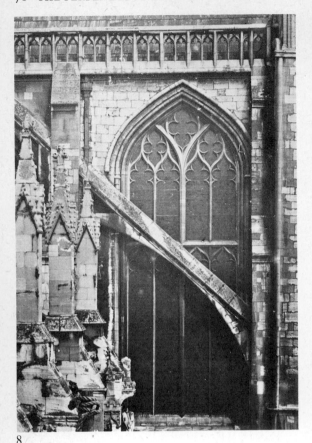

8

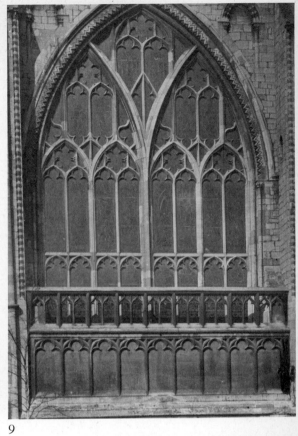

9

10

later the masters of a new generation freshly come to London, Yeveley among them, saw and studied the unfinished work. We know that Yeveley had the best of opportunities for viewing St. Paul's, since he leased from the chapter workshops for the monumental trade. The new cloisters and chapter-house, the most modern addition to the greatest cathedral in the country – indeed, a far bigger church than Old St. Peter's in Rome itself – were there for close study, and as inspiration. Three centuries later the Convocation House, as it had become, was to be the nerve-centre of another architect's operations and place of exhibition for his great model of a new St. Paul's. Patched up to form an office, Ramsey's chapter-house thus survived the Great Fire of London for nearly a quarter-century.

Like the chapters of York and Southwell before it, that of St. Paul's had no central pier, but offered a free and unencumbered dome. Though founded upon these still earlier exemplars, there is no doubt that Ramsey's design owed something to the more recent octagon at the heart of Ely Cathedral, still unfinished when the London work began. At Ely the masonry of the octagon was started late in 1322 and was ready for the timbers of the vault six years later. The vault took another six years to build, the lantern on top of that another six, until 1340. The most experienced carpenter in the country, William Hurley, was in charge at Ely and journeyed thither, one might say commuted, from London. Members of Ramsey's own family too were concerned in the work, and the relationship between London and Ely was evidently close.

It was close in another respect also, for in spite of the diversion of funds to the rebuilding necessitated by the fall of the Norman crossing tower, the works of the Lady Chapel continued alongside. This is the nearest surviving parallel to St. Stephen's Chapel at Westminster, and, though not yet Perpendicular, foretells the architecture of unity and light. As at St. Stephen's and at St. Paul's, giant windows take up most of the space, and the walls are reduced to a filigree panelling. This panelling is itself of interest to us, in that by what may well have been an accidental interpenetration, two series of wall ribs and canopies give the illusion of Perpendicular traceries. The dates of the Ely Lady Chapel are very precisely recorded: work began on Monday, 16 March 1321, and the formal laying of the first stone took place on 15 August. The structure was evidently complete and weathertight by June 1345, when Bishop Simon de Montacute was buried before the altar. In so far as Ely provided a precedent for Ramsey, it was there. The Lady Chapel also, in the longer term, provided the model for the great collegiate chapels including that of King's College, Cambridge.

The glasshouse-chapel seemed, in its extreme simplicity, to be the perfect solution to an architecture of light, that is of physical illumination casting into the church beams symbolically equivalent to the Heavenly Light itself. For purely collegiate services, when supplied with stallwork, it was entirely adequate, but it did not cater for monastic processions. Nor, in terms of mere snob value, did it give the grandiose impression of an aisled sanctuary, surrounded by the mysterious outer space of ambulatory and chapels. The question was, how to make the best of both worlds? In the major monastic churches, which included most of the English cathedrals, the single-cell

8 Gloucester Cathedral: south transept, side window 1331–36

9 Gloucester Cathedral: south window c. 1335–36, probably by William Ramsey

10 London: Old St. Paul's Cathedral, chapter-house and cloister from south, 1332–49, by William Ramsey

solution was not deemed acceptable. Nor, since enormous sums had been invested in the Gothic fabrics or still earlier Norman ones, was it practical to think in terms of rebuilding. It is this background, of a major problem to be solved both in structural and in aesthetic terms, that gives to the case of Gloucester its particular importance.

The abbey church at Gloucester was only turned into a cathedral by Henry VIII in 1541. It did not even share with Worcester, as Coventry did with Lichfield and Bath with Wells, in the title of the diocese. On the other hand, its mitred abbot – one of 27 – sat in the House of Lords along with the 17 bishops. Gloucester was always, as it had been since the Norman church was begun in 1089, one of the greatest ecclesiastical buildings of the realm. Gloucester, with its royal castle, was one of the places in the provinces where the Royal Household was wont to stay, and the King to wear his crown. Parliaments were held within the monastic buildings. Well before the fourteenth century the church contained the tomb of the royal prisoner, Robert Duke of Normandy. By the stroke of ironic fate, one of Edward II's few loyal friends was Abbot John Thokey who ruled from 1306 to 1329. Dining with the abbot on one occasion, the king asked whether his own portrait was to be added to the series of sovereigns painted in the hall. Thokey replied that he intended that *his* picture should be in a more honourable position.

After the king's murder in September 1327 his body was refused burial at the monasteries of Bristol, Kingswood and Malmesbury, for fear of Queen Isabella and her paramour Mortimer. Thokey, however, received the corpse and boldly gave it burial with due honour. He certainly risked his own liberty, perhaps his life, and it is an unjustifiable modern cynicism that suggests that he had the ulterior motive of acquiring the relics of a royal martyr for the financial betterment of his house. Popular revulsion from the appalling crime did, however, bring in immense sums in offerings within the next few years and made possible the extensive building programme which was to continue for a century and a half. To an unusual degree this long programme was determined by the character of designs made at an early stage yet not at the very start. Although there was remarkable continuity of detail and appearance under successive masters, there are at the beginning several stages of conflicting style to be disentangled.

Before the king's death there had already been one work of Gothic reconstruction. Rather surprisingly, this was the south aisle of the nave, where the Norman wall may have been overturned by unbalanced thrusts from the vaulting. The new aisle was built between 1318 and Thokey's retirement from the abbacy in 1329, and was in the western style, encrusted with ballflower. Bowtells treated as slender shafts, with their own capitals and hexagonal miniature bases, are the only detail that looks forward towards the Perpendicular. In every other respect this work – important because of its known date – is unrelated to London developments and also independent of the unusual group of styles being exploited at Bristol less than 35 miles away. Whatever may have been the later relationship between the works at Gloucester and those executed in the great churches of Bristol, there had clearly been no relevant contact down to the time of Edward II's deposition and death in 1327.

The master of the south aisle may have been brought from Hereford or somewhere else within the region of most intense addiction to ballflower. For the conversion of the south transept a very different architect came from elsewhere. The work is made up of several disparate parts: the side windows, the wall panelling, the south window, the vault. As an innovatory treatment the design is of great interest, but the aesthetic impression is disappointing. Internally a panelled screen covers the Norman structure, pierced by the four-centred side windows **8** and the very large south window **9**, all transomed but with differing forms of decorative cinquefoiled archlets beneath the transoms. It is evident that the tracery of the south window, including its transom, was designed separately from the rest, and by a master with personal experience of the ruling Canterbury style practised at Westminster and with knowledge of Ramsey's new Perpendicular details at St. Paul's. This is unlikely at any date before 1335, whereas the transformation of the transept had begun not later than 1331, shortly before the start at St. Paul's. In the other parts of the Gloucester transept, however, there is no sign of the coming change except for the generalised idea of traceried wall panelling, itself probably derived from St. Stephen's.

The vault in particular suggests not merely ignorance of, or even defiance of, what had been happening at the crypt of St. Stephen's in Westminster before 1323 and at Ely after 1321, but also complete independence of the Bristol style of net-vaulting without, or with intermittent, ridge-ribs. In the Gloucester south transept a strong emphasis is put on the cross-arches, diagonals, and wall and ridge-ribs, but between them is an awkward filling of straight liernes making up a gawky mesh. Furthermore this is not even disguised by bosses or carving at the intersections, and the panels of web are not enriched with cusping, as at Bristol, Wells or the presbytery at Tewkesbury. The setting-out of the rib pattern seems to have been done on the drawing board with squares, without regard to the optical results. It was long ago pointed out by Francis Bond that this method seems also to have been used for the roughly contemporary vaults of the south transept at Tewkesbury and that of the south nave aisle at Worcester. The shafts and mouldings do show an awareness of coming Perpendicular treatment, though they are not yet those of the choir and presbytery. In spite of the common factors between the south transept and the eastern arm, there seems to have been a break in continuity and a change in master after 1335.

This change in the direction of the Gloucester works may indicate active disapproval of the unsatisfactory vault, comparing so unfavourably with what could be seen within a few hours' ride; and a closer personal interest taken by the young king Edward III in what was being done. The fact that, under the tutelage of his mother and Mortimer, he had been forced to benefit for more than four years from the destitution, sadistic imprisonment and horrifying murder of his father, certainly left a lasting impression on his mind. He was keen to show reverence to his father's memory and mere lack of records cannot be regarded as evidence that there was no official intervention. The close stylistic resemblances, not merely between the bay-designs of the St. Paul's chapter-house and the eastern work at Gloucester, but also between their mouldings, indicates the direct influence of William Ramsey after he had become the king's mason in 1336. Another interesting possibility deserves consideration: that one of the local masters employed may have been John de Sponlee, later to be in charge of the royal works in Windsor Castle from 1350 onwards.

Master John's surname indicates that he came from Spoonley near Sudeley Castle and Winchcombe, and this suggests that he worked at some period of his early career at Winchcombe Abbey. He did not die until 1382, but had been pensioned by 1364; advancing years are also suggested by the promotion of his assistant Wynford to be joint master with him in 1361. Possibly born about 1310 and trained between 1320 and 1335, Sponlee might well have been, as Mr. Howard Colvin suggests, the Master John the mason who in 1336 carried out a survey of Gloucester Castle with one Master Nicholas the mason from (Chipping) Campden, who might even have been Nicholas Ramsey. At the funeral of Queen Philippa in 1369, when Yeveley and Wynford both ranked as esquires of lesser degree, Sponlee took precedence as 'of great estate'. There may therefore be considerable significance in the likeness between his shafting at Windsor (in the Aerary Porch of 1353) and the transept wall-shafts at Gloucester **fig. 10**. Sponlee's vaulting, too, had mitred ribs without bosses at the intersections, and in the course of twenty years he might well have outgrown the crudity – or merely juvenile inexperience – of the early job at Gloucester. Although this career remains entirely hypothetical, Sponlee's sudden emergence in 1350 as a valued successor to Ramsey implies some such previous occupation on buildings which, though not royal, were of the highest class.

Before returning to Sponlee's important work at Windsor we must cast an eye at what was going on elsewhere between 1335 and 1350. A major campaign of repairs, possibly comparable with that at Gloucester, was going on at the old Norman abbey of Bath after 1324, and the architect in charge was Master Richard of Farleigh, probably Monkton Farleigh. By 1334, when he obtained the reversion to the post of master in charge of the great steeple at Salisbury, he was also in charge of works at Reading. The tower at Pershore Abbey, closely resembling Salisbury though on a smaller scale, must also be assigned to him, and he was master of the works at Exeter Cathedral in the 1350s. As late as 1363 he and his wife Margaret are found disposing of land at Keynsham, between Bath and Bristol. In Richard Farleigh we have a notable instance of the mediaeval master with a large private practice, comprising works where he had constant charge along with others which he can only have visited from time to time as a consultant. His building at Bath and Reading abbeys is totally lost, that at Exeter not obviously identifiable: it probably consisted of the completion of the nave vaults to an earlier design. At Salisbury he was in charge of one of the greatest works of structural expertise of the whole Middle Ages, yet the design – pre-Perpendicular in style – has to be attributed to his predecessor Master Robert. Possibly the charming little chapel of St. Anne above the east gate of

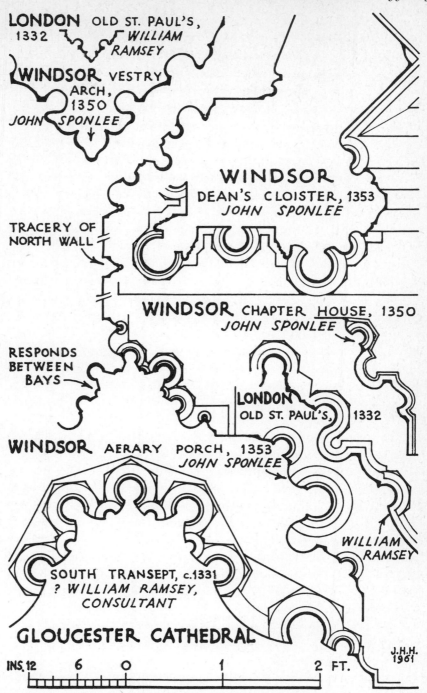

LONDON OLD ST. PAUL'S, 1332 WILLIAM RAMSEY

WINDSOR VESTRY ARCH, 1350 JOHN SPONLEE

WINDSOR DEAN'S CLOISTER, 1353 JOHN SPONLEE

TRACERY OF NORTH WALL

WINDSOR CHAPTER HOUSE, 1350 JOHN SPONLEE

RESPONDS BETWEEN BAYS

LONDON OLD ST. PAUL'S, 1332

WINDSOR AERARY PORCH, 1353 JOHN SPONLEE

WILLIAM RAMSEY

SOUTH TRANSEPT, c.1331 ? WILLIAM RAMSEY, CONSULTANT

GLOUCESTER CATHEDRAL

INS. 12   6   0   1   2 FT.

J.H.H. 1961

Fig. 10 Moulding profiles at Gloucester *c.* 1331, London 1332, and Windsor 1350–53

the Salisbury Close **13** may be attributed to Farleigh. It had recently been built in 1354, and its tracery shows the impact of Perpendicular on what would otherwise be normal reticulated work of ten to twenty years earlier.

At Wells, where the eastern Lady Chapel had been finished by 1319 with a remarkable vault of domical type, the master was probably Thomas Witney.

Witney, as we have seen, had been architect of the new presbytery at Winchester Cathedral and was called to Exeter. Like Farleigh he was a consultant with a widespread private practice. He was presumably the Master Thomas recorded as in charge of the building of the central tower at Wells from 1315 to 1322, since in its original form the tower was an enlarged version of that of Witney parish church, an important possession of the bishops of Winchester. At Exeter Thomas Witney built the nave in a last flourish of Decorated design, richly varying the tracery patterns of the windows. He was probably responsible for the central porch outside the west door, for its vault is much like a small version of that over the Wells Lady Chapel. The rest of the porches was completed later. Returning to Wells we find that, after 1329. Witney had been replaced by William Joy, who was in turn to follow Witney at Exeter for some years, before Richard Farleigh took charge.

Joy, who had undoubtedly trained in the Bristol school of masoncraft and used the net vault on a large scale, was still living in 1347 and probably died in the Black Death. The south porch of St. Mary Redcliffe, Bristol, of unknown date but probably designed not far from 1335, is markedly similar, with anticipatory 'Perpendicular' mullions rising to cut four-centred arches. At Ottery St. Mary (c. 1337–1345), again, there are vaults of a free Bristolian type, with the strong mullioned windows already mentioned and a four-centred west doorway. Whether this can be attributed to Joy is a moot point, but it is closer to his known work than to any other comparable building of the time. Joy's new presbytery at Wells, though utterly different from the transept at Gloucester, shows panelled treatment, and the great east window of the later 1330s was designed under the influence of London Perpendicular. A visit by Edward III with the royal household to Wells in the winter of 1332–33 may well have allowed personal contacts with masons and other artists attached to the Court.

As we saw, William Ramsey became a royal master in the summer of 1336, and thereafter his style dominated official work in the south of England. He was in direct charge of the fantastic tournament amphitheatre begun at Windsor in 1344, a circular building no less than 200 feet in diameter, but presumably containing a central arena open to the sky. The work was abandoned at the end of a single season and nothing remains, but the romantic concept of the Round Table gave Ramsey the chance to produce one of the most remarkable of architect's dreams. What still exists is his new presbytery at Lichfield Cathedral, seriously damaged in the Civil War, but displaying typically Perpendicular bases and the ranges of quatrefoils found in his other work. At Lichfield, however, he was largely bound by the earlier design of the new Lady Chapel to the east, and of the old choir bays to the west. Both the high and aisle vaults are conventional, and the bay design is a somewhat modified version of that in the nave. Ramsey did, none the less, eliminate the triforium and carry a panelled screen down below the clerestory windows.

The plague came, and the face of the earth was changed. Ramsey was succeeded in the King's Works by John atte Grene from Ely, and he soon afterwards by John Box from Canterbury. At Windsor Castle we find John Sponlee already in charge in 1350, and thereafter until his partial retirement in

11 Windsor Castle: Dean's Cloister, Aerary Porch 1353–54, by John Sponlee

12 Oxford: New College, vault of staircase to hall c. 1385, by William Wynford

13 Salisbury: St. Anne's Gate and Chapel –1354. Note Perpendicular detail in tracery of east window

14 Durham: vault of Priory kitchen 1366–71, by John Lewyn

11

12

13

14

1364. The chapter-house of 1350 has a beautiful early Perpendicular window opening on the Dean's Cloister, looking as if it had been detailed by Ramsey before his death **16**. This is more sharply classical than Sponlee's later work in the Aerary Porch **11** of 1353–54 and the cloister **17** built from 1353 to 1356. These too are completely Perpendicular, though the blind traceries on the porch walls amount to straightened reticulated, with echoes of the south transept at Gloucester. The cloister, with two-light Perpendicular sub-arcuations beneath round arches, forming four-light bays, has double-cusped quatrefoils. In this respect it comes fairly close to the new design for the south walk of the Westminster Abbey cloisters **22**, begun in 1349. At Westminster, however, each window on the garth was of three lights, with lobed quatrefoils set X-wise in a pair of straightened reticulations above. Though now an apparently accurate Victorian renewal, the Westminster cloister has some claim to be regarded as the earliest surviving work of the pure Perpendicular style, taking precedence of a year over the Windsor chapter-house. With the claims of Gloucester we shall deal shortly.

At this point something must be said of two important builds, both of them having for patron William Edington, consecrated bishop of Winchester in 1346. A king's clerk in 1335 and holding important offices of state from 1341, culminating in the chancellorship in 1356–63, Edington was one of the chief servants of Edward III and well placed to obtain architectural advice from the best masters. Well before his death in 1366 he had caused the Norman west front and tower of Winchester Cathedral to be demolished, and a start to be made on Gothicizing the Norman nave. An aisled front with tall turrets and a set of three projecting porches with four-centred arches, this is an enigmatic work **21**. Just how much was designed at the start, and when that start was, is a problem compounded by the question of what was under construction for Edington's successor Wykeham in 1371, and how much of the front itself was designed by Wynford in or after 1394. In spite of the manifest fact that the lower parts of the front, the aisle windows on each side, and at least the lower parts of the west window, are to a design quite different from that of Wynford's reconstruction of 1394, and with very distinct mouldings, the real dates of design elude us.

On a basis of stylistic evidence the western porches are very closely related to the undercroft of Ramsey's St. Paul's chapter-house, while their shafting internally, with its bases and caps, is in the style of Gloucester. The motive of a projecting western porch is a very old one, ultimately derived from the narthex. A low porch formed part of the west front of St. Albans Abbey, built in 1195–1214, and something of the sort was probably attached to the west end of Lambeth Palace chapel, planned before 1240. Henry III's chapel in the Lower Ward of Windsor Castle, now incorporated in the Albert Memorial Chapel, still preserves its porch of 1240–43, slightly earlier than that of the French Sainte Chapelle in Paris. Cloaked with a screen of statuary, a similar series of three porches runs across the base of the west front at Exeter and was, as we have just seen, probably begun by Thomas Witney before 1342.

Though the date of Edington's work at Winchester remains uncertain, we can place within ten years (1352–61) the eastern arm and transepts of his church at Edington in Wiltshire **18**. Intended in 1351 to be a college for secular priests, it was changed a year later at the request of the Black Prince into an establishment for canons of the order of Bonshommes. This royal intervention not merely links the building with the Court style but specifically with the architectural programme at Windsor. The Prince was an integral part of his father's foundation of the Order of the Garter in 1348, and Edington as bishop of Winchester was officially prelate of the Order. It comes as no surprise that the side windows of the chancel, and the transept windows, at Edington are of the same sort of straightened reticulated tracery as that in the Aerary Porch at Windsor. Whoever may have been the mason in charge at the site, there can be no doubt that architectural advice and probably drawings were coming from John Sponlee. The resemblances of mouldings: the double-ogee, the casement and the pear-shaped version of the bowtell-and-fillet, tell the same story. The masons' marks at Edington show that a dozen men worked on the chancel. Of them, seven also worked on the north transept and eight on the south. Four of these eight, with one other mason, produced the western end of the south nave aisle. The details of the west front are thus linked to the eastern parts of the church and were probably designed by 1360.

From the well fixed dates of Edington we return to the uncertainties of Gloucester and Winchester. The demolition of the very large Norman front at Winchester, begun at the earliest in 1346 or 1347, is likely to have occupied more than a single year, and considering the incidence of the plague it is most unlikely that designs for the new work were prepared before 1350. By 1355 the cathedral priory was paying an annual fee of £1 to Thomas Le Masson, and it is reasonable to think that this may well have been a retainer paid to him as a consultant or designer. He cannot be Thomas of Witney, certainly dead by this time, but an identity with Thomas of Gloucester is quite possible. The latter was warden of the masons at Westminster Palace, under Master John Box, in 1354–55; in 1356 the principal mason working at St. Stephen's Chapel; and in the same year one of the six hewers representing the freestone masons upon a commission for regulating the craft of masons in London. He was still warden in charge of the masons in Westminster Palace in 1357–58.

If the mason concerned was not this Thomas, at least he is likely to have had some close association with Gloucester. The blind tracery in the western porches uses the sixfoil reticulation, and the vertical panelling has trefoiled cusping. The vaults, small as they are, display characteristics related both to work at Westminster and to the choir vault at Gloucester. The side and west windows of the aisles, though employing cinquefoil rather than trefoil cusping, agree with the great east window at Gloucester in being divided by strong mullions into central and side panels; yet the effect is quite different from that in the Gloucester sanctuary. Nor does it, except in a certain period flavour, come very close to the church at Edington. The body of rather confusing evidence is increased by the style of bishop Edington's chantry chapel, markedly of the type of Gloucester south transept, late reticulated Decorated and not at all Perpendicular in effect except from its arcaded transoms, cinquefoil-cusped.

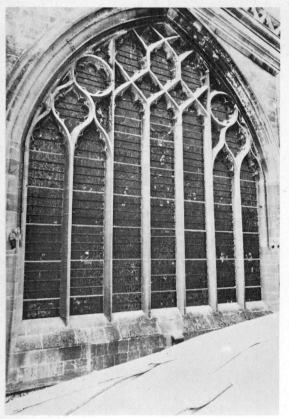

15

16

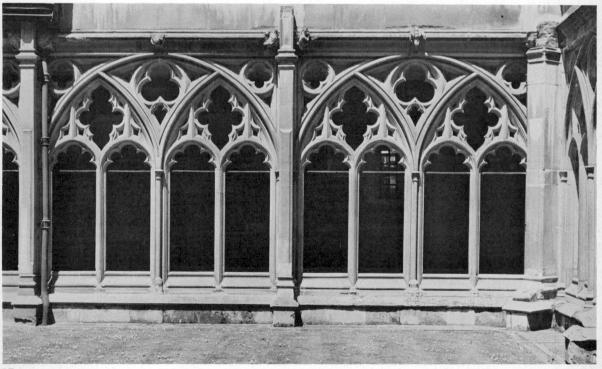

17

18

19

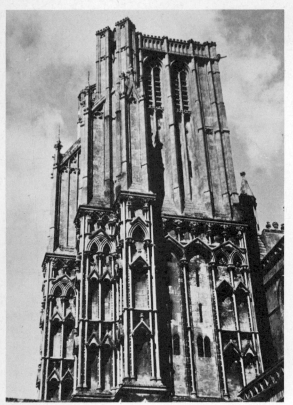

20

21

22

23

24

25

The main lights are trefoiled, and this ambivalence is again that of the Gloucester work of 1331–35. Yet we know that this chantry cannot have been undertaken before 1346 at the earliest. It is finished off with a band of quatrefoils in square panels, hinting at Court influence, and above that a cresting uniquely complex (though dismissed by one authority as 'simple'). It is as though two separate series of inverted trefoils, terminating in scrolled leaves, were seen staggered or 'out of step', yet coinciding from time to time like a 'beat' in musical discord. Here is a conceit so entirely Decorated as to seem a positively anti-Perpendicular manifesto. How can we, within the common ambit of Gloucester style of the overall period, reconcile Edington's chantry with the architectural design of the western nave and front?

Referring back to the east window at Edington, likely to have been designed in 1352, pre-Perpendicular elements are there seen in a state of transition. Cinquefoiled ogee archlets, double-cusping, and daggers, falchions and lobed cruciform fillings jostle with strong mullions, lateral subarcuation, and a crested (or brattished) supertransom looking far later than it is. Unless bishop Edington was at one and the same time employing several designers completely out of step with one another, the sequence seems to be: Gloucester south transept; Winchester chantry chapel (c. 1347?); west front and aisles perhaps 1350 or soon after; the detailing of the porches probably rather later; Edington church 1352, including the detail of its east window; the side and transept windows c. 1353 and close to Sponlee's works of that date at Windsor. It is difficult to imagine that any mason trained even in part at Gloucester, as the Winchester designer(s) must have been, could have produced these details if he had seen the Gloucester east window drawn out on parchment, let alone built.

This brings us back to the major problem of the real dating at Gloucester itself. From the chronicles there is certainty as to the time-brackets into which the divisions of work fall, but room for doubt over definition. We have seen that the transformation of the south transept, in the six seasons 1331–36, can be broken down into sections, with the south window coming as late as 1335. Moving on to the end of the main works on the church, accurate dates are recorded for the north transept, begun on 7 January 1367/8 and finished on 24 December, Christmas Eve, 1373. We shall later have to consider where to fit in the design of the first section of the fan-vaulted cloisters, somewhere after 1351 and before 1377. Disregarding this, the eastern arm is likely to have been completed immediately before the undertaking of the north transept, that is the end of 1367.

What we are told concerning the eastern arm is, as far as it goes, explicit. The vault of the choir and one half of the wooden choir-stalls were made in the time of Abbot Adam de Staunton, 1337–51, or fifteen years at most, less a virtually certain gap or slowing down due to the plague. Each of the transepts took six years, and consisted of two bays, so that four normal bays would involve the work of 12 years. The ritual choir, mostly beneath the crossing tower, was equivalent to about three bays, counting the whole crossing and eastern arm together as eight rather than seven. The engineering problems of carrying the choir vault over the crossing, ingeniously surmounted by the famous flying arches and stone 'king-posts', would mean an expenditure of time above the average. Completion of this section of the whole work, the choir in the strict sense, might well be all that could in the circumstances be accomplished before Abbot Staunton's death. In other words, neither the east window, nor any part of the eastern arm as we see it now, existed until after 1351.

The design of the shafting, wall-panelling, and side window traceries was indeed settled in or soon after 1337, but stylistically these followed closely upon Ramsey's London scheme of 1332 and upon local Gloucester tradition for the shafts with their bases and capitals. The impact upon the outside world and upon progressive architects did not come until later. This is strictly in accordance with the wording of the chronicle, that it was not until the time of Abbot Thomas de Horton, after 1351, that the work of the presbytery, with the high altar and the second half of the stalls, was undertaken. The five bays, at the rate of the transepts, would need 15 years; and from 1352 to 1367 inclusive there are 16, an extra year easily accounted for by the structural problems of the ambulatory and the east window. As a model for the future of Perpendicular, the eastern arm of Gloucester Abbey was not available until somewhere near 1365. The great differences between the south and east windows fall naturally into place, and it is unnecessary to find anything extraordinary in the late arrival, outside London and Gloucester, of fully developed Perpendicular on a monumental scale.

At Glastonbury, regarded as the premier abbey of England, a similar scheme of rebuilding and transformation took place under Abbot Walter de Monington between 1342 and 1374. Little is left to show the form of the work and the dates are too vague to indicate how far Glastonbury may have been a pace-setter in style. In an opposite sense it does seem to be significant that there were few major building schemes with fully Perpendicular detail until after 1375, and that conspicuously Decorated details were still employed until then in churches of outstanding quality. The large and fine Curvilinear windows of the London Austin Friars, destroyed in the Second World War, were made in 1354–60, the east window of the Ely Lady Chapel was not inserted until 1371–74, and the central tower at Worcester **26**, built in 1357–74, does not employ strictly Perpendicular detail, though it has bands of tangential quatrefoils and trefoiled cusping of the same type as at Gloucester. The chancel at Castle Bytham, built for the dean and chapter of Lincoln in 1368–69, is Flowing and Reticulated without any sign of the coming change.

At Hereford, on the contrary, one of the most vital buildings in the development of the new style was completed in the seven years 1364–70. This was the upper part, with vault and windows, of the octagonal chapter-house, only known to us from slight fragments and from a drawing by William Stukeley made in 1721. From the detailed study of these made by Mr. Norman Drinkwater it is certain that there is a very close link, both stylistic and chronological, between the Hereford chapter-house with its fan-vault on a grand scale, and the smaller vaults and traceries of the east cloister at Gloucester. The question of precise dates once more becomes important. At Hereford the construction was undertaken by Thomas de Cantebrugge, mason and citizen of

Hereford, from 13 December 1364 within seven years. Cantebrugge is almost certainly the Cambridge in Gloucestershire 12 miles south of Gloucester on the main road to Bristol. The work was carried out under the contract, for a receipt survives from 1367 for an instalment covering payment for the fourth quarter of the third year.

It is rather less certain that Cantebrugge was the designer, for on 9 April 1359 the dean and chapter of Hereford had appointed John of Evesham, mason of Worcestershire, to have complete control over the works of the cathedral both in masonry and carpentry, for his life. He may have died within the next five years, but it is also possible that he provided the designs from which Cantebrugge was to work. At the outside the design can be placed within 1359–64. Turning to Gloucester, the six bays of the east cloister from the transept to the door of the chapter-house **29** were built under Abbot Horton, but this merely fixes them between 1351 and 1377. In spite of their smaller scale, the traceries and fan-vaults of the cloister correspond so exactly with the style and details used at Hereford **fig. 6.12** that there can be no doubt that the designer was one and the same man. He might be Cantebrugge, the presumably Gloucestershire contractor of 1364; or Evesham, if he still lived; or the master mason of Gloucester Abbey if he were not identical with either of the others. As we shall see later, the Gloucester style in precise detail was carried to Exeter Cathedral from 1376 onwards to 1394, by Robert Lesyngham, who was by then evidently the master mason of Gloucester. No doubt Lesyngham had held his appointment there for some time to obtain the reputation which reached Exeter, but fresh difficulties arise.

There is a sharp distinction, certainly implying the advent of a different architect, between the east walk of the Gloucester cloisters, finished by or soon after 1377, and the other three walks, not begun until after 1381, and not completed until perhaps as late as 1412. The style of the north transept work of 1368–73 seems closer to the later walks of the cloisters; that of the northern porch in the west front of Exeter Cathedral **32** looks intermediate between the two phases of the Gloucester cloisters. As a working hypothesis it might be suggested that Thomas de Cantebrugge was in charge at Gloucester for some time before 1364 and built the early bays of the east walk; that he then left to take on the important contract at Hereford and set himself up there by investing in the freedom of the city; and that Robert Lesyngham was thereupon appointed master at Gloucester. In this case Lesyngham would be the designer of the north transept and of the remainder of the cloisters; presumably also of the Tewkesbury cloister, identical but for its four-centred arches.

The central tower of Worcester Cathedral **26** has been mentioned for the non-Perpendicular character of its detail, in spite of a start to the work as late as 1357. This supports the dating of the presbytery clerestory and east windows at Gloucester to somewhere near 1360, and this in turn tends to identify the Gloucester master of the east window with the east cloisters as well – hypothetically Thomas de Cantebrugge. At Worcester there is a general use of trefoil cusping in the Gloucester manner, and the overall effect is of Perpendicular panelling. The one master evidenced is John Clyve or Cleve,

26 Worcester Cathedral: central tower 1357–74; and chapter-house restored 1386–92, by John Clyve

27 Great Grimsby Church: central tower 1365–

28 Wymondham Abbey: central tower 1390–1409; nave clerestory 1432–45; west tower 1445–78

26

27

28

29

30

31

32

otherwise employed as a contractor for mason's work at Windsor Castle in 1362–65. At Worcester he appears only between 1376 and 1392, but his surname probably means that he came from Cleeve Prior, five miles from Evesham, and in the absence of records it is quite possible that his work at Worcester began long before 1376. The tower, with its tall transomed panelling, turreted angles, and bands of quatrefoil, has to be considered a Perpendicular design even if – as happened elsewhere – its fenestration is exceptionally conservative. The mouldings of the belfry stage, with pear-shaped bowtells and wide casements, unquestionably belong to the style.

We know very little of the penetration of Perpendicular to other parts of England before 1360. One interesting case is the church of Donington in Lincolnshire, where there were in 1351 works in progress to which Henry, Lord Percy, bequeathed £8. There are clerestory windows of early Perpendicular, yet not so early as this, but in the north aisle occurs a curious pattern with stilted segmental-pointed head, trefoiled ogee lights, and most unusual but definitely Perpendicular tracery **fig. 6.7**. The early treatment of the jambs and mullions as shafting, with capitals at the springing, renders the date plausible, while Percy moved in Court circles and could well have favoured an advanced style.

The church at Ingham in Norfolk is of greater importance; in 1360 it was to be rebuilt for a Trinitarian priory. The east and north windows of the choir have Flowing tracery and may survive from work of c.1343 associated with the notable tomb of Sir Oliver de Ingham against the north wall. The original forms of the later tracery are doubtful, as an engraving of 1824 (in J. P. Neale and J. Le Keux, *Views of the most interesting ... Churches*, vol. I, 43) shows that the present fillings are drastic alterations. The surviving west window of the south aisle, however, agrees with what is shown as the ruling pattern, early Perpendicular of three lights with two quatrefoiled reticulations **fig. 6.8**. This is acceptable as dating from the 1370s, along with the arcades.

We have to lament the loss of a large proportion of the most important works of this period, especially those built under royal auspices. These would certainly have revealed a whole chapter of the early history of the style, now gone for ever. Even at Windsor, where much remains, alterations and restoration have left little stylistically distinctive in the three great gatehouses: the Spicery Gate of 1357, the Great Gate of 1358, and the New Gate of 1359, all built by John Sponlee. At Vale Royal Abbey in Cheshire we now know, thanks to the excavation by Mr. Hugh Thompson in 1958, the unusual plan of the eastern ambulatory and chapels designed in 1358 and completed by 1374. The master, William de Helpeston, produced an ingenious version of the much earlier plan of Toledo Cathedral in Spain. Whether this was derived from personal study or from contacts at Bordeaux or elsewhere during a period of diplomatic activity between England and Castile, is so far unknown. Hardly any architectural fragments have been recovered, but the few pieces of jambs, mullions and ribs indicate very late Decorated rather than Perpendicular details.

Nothing whatever is left of the great Cistercian abbey founded on Tower

29 Gloucester Cathedral: east cloister c. 1360–, here tentatively ascribed to Thomas Cambridge

30 Gloucester Cathedral: south cloister c. 1385–, probably by Robert Lesyngham

31 Exeter Cathedral: east window 1390–92, by Robert Lesyngham

32 Exeter Cathedral: north porch of west front c. 1380, by Robert Lesyngham

Hill by Edward III in 1350: New Abbey, St. Mary Graces, or Eastminster, the site of the later Royal Mint. John Tyryngton, a mason who had worked for the Black Prince at Kennington in 1351 and still earlier on the Tower of London, was in charge in 1353 and 1361. He was, like Thomas of Gloucester, one of the principal freestone hewers of London on the commission of 1356. Outside London, at King's Langley, substantial royal works were carried on after 1359 at the Dominican friary beside the king's manor-house; but there again nothing is left even to give a stylistic clue. Likewise we are left in the dark as to the architectural content of the daughter house of Dominican nuns, subject to Langley, which had been founded by the king at Dartford in Kent in 1346. From 1349 until 1362 the buildings were erected with royal help, like those of Eastminster. All these works were undoubtedly among the earliest to be designed from the start in the Perpendicular style. Of this galaxy of metropolitan and royal buildings nothing now stands but Sponlee's works at Windsor and, in its state of melancholy renewal, the south cloister walk of Westminster Abbey.

CHAPTER FOUR

The Age of Henry Yeveley

1360–1400

The great age of Perpendicular, in which it received its essential form and attained its outstanding triumphs, was the last generation of the fourteenth century. The parallel which English architecture thus finds in English literary development under Chaucer is so precise as to be startling. Geoffrey Chaucer and Henry Yeveley, his fellow servant under the Crown, died in the same year 1400 and within a few weeks of each other: Yeveley on 21 August and Chaucer on 25 October. The architect was a considerably older man than the poet, certainly born by 1330 and perhaps as much as ten years earlier. Coming from a family of Derbyshire stonemasons originating in Yeaveley, his father Roger had settled seven miles away at Uttoxeter in Staffordshire where he held land and burgage tenements. Henry Yeveley and his brother Robert, both masons, probably journeyed to London together soon after the Black Death, when the shortage of skilled craftsmen in the South attracted men from long distances, lured by unwontedly high pay and great opportunities. Of their work and lives we know nothing until 1353, when Henry obtained the freedom of the City of London on 3 December.

Presumably the brothers had some working capital, for within little more than two years Henry had been chosen one of the six freestone hewers on the commission of 1356 already mentioned along with Thomas Gloucester, John Tyryngton and three others; together with six representatives of the layers and setters. The regulations then made have an important bearing upon the necessary standing of such craftsmen as the Yeveleys. No one was to take work in gross, i.e. by contract, unless he had the ability, financial as well as in craftsmanship, to complete it. A man wishing to undertake a contract had to bring at least four 'ancient men' of his trade to swear to his ability and ready to undertake completion of the work themselves if he should fail. Without substantial means it is difficult to see how newcomers could break into the charmed circle. Contrariwise, we may safely assume that for some years before 1356 Henry Yeveley had been able to satisfy these requirements and to undertake contract work.

By 1357 he was introduced, possibly by John Tyryngton, to the service of the Black Prince. During the next two years he carried out substantial contracts at Kennington, where similar work had previously been done by Tyryngton, now master at Eastminster. By 1359 Yeveley was being described as 'the prince's mason', with the implication that he had become a good deal more than a successful contractor. He obtained a special licence from the Crown to discharge victuals at Calais, presumably a profitable side-line run in connection with cross-Channel trade in building materials. Next year Yeveley was appointed, on 25 June 1360, to be disposer of the King's works of masonry in the Palace of Westminster and Tower of London, during pleasure, taking 12*d*. per day. On 13 August he was authorised to impress masons for the works, and on 20 August was described as the King's deviser (i.e. designer) of masonry. The phrase used: '*deuisour de la maceonerie de noz oeueraignes*', deviser of the masonry of our works, is of cardinal importance. It proves that, from the very start of his long royal career, Henry Yeveley was employed in an architectural capacity, and not as an administrator nor as a merely efficient builder. It remains an open question, likely to be solved only by very detailed study of every scrap of stylistic evidence, how far Yeveley's responsibility for design extended at any given point in his career.

In 1360 it is certain that the architectural aspect of whatever was done in the royal palace at Westminster, and at the Tower of London, came within Yeveley's purview, and the general scope of the phrase 'of our works' may have tended very soon to spread through official building in a wider field. As we have seen already, the important works at Windsor had been carried on ever since 1350 by the senior master John Sponlee. From this very year, 1360, William Wynford was working under Sponlee and became joint disposer (*ordinator*) with him from 12 April 1361. Wynford was already referred to as 'Master' in 1360, and there is no doubt that he was brought in as Sponlee's eventual replacement. There is thus a strong presumption that all the major works carried out in Windsor Castle for Edward III and mostly finished before the end of his reign, were carried on independently of Yeveley. The position elsewhere is less clear. As we know, the Canterbury master, John Box, had been called to Westminster in May 1350 and from 20 June 1351 until 9 October 1357 he was paid 12*d*. daily as master mason in charge of the works at Westminster and the Tower, and was said to be working at ordaining the King's works (*super ordinacione operum Regis*) there. In May 1356, however, he was sent to Calais, where he remained for two years. On his return he was not reinstated, and the office of master mason for the works of the metropolitan area was left vacant until Yeveley's appointment in 1360. A new job was found for Box in the following spring, as chief mason of the new Queenborough Castle in Sheppey.

The fact that Box's regular allowance of 12*d*. a day was withdrawn in the autumn of 1357 could be due simply to his absence at Calais, but the failure to reinstate him and the bringing in of Yeveley two years later, must indicate royal dissatisfaction. In the absence both of official records and personal gossip, we can but surmise that Box, in the months after Yeveley's appointment, pressed his own claims and managed to obtain the equally well paid job at Queenborough as compensation. Whether he was completely independent there as designer of the castle remains doubtful. Gone were the days when the real architect of every large work was also the resident master in day-to-day charge on the site. From even before 1300 the trend of architecture at the higher levels was towards the modern system of more designs produced by fewer individuals. Consultancy and advice, amounting in some cases to architectural dictatorship by remote control, were increasingly responsible for the spread of a single style over the whole country.

This pattern, intensified by England's insular position, was by no means peculiar. Yeveley's contemporary in France, Raymond du Temple, had immense prestige from 1362 until his death in 1404, when his mantle was divided between his sons Charles and Jean. In Germany and central Europe the preponderant part played by Peter Parler from 1353 until he died in 1399, both in directing the works of Prague Cathedral and in creating and inventing Sondergotik, the continental counterpart to Perpendicular, has long been recognised. In Spain the wide sphere of architectural influence exercised between c. 1325 and 1362 by Raynard dez Fonolly, who as we know was English, was studied in detail by the late Josep Vives i Miret. Not only was Henry Yeveley a phenomenon of a known type, the co-ordinating genius, but the state of Perpendicular style by the opening of the fifteenth century, as compared with 1360, would demonstrate that such a master must have been concerned.

Just as the main provincial schools of later Decorated can be traced to named individuals who had worked under Master Michael of Canterbury at St. Stephen's Chapel, so at a later date progressive stages of style were carried outwards from London and Windsor by men who had been engaged on the royal works. To such direct stylistic influence must be added that of sedulous imitation of fashionable details, and the less tangible effects of the interchange of ideas at the regular congresses of masons in the various regions, and of personal notes and sketches jotted down by masters in the course of their journeys. In the forty years from 1360 there is a progressive dominance of the scene by Yeveley himself and by the designs of the official architects associated with him, William Wynford and the carpenter Hugh Herland. Possibly the most noteworthy feature of development was the abandoning of panelled treatment of walls in favour of simple expanses of plain ashlar, the 'big and bare style' of Lethaby's memorable phrase.

A crucial problem which at present seems incapable of definitive solution is the authorship of the several successive phases of early Perpendicular work at Westminster Abbey. This is highly relevant to the adoption of certain motives, both by the Court masters including Yeveley, and elsewhere. While Ramsey was building his cloister at St. Paul's with Perpendicular detail, it was decided at the Abbey to proceed with a general rebuilding of their cloister. Before the Black Death the four southern bays of the east walk had been completed under the mason Walter le Bole, in charge of the works from 1341 onwards. The cloister bays seem to have been built in 1344–49, and by July of that year Bole had died, along with Abbot Byrcheston who had given £80 to the work, and 26 of the monks. Three bays have Curvilinear reticulated tracery, two of them with eight-foil cusping, the southernmost bay with ogee quatrefoils. Opposite to the chapter-house entry is a larger bay filled with magnificent 'Kentish' reticulated tracery above four open lights with tall double-cusped heads. This is the last fling of the Canterbury school. Notwithstanding the plague, a beginning seems to have been made on the south walk almost at once. The leading mason, not named from 1349 to 1351, received the same fees and perquisites that from 1352 were paid to John Palterton, who continued in charge until the completion of the west walk in 1365.

Palterton had been a working mason at Westminster Palace in 1344 and to that extent had been trained in the official style when William Ramsey was chief mason; but it is curious that Palterton was never described as master until 1361, and his emoluments do not suggest that he was of very high rank. The design of the work was probably provided by an outside architect, as indeed seems likely in the time of his predecessor Walter le Bole. Now it is at least plausible that the window with Kentish tracery had been designed by Master John Box, since he had worked at Westminster Palace in 1333–34 and was known to the king, who sent for him in 1350 to replace John atte Grene. Box was then in the service of the Prior of Christchurch, Canterbury, but he might well also have designed the tomb of Archbishop Stratford who died in 1348. The detail of this tomb seems to be the closest parallel to the great bay of the Westminster cloister.

The east walk followed in scale the original work of the thirteenth century, which included also the whole of the north walk. The south and west walks were built more economically, several feet lower. But there was also a difference between the south and west walks, though both were built under Palterton. The vaulting of the south walk was taller, that of the west walk relatively depressed. The bay design was different, and again the traceries of the west walk were of a broader, squatter proportion than those on the south side, having four lights each instead of three **25**. The mouldings of south and west walks are virtually the same, and follow fairly closely the scheme of Ramsey's cloister at St. Paul's, with casements, double-ogees and triple shafts to the walk. In the south walk at Westminster Abbey are tall heads to the lights, handsomely double-cusped and rather nearly resembling those of the 'Kentish' bay in the east walk. In the west walk the archlets are much lower, though similarly treated with double cusping.

Even if not actually administered by the royal works, the Abbey remained a royal foundation, and a close association with the adjacent Palace was always maintained. The details, particularly those of the south and west cloisters, clearly belong to the official school as practised by Ramsey and his followers. Was the south walk sketched out, or even detailed, by Ramsey himself before his death? Who was responsible for the fresh design introduced in the west walk, not begun until 1362? Lethaby gave a tentative answer to this second question. Pointing out that the detail of the Infirmary, built under Palterton as master from 1365 and including the doorway to the Little Cloister precisely dated to 1371–72, 'looks earlier than the great Cloister', he went on to say: 'I am drawn to think that Henry Yevele ... may have been concerned with the design of the Cloister. In any case, Yevele was the master of the work in building the new Nave, and the Cloister may well have been planned in connection with that.' Lethaby showed that the plan of the new nave and western towers must have been set out with precision before the building of the west cloister and the Abbot's House, and this is no mere hypothesis but a firm conclusion which can be demonstrated on the site. The date of the plan for the Gothic nave is thus set back to 1362 at latest, the last year of the abbacy of Simon Langham, who is with reason regarded as the active promoter of the work not actually begun until 1375.

It now seems all but certain that Lethaby was right in suggesting that Yeveley was concerned with the cloister. The changed design of the west walk can best be accounted for, along with the close association between it and the planning of the nave, if he took over as architect by, or possibly rather before, 1362. It will be seen that this fits very well with his assumption of architectural control at the Palace in the summer of 1360. Within the next year or so what can be more likely than that the new chief architect, favoured by the king, should have been called across to advise Langham upon his cherished programme for replacing the old Norman nave with a splendid Gothic continuation of the monastic choir, which already stretched five bays to the west of the crossing. The late R. P. Howgrave-Graham, in an exhaustive study, was able to show that, contrary to earlier beliefs, the two western bays of the north cloister had been built in the thirteenth century, outside the Norman south aisle; and that the three bays of the new south nave aisle, corresponding to these two bays and the north-west angle bay, must have been built in 1375–87.

It is thus impossible to separate the later work on the nave, vouched for by the *Novum Opus* rolls after 1387, from the earlier work on subsidiary buildings that had gone on ever since 1362. That Yeveley had been prepared to accept the pre-existing mouldings of the south cloister, and simply to modify the tracery design, helps to explain the character of early Perpendicular. Yeveley was not an innovator and tended to be a moderately conservative adherent to existing orthodoxy. From this attitude stems the predominance of adaptation of pre-Perpendicular forms; and also the variety of tracery patterns found within the Court style before the end of the century. For instance, it might at first sight be thought that the three-light windows of the Black Prince's Chantry under Canterbury Cathedral **35**, designed in 1362, were incompatible with the known output of Yeveley at a later date in his career. Yet the combination of a pair of strong mullions with subarcuation of the side lights, treated with rich double cinquefoil cusping, can be put into its proper perspective when it is considered in its chronological place. It is the vital link in development from a type of Decorated window used early in the fourteenth century. A fine example, illustrated long ago by Freeman, is in the Mayor's Chapel at Bristol; its rich incrustation of ballflower shows that it is unlikely to be later than 1330.

The earliest of Yeveley's surviving official works include the vault in the Bloody Tower of the Tower of London, part of a large contract carried out by his brother Robert in 1361–62. This was followed in 1365 by the Palace Clock Tower, a pioneering functional building of great simplicity; and by the Jewel House which still survives. The vaulting, virtually identical with that of the Abbey west cloister, provides stylistic confirmation of Yeveley's overall responsibility. These simple tierceron vaults show an inherent conservatism and a withdrawal from the exotic and bizarre fantasies of Curvilinear: fundamental characteristics of the strong and noble style which was to be the outcome. Yeveley experimented with the conversion to Perpendicular of other earlier motives. In the Abbey parlour or entry to the cloister there are two-light windows **fig. 11.7** built in 1363–65 which borrow the eight-foiled reticulations of the east walk but set them between vertical supermullions after the manner

33

34

35

36

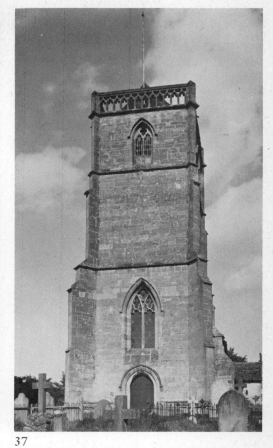

37

38

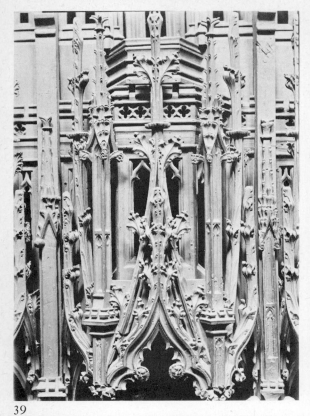

39

40

41

42

of the Buckland nave windows (before 1348) and the east window of St. Anne's Chapel at Salisbury (before 1354) **13**. The straightened reticulations of the west cloister were based on those of St. Paul's chapter-house, but filled with double-cusped quatrefoils in the manner of the south walk. Later Yeveley adopted the quatrefoil lobing with daggers as a filling for the oculus of the windows of the otherwise plain, but exquisitely proportioned Abbot's Hall of 1372–75 **24**.

Most of the freestone used at Westminster came from the greensand quarries near Reigate, and this probably accounts for the dissemination of a similar but transitional pattern found at Etchingham church in Sussex **fig. 6.4**. Windows for the church were made in 1363 by Thomas Esshyng, mason of Betchworth, Surrey, who may well have been employed earlier to make traceries to order for the south cloister at the Abbey. Another route for the migration of detail of this kind was provided by the move from Westminster to Norwich of the mason Robert de Wodehirst. He had worked at the Palace as a junior man in 1351–52, but by 1355 was getting the full standard rate. In June 1357 he appeared at St. Stephen's Chapel as a specialised carver and continued there for a year, when he transferred to the Abbey and received the highest specialist's pay of 3s. 4d. a week carving vault bosses for the south cloister.

By 1385 Wodehirst is evidenced as master of the work for the Norwich Cathedral cloister; he was a man of high standing as a property owner and a feoffee of the manor of Earlham until he died late in 1401. Between 1387 and 1393 he was also called to Ely Cathedral as master mason. The stylistic evidence of traceries and lobed fillings **Map X** with double cusping of the Westminster type and the use of double-ogee and other 'modern' mouldings leaves no doubt that among the works of Wodehirst's middle career were the new presbytery windows at Norwich Cathedral (1362–69) **33**, the magnificent parish church at Swanton Morley **47, 48** in progress in 1378, and the choir of the Great

39 Chester Cathedral: choir stalls c. 1390, here attributed to Hugh Herland

40, 42 Durham Cathedral: details of the Neville Screen made in London 1372–80, here attributed to Henry Yeveley

41 Canterbury Cathedral: pulpitum c. 1410, here attributed to Stephen Lote

Fig. 11 Details used by Henry Yeveley: 1. Canterbury c. 1376 and c. 1391; Westminster c. 1375 and 1394; 2. Layer Marney c. 1360; St. Bartholomew the Great c. 1400; Westminster royal tombs; 3. Durham 1372; Westminster c. 1372 and c. 1375; Canterbury 1378; Oxford, New College 1380; 4. London Charterhouse c. 1372; Westminster c. 1375 and 1377; St. Albans before 1396; 5. Westminster, tomb of Edward III; Cobham, Kent, c. 1370; Arundel c. 1380; St. Paul's, tomb of Burley c. 1389; Canterbury c. 1391; Maidstone c. 1395; 6. Westminster, royal tombs; St. Paul's, Burley tomb c. 1389; 7. Westminster Abbey, windows in Parlour 1363–5

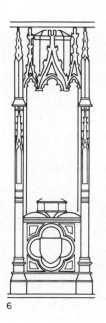
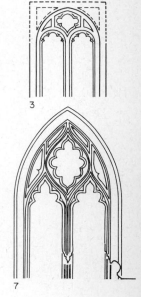

43

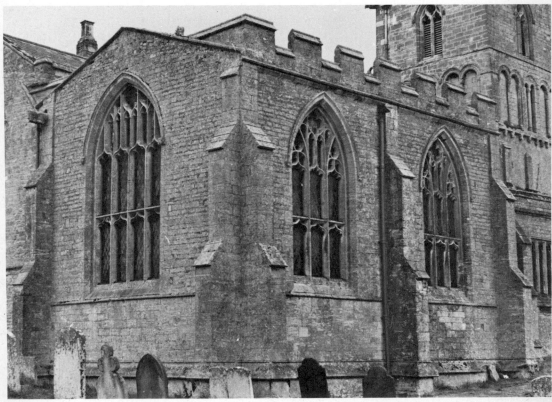

44

Hospital at Norwich (c. 1380–84) **46; fig. 6.13**. He may also have been concerned with the works of Ingham church **45, 49** already mentioned (1360–), of North Walsham rebuilt from c. 1382 **66, 67**, and with the east window of the Ely Lady Chapel (1371–74). The most remarkable feature of Wodehirst's designs is his perpetuation of the late Decorated principle of variety rather than uniformity in traceries. In the rich choice of the Norwich presbytery there is even one Flowing window without any strictly Perpendicular detail. All these works were done for very high-level patronage and interpret the Court style of Westminster in the mid-century to provincial East Anglia of 1360–1400.

It is instructive to contrast with this old-fashioned exuberance the more sober versions of the same motives, gradually shorn of such enrichments as double cusping and the use of Curvilinear falchions, employed by Sponlee and Wynford at Windsor (presumably also for the great west window at Edington of c. 1365–70), by Lesyngham at Gloucester in 1368, and by Yeveley himself. Yeveley's aisle windows for the new nave of Canterbury Cathedral **34**, designed about 1378, make use of the same vocabulary as Wodehirst's traceries for Norwich and Swanton Morley, but in a rather severe and uniform way. Only in his later Canterbury cloister, not begun until 1397 though probably designed some years earlier, did Yeveley revert to an extensive use of double cusping **91**. Where money was available, however, Yeveley continued to use such enrichments, both in his monumental practice including the Neville Screen **1, 40, 42** made for Durham Cathedral in London in 1372–80, and on the royal porches at the west end of Westminster Abbey **87** and the north front of Westminster Hall **86**.

Although a conservative in detail, Yeveley was an innovator in planning. He seized upon the small-scale precedent of the Dean's Cloister at Windsor as a basis for co-ordinated quadrangles in military and domestic buildings, as well as in the lodgings of collegiate churches. The late Christopher Hussey argued an overwhelming case for his design of Cobham College in Kent **fig. 6.9**, apparently the first instance of independent planning of this kind on a free site. This probably goes back to 1370 and is quite small, but in the next year he laid out the gigantic cloister of the London Charterhouse, where slight remains of detail confirm the documentary attribution to him. Various combinations of structural evidence and records indicate that Yeveley himself or his close associates were responsible for Nunney Castle in Somerset (1373) **53**, Norrington Manor, Wiltshire (1377?), Shirburn Castle, Oxfordshire (1377), the West Gate of Canterbury **50, 51** and the new Holy Cross church beside it (1378–80), Cowling Castle in Kent (1380), the great gatehouse of Saltwood Castle (c. 1383), and Bodiam Castle in Sussex, begun in 1385. Yeveley's major church works will be dealt with later.

We must now turn to the course taken by provincial work remote from Court influence. As has been seen, there was a long overlap in which Curvilinear and even Flamboyant detail continued in fashion. This occurred sometimes where more rapid adoption of fully Perpendicular detail might have been expected, as with Wodehirst's building in East Anglia. The category also includes the octagonal lantern added to the west tower of Ely Cathedral,

45

46

47

48

49

50

51

52

53

54

55

56

probably in 1369–72. Little that can be regarded as specifically Perpendicular remains in the Merton College Library at Oxford, built in 1371–79 under William Humberville, notwithstandng that he had worked as a mason at Windsor Castle in 1351–54, and that he travelled to London and elsewhere to view libraries. The library does, however, close Mob Quad in regular form and to this extent borrows from Yeveley's up-to-date practice. A good deal more puzzling is the quite opposite case of the church of St. James at Great Grimsby in Lincolnshire, where crossing and tower **27** are of 1365. The style is as fully Perpendicular as anything in the royal works. Other instances of precocious detail, but with less certain chronology, occur at Maxey church in Northamptonshire where the north chapel **44** of the chancel is a chantry founded in 1367, and the choir of Cottingham **36** in east Yorkshire in progress in 1374 and completed before the death of Nicholas de Luda ten years later.

An inscription recorded by Dugdale showed that the splendid steeple of St. Michael's, Coventry **3**, was begun in 1373 and the tower finished by 1395; the spire took another 38 years to build. Not only is the composition superb, but the variation in tracery designs and in the size of windows at different levels indicates that the whole effect was planned from the start. This is not to say that there may not have been adjustments, but every main proportion is satisfactory to a degree that excludes major afterthoughts. Here is a work of genius fit to rank, as I have remarked elsewhere, with the Wonders of the World. Analysis cannot add to its impressive beauty, but may demonstrate the sophisticated eclecticism already attained by Perpendicular architects within a single generation. The west doorway is steeply four-centred, as in John of Gaunt's hall at Kenilworth Castle, and the general character of the mouldings resembles both Kenilworth and the choir of St. Mary's, Warwick (1381?) **72, 73**. On the other hand the five-light west window above comes close to Robert Lesyngham's east window of Exeter Cathedral (1390) and his presumed work at Gloucester, notably the side windows of the north transept (1368) and the later walks of the cloisters, built after 1381 **29–32**.

Two markedly different personal variants of the new style occur at York Minster in the Lady Chapel **6**, of which the first stone was formally laid on 29 July 1361, while the fabric was structurally complete at the death of Archbishop Thoresby on 6 November 1373. The windows of the aisles, whose full-size setting-out can be seen on the surviving plaster tracing-floor, were designed within the term of office of William Hoton junior as master mason. Appointed in October 1351, he had died before the appointment of Robert Patrington on 5 January 1368/9. Whereas Hoton's tracery is a somewhat clumsy mixture of perpendicularised panels and reticulations, Patrington's design is extremely elegant. He combined the Flamboyant flourishes of falchions with vertical panels and arcaded supertransoms, and provided the unusual feature of an external masonry screenwork outside the clerestory windows. This is closely paralleled by the curious arcading which surrounds the base of the spire of Patrington church in the East Riding, very likely Master Robert's birthplace. He had, however, settled in York by 1353 and apparently resided there until 1385 at least. Apart from his post at the Minster he was concerned with making

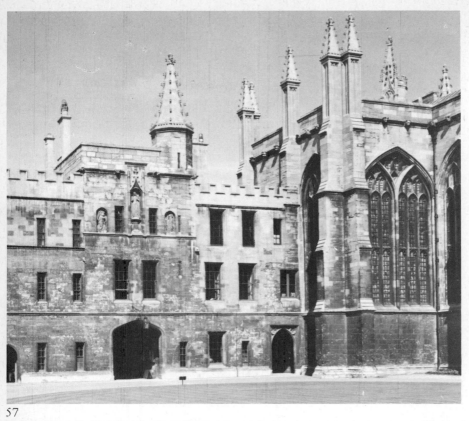

57

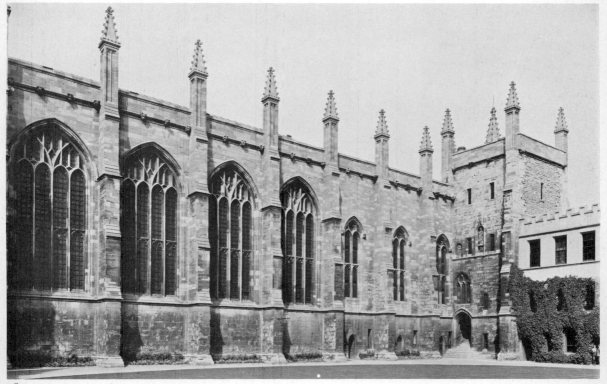

58

59

60

61

62

59 Oxford: New College, west front of ante-chapel 1380–86, above cloisters 1396–, by William Wynford

60 Arundel Collegiate Church from north-west 1380–, probably by Henry Yeveley and William Wynford

61 Arundel Collegiate Church, choir from south 1380–, probably by Henry Yeveley and William Wynford

62 Canterbury Cathedral, south side of nave 1379–, by Henry Yeveley

tombs and monuments, including in 1385 the memorial Cross set up at the command of Richard II on the spot where his half-brother Sir John Holland had killed Sir Ralph Stafford in a brawl.

It is likely, from the use of falchions near its head, that Patrington designed the great east window of the Minster, though some details were altered in execution and it may not have been finished until 1405, when the glass filling was commissioned. The window, although not quite so large overall as that at Gloucester, contains a bigger area of glass and is the most magnificent masterpiece of its kind to survive in Europe. Unlike the Gloucester design, it contains no strong mullions but consists of a single panel divided into a major plane of three 'great lights' and two reticulations, subdivided into three lights each and strengthened by an extensive use of supertransoms. In this combination of supertransoms with falchions Patrington was followed by a school in eastern Yorkshire: at Cottingham church *c*. 1374 **36**; in the nave of Holy Trinity, Hull, *c*. 1389 **65**; at Skirlaugh Chapel (1401) **105**; in Robert Playser's tower at Hedon (1427) **84**; and *c*. 1431 at Thirsk church **137, 140** and also in the south-west tower of York Minster **101**.

Besides the important regional school of architects who practised in York and eastern Yorkshire, there was in the North another major centre at Durham. For over 30 years until his death about 1398 John Lewyn was the chief architect to Durham Cathedral and to the Palatine Bishop. He also had a wide private practice which included work for the Crown at Bamburgh Castle in 1368–72, Carlisle Castle in 1378–83, and at Roxburgh Castle in Scotland (but in English occupation from 1346 to 1460) from 1378 to 1387 and again from 1392, as well as at Berwick-upon-Tweed in 1384–86. He worked at Dunstanburgh Castle for John of Gaunt in 1380–81 and at Bolton Castle in north Yorkshire for Sir Richard le Scrope *c*. 1375–80. On documentary and stylistic grounds it also seems likely that he was concerned with large building programmes at Raby Castle from 1378, and at Sheriff Hutton Castle in Yorkshire from 1382, both for John lord Neville, and later for his son Ralph at Brancepeth Castle. For Durham Cathedral he built the priory kitchen with its oriental vault of intersecting ribs **14** in 1366–71, and in 1395–98 was working at the subordinate priory of Finchale.

Most of Lewyn's known output was of a severely practical kind, and it is difficult to see how he could have had time to do much else. There is, however, one question of attribution to which he appears to be the logical answer. To the palatinate of Durham belonged Howden and its district, Howdenshire, in east Yorkshire. The collegiate church of Howden, now partly in ruins, with its octagonal chapter-house and noble central tower, was architecturally of cathedral rank. The chapter-house, begun in 1380, is in an unusually rich style, with varied traceries and much use of embattled supertransoms **64**. So far the only other traceries which seem at all closely comparable are those of the Perpendicular windows at the east end of Melrose Abbey **fig. 6.14** in Scotland, largely rebuilt during the English occupation of 1385–89. Since Lewyn was certainly in charge at Berwick during this campaign, there is no reason why he should not be the personal link between these buildings over 200 miles apart.

63 Arundel Collegiate Church: choir (Fitzalan Chapel), interior looking north-east 1380–, probably by Henry Yeveley and William Wynford; the timber vault by Hugh Herland, rebuilt 1880.

The Howden tower **83** is a very different matter, having tall transomed windows with tracery of a southern type found at Combe church in Oxfordshire by *c.* 1395 and in the fine rebuilding of Great Shelford church near Cambridge, *c.* 1396–1411 **76, 95**. Internally there are double-ogee and casement mouldings characteristic of the royal works under Yeveley. This main stage of the tower was certainly built with the aid of Bishop Skirlaw (1388–1406), and is said to have been started *c.* 1390. On the other hand he left a legacy of £40 to the fabric of the tower, which might imply that work did not begin until 1406 or later. The detail, however, looks earlier than that.

At this point it is necessary to return to the works of Yeveley and of his colleague Wynford. During the period after 1380 the Perpendicular style came to maturity in their hands, and its principal triumphs were built. The number of important building works greatly increased in the last quarter of the century as compared with the first three-quarters, rising between 1380 and 1395 to a peak never equalled during the Gothic age. For this there were several reasons, of which the chief was the special love of the young king, Richard II, for art and architecture. The opening of the century had been overshadowed by the war with Scotland and then by the great European Famine, by civil strife under Edward II, by the costly campaigns at the start of the Hundred Years War with France, by the Black Death. The apparent victory of England consolidated by the Treaty of Bretigny in 1360 proved to be illusory and in the upshot another invasion of France was undertaken. Only after the deaths of the Black Prince and of his father, Edward III, was there in the new reign of a boy, paradoxically perhaps, a fresh surge of hope and a feeling of renewed prosperity. In spite of the setback of the Peasants' Revolt of 1381 and the threats of French invasion, investment in building began on a very large scale.

To a substantial extent this was due to the fear of invasion. Many castles were built or greatly modernized within a few years, and town walls and gates strengthened. Several castles with which Yeveley was concerned have been mentioned, and others can be added. In March 1378, a few months after the beginning of the new reign, Yeveley and the aged Sponlee were sent to Southampton to advise upon the foundation of a defensive tower, and the work proceeded under Wynford who, in that year and the next, was paid for 380 days spent at Southampton. From 1385 much was done at Portchester Castle under Yeveley's direction, and again in 1396–99 when a minor palace was formed within the castle **52**. At the private castle of Donnington in Berkshire a great gatehouse was built in 1386, completely in the official style and very likely to the design of Wynford **54**. As the threat receded a beginning was made upon the aggrandisement of the civilian house: in the ten years from 1389 was built Dartington Hall **55** in Devon for the king's half-brother John Holland, the first of the great unfortified mansions of our countryside. Old Wardour Castle in Wiltshire **56**, begun in 1392, had both civil and military aspects. Dartington and Wardour were architecturally dependent upon the official style and may be ascribed to Wynford. Dartington's important hammer-beam roof can only be regarded as a trial-piece by Hugh Herland, who certainly designed another for the chapel of New College, Oxford, a half-scale model for Westminster Hall.

64 Howden Collegiate Church: chapter-house 1380–(1400), perhaps by John Lewyn

65 Hull: Holy Trinity Church, nave 1389–1418, from south

66, 67 North Walsham Church: south porch and porch windows *c.* 1382–, possibly by Robert Wodehirst

64

65

66

67

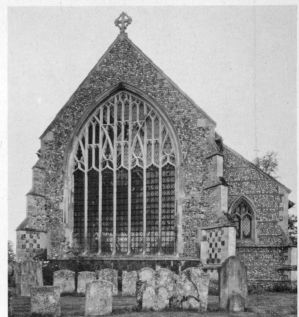

68

69

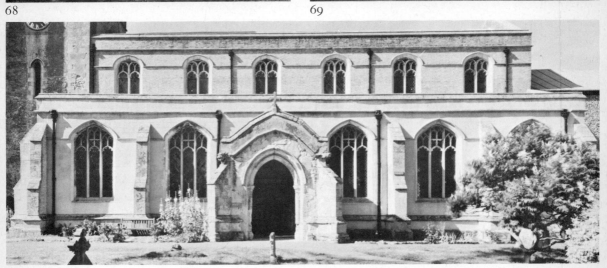

70

More must be said later on details of Herland's style (p. 170).

Yeveley's office, in 1360 granted during the king's pleasure, was in 1369 regranted for life, and in 1378 the new sovereign did not merely confirm this but extended its scope 'throughout England'. For the last 22 years of his life Yeveley was, therefore, as much of an architectural dictator as this country has ever seen. His responsibility for official works of all kinds was limited only by the primacy of the carpenter's craft in a few instances, notably at Westminster Hall, and by purely practical limitations. With the drawing to a close of the works in Windsor Castle by the end of the old king's reign, William Wynford could no longer be maintained as a chief mason more or less co-equal with Yeveley in London. Edward III had granted Wynford a life pension of £10 a year at the end of 1372, and there is no sign that he worked full time for the Crown after the Southampton campaign of 1378–79. He became free to act in a private capacity, chiefly for William of Wykeham, bishop of Winchester.

Stylistically it is not easy to lay down the precise distinction between the designs of Yeveley and those of Wynford. On several occasions they were given joint commissions for royal works, such as the survey of Winchester Castle in 1390, and Yeveley as well as Wynford and Herland was a frequent visitor to Wykeham and also to New College. One obvious difference is that Yeveley rarely employed the four-centred arch, and when he did as at the Canterbury West Gate **50, 51** and Cowling Castle, it was of a low and rounded form. Wynford, on the contrary, made substantial use of the sharper type with the larger arcs almost straight lines. Both masters used normally a pointed arch with centres placed at thirds of the span, a much lower form than the equilateral arch. Notwithstanding the marked differences between the naves of Yeveley's Canterbury **62, 85** and Wynford's Winchester **193**, the tracery systems of their clerestory windows and associated triforium panelling are almost identical. So far as study of their works may yield a subjective impression, one might say that Wynford was the more elastic designer of the two, prepared to adapt himself to regional style and capable of a wide range of variation. Yeveley, though in his early career ready to use pre-existing motives, became more firmly set in his ways, and stamped his later work with a dominant personality.

As if by some magical conjunction the first year of the new reign, 1378, did not merely widen the official scope of Yeveley's architectural authority. By December Archbishop Sudbury had announced his proposal to rebuild the ancient nave of the metropolitan cathedral at Canterbury and called for subscriptions. Work had, he said, already begun, so we may suppose the design to have been made in outline in 1377–78. The details of the aisles, such as the window tracery already mentioned, and the mouldings, leave no doubt that Mr. Arthur Oswald was right in seeing Yeveley as the architect. The fundamental resemblances to the Perpendicular transformation in progress at Westminster Abbey, where Yeveley was already engaged, go far beyond the power of mere imitation and manifest a forceful immediacy attained only by the greatest artists. In the panelled triforium and the patterned spandrels to the arcades **85** Yeveley showed not merely his absorption of the older Court style, but recorded a reminiscent echo of Lichfield Cathedral, which he must have

71

72

74

75

76

77

78

74 Thornton Abbey: gatehouse from east 1382–89

75 Ely Cathedral: gatehouse from east 1396–(99), by John Meppushal

76 Great Shelford Church: east front c. 1396–1411

77, 78 Colmworth Church c. 1390–96: east front; and view from south–east

79

79, 80 Winchester
College 1387–94, by
William Wynford:
chapel and muniment
tower from north–east;
and Middle Gate from
south

81 Oxford, New
College: bell-tower
1396–1400, by William
Wynford

82 St. Albans: clock-
tower c. 1405–10, by
Thomas Wolvey

80

81

82

83

84

known well in the days of his youth. In the exquisitely modulated high vaults he re-stated the views on pattern which he had announced years before in the Black Prince's Chantry.

The building at Canterbury was interrupted by the murder of Archbishop Sudbury during the Peasants' Revolt in 1381, and was not resumed for some ten years. Apart from official business Yeveley probably designed Arundel church and college (*c.* 1380–90) **60, 61, 63**, perhaps in collaboration with Wynford; work at Meopham church in Kent for Sudbury's successor Courtenay; and the chapel on London Bridge (1384–). For Courtenay he evidently designed the church and collegiate buildings at Maidstone **38**, begun about 1395 and largely finished in three years. A variety of window traceries and of mouldings falls within the norm of the official style, but one may assume the association of a competent site architect who was used to working for Yeveley. Such arrangements are on record in the case of the palace built within Portchester Castle **52** in 1396–99. The everyday supervision of the men was in the hands of Walter Weston the sub-warden, but Walter Walton, Yeveley's deputy and coadjutor, visited from time to time to ordain and survey the work. Yeveley's official responsibilities for the repairs of Canterbury Castle and city walls took him into Kent and the high military quality of his work has recently been demonstrated by Colonel J. G. O. Whitehead. Like many other architects of the Middle Ages, he displayed complete mastery over ecclesiastical, civil and military work alike.

Yeveley's use of modified Westminster traceries for the Canterbury cloisters **91** has been mentioned. These were begun in his time, but the renewal of the upper part of the chapter-house **90**, to a closely similar design to the cloisters and the nave aisles, was carried out after 1400 by Stephen Lote. Yeveley's last official work, the reconstruction of the Norman Westminster Hall, gave him his supreme opportunity to design a show-front **86**. The north gable of the hall, surmounted by its pinnacled niche and flanked by two simple towers, rests upon the finest of his welcoming porches in the midst of a long range of nichework. The plain towers were a minor reflection of his tall Clock Tower opposite, and the whole composition of Palace Yard proves Yeveley to have been a town-planner before his time. Conversely, his work inside the hall modestly awards the palm to Hugh Herland's amazing roof **7**. In spite of Richard II's political failure and death, and that of his chief architect a few months later, they left to us the finest achievement of the Middle Ages.

It might be expected that, in comparison with Yeveley's final works, at metropolitan cathedral and royal palace, anything else would be an anticlimax. Yet so far is this from being the case that many have preferred Wynford's nave of Winchester **193** to that at Canterbury, have regarded his design for the western towers added to Wells Cathedral as producing the noblest front of the whole mediaeval period, or have considered his Oxford and Winchester colleges as the finest architectural flower of the fourteenth century. And there is no mere exaggeration or perversity in such judgments. Each one of the greater works of Yeveley, of Herland and of Wynford would be sufficient to rank with the Coventry steeple as Wonders of their age. Changing one art for another, we

PREVIOUS PAGES

83 Howden Collegiate Church: central tower *c.* 1390–, with later belfry stage

84 Hedon Church: central tower 1427–37, by Robert Playser

85 Canterbury Cathedral: nave looking east 1391–1405, by Henry Yeveley

86 Westminster Hall: north front 1397–99, by Henry Yeveley

87 Westminster Abbey: west porch *c.* 1390–1400, by Henry Yeveley

88 Oxford: New College cloister 1396–, by William Wynford

86

87

88

89

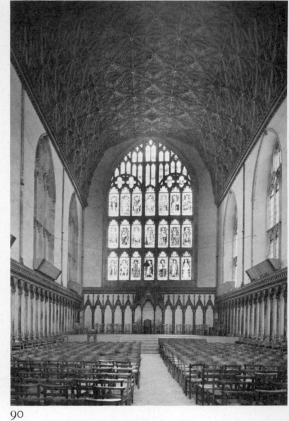

90

91

may fairly consider Yeveley and Wynford as Bach and Handel, Haydn and Mozart. Even if, attaining the higher official position as a national architect for all England, Yeveley is our greatest architect, still in intrinsic creative achievement he is not to be preferred to Wynford. Each to his taste: let both divide the palm.

Wynford's experience at Windsor Castle, where he had the Dean's Cloister as a model, and was concerned with the design of new ranges of royal apartments, underlay his capacity to plan Wykeham's two colleges. New College, begun in 1380 and no doubt designed in 1379, was on a lordly scale, beyond anything hitherto imagined at Oxford. Even now, after six centuries of various design, it is an impressive work **58, 59**. Its internal size is 177 by 125 feet, and before the addition of a third storey to its residential ranges in the seventeenth century, the courtyard would have looked even bigger. The deliberately impressive quality of the internal design was carried through to the outside world by the building, for the first time at Oxford, of a massive gate-tower **57** of defensive aspect and potentiality. This was derived from Wynford's experience at Windsor Castle, and served both the need for security and quiet, and the less tangible desire that the buildings should look imposing. The great height of the gatehouse may even have been a practical afterthought due to the dangers manifested in the Peasants' Revolt, during the second year of building.

Winchester College marks an advance upon New College in organisation. Wykeham and his architect Wynford had learnt a great deal in the course of creating the pioneer of all deliberately planned university colleges. Although Winchester was on a smaller scale it consisted of two courtyards instead of one, with the warden's residence high in the Middle Gate tower between the two **79** surveying all that went on in the outer court of the servants and the inner quadrangle of the boys. Both colleges eschew panelling and other enrichment of the masonry, which follows the normal usage of Yeveley and the official school. Window tracery is more interesting and better organised at Winchester than at New College. Substantial use in the great windows is made of the device of the latticed transom **80, 89**, and the side windows of the chapel have a level supertransom above the central archlet. The latticed usage apparently derives from Gloucester **29** and Hereford **fig. 6.12**, the supertransom from the east window of Edington church **18**, though it had been used by Patrington at York as early as 1369. Simple windows of what was by now standard Perpendicular two-light design were used, and also the less common three-light version with a pair of straight reticulations. One of these occurs in the New College muniment tower **58**, another lights the Winchester vestry, and an almost identical window is found in the chancel of Effingham church in Surrey, repaired by Wykeham's injunction in 1388, at the costs of Merton Priory.

At both New College and Winchester the cloisters **88, 145** were added a few years after the first build, and it is likely that they were functional rather than merely ornamental. At Winchester they were certainly used as supplementary classrooms over a long period, and at Oxford they may have served as a place for study even if not as additional lecture rooms. It is worth recalling that in

89 Winchester College Chapel: interior looking east 1387–94, by William Wynford; timber vault by Hugh Herland

90 Canterbury Cathedral: chapter-house c. 1400–12, by Stephen Lote; timber ceiling probably by Hugh Herland

91 Canterbury Cathedral: cloisters 1397–1414, by Henry Yeveley, completed by Stephen Lote

Spain (with a far more severe winter climate) the cloister was always the normal place for teaching, and the word *claustro*, besides its literal sense, also has the meaning of the whole body of masters. As a dictionary word it is still the Spanish equivalent for 'convocation' in its Oxford significance. New College also built a tower **81** standing by the cloisters, instead of beside the chapel as the original Winchester belfry did. At Winchester there was a tall lead-covered spire, but at New College it appears that Wynford designed a square-topped unbuttressed tower from the start in 1396. By that time he had himself already created the precedent of the south-west tower of Wells Cathedral **20** begun about 1385 and ready for the bells in ten years or less. From structural evidence it is certain that the Wells tower was never intended to have a spire, presumably to rhyme with the strongly horizontal emphasis of the thirteenth-century front below. Yeveley's Clock Tower at Westminster, undoubtedly the architectural precedent for the New College example, did have a small spire.

To Wynford then must be given the credit – or not – for introducing the typical English church tower of the later Middle Ages. The abolition of the spire was surprising and both aesthetically and spiritually a grave step. The intention of the square-topped towers at Wells, in harmony with the old front, is intelligible enough. The deliberately blunt finish, possibly hinted at by Ramsey's unfinished chapter-house at St. Paul's **10**, is in its own way effective. Yet one can hardly suppose that it was Wynford's intention to start a fashion which would end by sweeping away the spire as part of the normal equipment of every church great and small. At Shepton Mallet, only five miles from Wells, the fine western tower of the parish church was probably in course of erection more or less at the same time as the cathedral tower. A stone spire was actually begun, but was not continued and remains as a stump, apparently in response to the new fashion. At Yeovil in the south of Somerset the church was built by a canon of Wells, rector from 1362 until his death in 1382 when he left a major legacy to complete the works. The western tower, spireless, and other features in the church strongly indicate the intervention of Wynford **5**. This is not surprising, as he was already master mason of Wells Cathedral by 1365; but, unless his design for the tower came rather late in the proceedings it is remarkable that it should so closely foreshadow both his decision in favour of topless towers, and the impression of his collegiate style, more especially at Winchester.

That Wynford must have provided designs for parish churches is evidenced not only by the parallel between the windows at Winchester College (1387) and Effingham (1388), but also by the new chancel built at Harmondsworth in Middlesex in 1396–98. The work was done for Winchester College and cost just over £68 inclusive of the glazing of four windows and the fees for dedication. The window design is almost identical with that of the Winchester chapel side windows, except for omission of the supertransom **93, 94**. This tracery design, in one form or the other, was to become a standard feature of later style. It occurs, for example, in the supertransomed form at Tong collegiate church in Shropshire **118**, begun in 1410. Without a supertransom it appears in Yeveley's Holy Cross church at Canterbury (1380), and in the nave of Arundel church (?c. 1390) **60**; about the same time in the cloisters at New College **59, 81**. Enriched with falchions filling the lateral spandrels it was used for the Winchester College cloisters **145**, where the bays are internally framed in squares with intersecting bowtells and blind tracery filling the spandrels.

We have reached William Wynford's, and the century's, last great work, the nave of Winchester Cathedral **193**. It is considerably less satisfactory externally than Canterbury, but this is hardly Wynford's fault. His work was inevitably conditioned by the decision, no doubt dictated by Wykeham's depleted purse and desire to hurry – he was already 70 – not to demolish but to recut the Norman arcades. The work already done under Edington at the west end looked then, as it does now, dreadfully old-fashioned. Even to give moderately satisfactory proportions to the front, Wynford had to add a second parapet above the raking ends of the aisles **21**. Panelling and panelled parapets brought about some kind of unity. Once inside, it is a very different story. Here too the design was hampered by the maintenance of the roof, keeping the crown of the high vault at an exceptionally low level. Yet this limitation was turned by Wynford into the excuse for a design of unique power and exuberance. The need to create an optical illusion of height led, not to the thinning of the vault-ribs as at Canterbury, but to an unparalleled upward surge of cross-arches, diagonals, tiercerons and liernes. Fountains of stone jet upwards, crossing each other's paths with the effect of a cascade inverted. The strong shafts on which the vault is carried might even be pipes or conduits directing the concentrated vertical gush from some reservoir in the foundations.

In the eyes of Freeman, writing in 1849, this work took precedence of everything else produced by our national style. 'Among the superb monuments of the complete Perpendicular style, the first place is undoubtedly due to the nave of Winchester. Making every allowance for the feelings with which one approaches the Cathedral-church of that mighty bishopric ... and endeavouring to pass a calm judgment upon a work hallowed by such associations, and farther allowing every due merit to those who first designed the pile which Wykeham did but re-model, no one can deny to that glorious temple a place in the very first rank, even in the land of Westminster and Lincoln. Nothing among all the products of architecture can be more overpowering than the series of tall shafts and arches, all pointing heavenwards, and extending along its interminable length a succession of the same glorious forms.' Whatever our personal preferences, we dare not disagree.

93, 94 Harmondsworth Church: chancel from south-east and side window 1396–98, here attributed to William Wynford

95 Great Shelford Church: interior looking north-east
c. 1396–1411

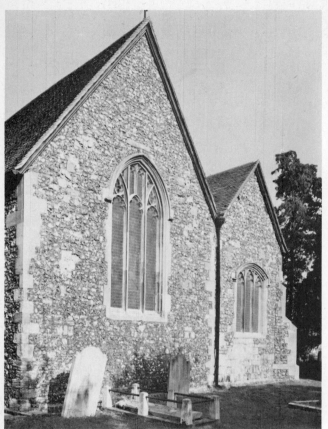

93

94

95

The National Style around 1400

When Henry Yeveley died in the summer of 1400, a few months after King Richard II, the great triumphs of the first pure Perpendicular were well on the road to completion. Westminster Hall, the transformation of the Norman aisled building, was all but finished; the nave of the Abbey nearby much more than begun. Yeveley's own masterpiece, the nave of Canterbury Cathedral, was nearly complete; and much had been done in his colleague Wynford's companion nave at Winchester. Wynford's two colleges held their full complements of fellows and students. The great tower of St. Michael's, Coventry, had reached its coronet and preparations for the spire had started. The rich and highly personal version of official style used by Robert Wodehirst had made its mark on Norwich and East Anglia.

These great buildings, with many smaller works designed by official architects, under their influence, or imitated from their practice, made up the Perpendicular which ruled throughout southern England. Even at York and further north the distinct forms of provincial masters were a parallel stream giving a similar general impression. This was something different indeed from the late Decorated of two generations earlier and from the style in vogue across the Channel and in Scotland. England was going it alone architecturally and its characteristic features were to diverge still more notably from the European norm for another 60 years. In places there were, it is true, pockets of resistance. We have seen the belated retention of Curvilinear details at Norwich and Ely. At Great Shelford church near Cambridge, too, built for Thomas Patesle, archdeacon of Ely, between 1396 and 1411, the spandrels of purely Perpendicular windows are sometimes filled with rosettes of vesica-shapes treated as daggers **76**. Throughout the fifteenth century this was to be a characteristic, revived again and again by some masters, of buildings mainly in the dioceses of Norwich and Ely. Even more noticeably belated were some churches of high quality in the diocese of Lichfield. Bunbury in Cheshire, made collegiate by Sir Hugh Calveley in 1386, indulges in traceries almost purely Flamboyant and with no sign whatever of Perpendicular. Work of this sort was in progress as late as the last few years of the fourteenth century. In a church as important as Holy Trinity in Coventry (1391–), rivalling St. Michael's, the six-light east window with Perpendicular subarcuations has nevertheless a spandrel filled with conjoined daggers.

In the country as a whole, such phenomena are exceptional, and it remains to consider the types of design which arose within the orbit of a national style. There is first of all the trend towards the wider use of the four-centred arch, including with it such related shapes as the segmental-pointed window filled with drop tracery. Although some of the very earliest of four-centred arches in England, in the south transept of Gloucester designed in or very soon after 1331, had been filled with Curvilinear tracery, four-centred traceries were uncommon until after 1400. Both Yeveley and Wynford used the four-centred arch for openings such as gateways, the latter extensively, but very rarely for windows. At Windsor there had been the blind wall-tracery filling the four-centred arches of the Aerary Porch 11, a symptom of Sponlee's adherence to the Gloucester sphere. Outside Gloucester we find Wynford making an exceptional use of four-centred windows in the New College antechapel 57 of 1380, and to about the same date belong the great east window of Arundel church (the Fitzalan Chapel) 63, and some windows in the Great Hospital at Norwich 46. In Wynford's designs for the Winchester nave, after 1394, the combination of clerestory windows and wall-tracery is grouped into a four-centred form of five lights with the outer, blind, lights divided off by strong mullions.

Outside the usage of the official school there was, however, a limited move in the direction of four-centred traceries in two distinct areas. One of these was that of influence from Gloucester: the east window of the chancel of St. Mary's, Warwick (c. 1381–96) 73, the new windows inserted into the Worcester chapter-house in 1386–92 26. The other area of four-centred experimentation lay to the east, and the types of tracery were quite different. At Balsham in Cambridgeshire the church was rebuilt by John Sleford, rector from 1378 until his death in 1401. He had been master of the wardrobe to Edward III, was chaplain to Queen Philippa, prebendary of St. Stephen's Westminster, archdeacon of Wells, and canon both of Wells and Ripon. Hence he moved in exalted circles and might be expected to patronise the official style. The traceries of the nave aisles 70, however, move distinctly away from metropolitan practice towards what was happening at Thornton Abbey in the north of Lincolnshire, and in Howden chapter-house (1380–) 64. The gatehouse at Thornton Abbey is the most precisely dated, begun in 1382 and probably finished by 1389 74. All these share an unusual treatment of horizontal supertransoms, not arcaded or supported by normal cusped archlets, but with small sharp cusps set vertically and horizontally to form a quatrefoil with straightened sides. The motive occurs beyond the border in the English work at Melrose Abbey of 1385–89 fig. 6.14, in an unobtrusive way at Combe church in Oxfordshire (c. 1395) and at All Saints Pavement in York in the west window of about 1395 100.

At Balsham and Thornton this cusping is associated with the four-centred arch, and with the stilted segmental-pointed opening at Catterick church fig. 12.13, Yorkshire (1412–15). In two-centred windows it is also found at Sleaford church, Lincolnshire (before 1403) 104 and at Croyland Abbey in work of 1417–27. Versions survive to a later generation in the tower of St. Margaret's Leicester (–1448–) 165 and in the Trinity (north) chapel of Louth church 139, again in Lincolnshire (c. 1460–65). At Thornton Abbey the issues are much more complicated, as some of the detail and the mouldings 74; fig. 22 come close to the official style of Yeveley, with extensive use of the double-ogee

96

97

98

99

100

101

96 Edington Priory
Church from south
1352–

97 Lingfield Collegiate
Church from north-east
1431–45

98 Canterbury
Cathedral: south-west
tower 1423–34, by
Thomas Mapilton

99 Beverley Minster:
west front c. 1400–30

100 York: All Saints
Pavement, tower
1395–(1425)

101 York Minster:
south-west tower
c. 1431–, here attributed
to William Waddeswyk

mould on a large scale, as at Canterbury. The magnificent gatehouse is a most unusual work, apparently built in response to the threat to monasteries posed by the events of the Peasants' Revolt and related movements of 1381. It is not simply defensive, but designed to impress aesthetically as well as to dominate by sheer scale. Its octagonal turrets, four on each side but differently arranged, are derived from Battle Abbey (1339–); the domestic windows including an oriel on the inner face are suitable for a nobleman's lodging.

The handsome aisleless church of Colmworth in Bedfordshire **77, 78**, unitary in design, was built for Sir Gerard Braybrook (? after 1389–) and ready for consecration in 1396. It shows most of the marks of official style but has also a most unusual window, segmental-pointed with complex drop tracery **77**. The great gatehouse or Porta of the monastery at Ely **75**, built by John Meppushal in 1396–1400, combines extensive use of steep four-centred arches with mostly square-headed windows and also a four-centred type with intersecting tracery crossed by strong mullions. The contrast stylistically between this and the almost exactly contemporary gatehouse at Maidstone College, by Yeveley or his associates, is marked and clearly points to a line of independent development. This is also shown in a less striking way by the character of the south chancel chapel added, as Dr. Eileen Roberts has shown, to Henley Church by Thomas Wolvey in 1397–98. Two varying types of stilted four-centred window were used, one with strong mullions, the other with supermullioned 'top-panelling' of narrow lights. Wolvey was on close terms with Walter Walton and John Swallow, associated with Yeveley's work at Westminster Hall, where Wolvey himself carried out a contract on the towers of the north front. The mouldings at Henley show that he was imbued with the details of the royal school, yet his traceries in spite of their extreme simplicity, belong rather to the new fifteenth-century outlook becoming typical outside official circles.

Within the first ten or fifteen years of the century this new look was spreading widely, even in quite modest churches. Four-centred supermullioned windows are found in the chancel of Lowick church, Northants., built c. 1406–15; a northern version, with crested supertransoms, was employed by a local mason, Richard of Cracall (Crakehall) or Newton, on the south aisle of Hornby church (1410) and for the chancel and east nave at Catterick (1412–15), both in the North Riding **figs. 12.3, 12.13**. Other variants, including traceries of complex design under segmental (unpointed) arches of flat outline, and also unusual four-centred designs, were combined in 1414–19 in the large church – legally a mere chapel-of-ease – of St. Nicholas at Lynn in Norfolk **112**. This also contains two of the finest early examples of subarcuated intersecting tracery as its east window of nine lights and its west, of eleven **113, 114**. This type, employing supertransoms, has an eastern distribution, and seems to have been invented by Robert Wodehirst, as it is first found in the east window of the choir **fig. 6.13** of the Great Hospital at Norwich (c. 1380–85) and in his traceries in the north cloister of the Cathedral (1385) **158**. It was used at Great Shelford church (c.1396) **76**, and had reached the East Riding in the nave of Holy Trinity, Hull (1389–1418) **65** and at Skirlaugh Chapel (1401–5) **105**. In east Yorkshire an

102, 103 Nottingham, St. Mary's Church: from south-west; and interior looking north, 1401–

104 Sleaford Church: chancel from south-east c. 1400–(03)

105 Skirlaugh Chapel from west 1401–05

102

103

104

105

106

107

108

enormous east window of nine lights of this kind was inserted in Beverley Minster (1416) **115**. In Lincolnshire such traceries were used at Sleaford **104** before 1403, and for the east window of Louth by *c.* 1430. As a somewhat unexpected final fling, they appeared in the side windows of Eton College Chapel (1448–60) **179**.

Segmental-pointed arches with drop tracery were used in the exquisite De la Pole Chapel in Wingfield church, Suffolk **figs. 12.6, 12.7**, in progress in 1415. The traceries are of two very different types, which have sometimes been regarded as of two periods. The details and mouldings are, however, the same, though we have the four-lobed rosette with daggers of Curvilinear appearance cheek-by-jowl with strong mullions, crested supertransoms, and the rather stark impression of typical Suffolk work of the time. It should be added that the gaunt, taut look of much East Anglian work is produced by economy in freestone, there an expensive imported commodity. Slightly earlier (1407–11) is the Guildhall at Norwich **109**, built by a local mason John Marwe. This has extremely simple windows, four-centred, with four lights: two have two-centred heads, two are ogee. These, long before the Tudor period, have 'squash' tracery above the springing, in spite of the very flat arches. Moving westwards into the great quarrying belt, where a more lavish use of stone was possible, four-centred arches with a large well rounded profile are found, filled with tracery originating in the Gloucester style as modified by Robert Lesyngham towards the end of the fourteenth century. Of this type are the rich windows of the south cloister at Hereford Cathedral **figs. 12.9; 19**, built by Thomas Denyar in *c.* 1412–18.

The steeper four-centred arch of the Kenilworth Castle pattern continued to be used in the Midlands, and spread as far north as Nottingham. There the very large parish church of St. Mary **102, 103**, the finest non-cathedral church of a wide region, had just been begun in 1401, when a petition produced an indulgence from Pope Boniface IX for ten years to those giving alms for the fabric. It had been described in the petition as 'newly begun, with solemn, wondrous and manifold sumptuous work, towards the consummation of which a multitude of workmen with assiduous toil fervently strive daily.' Some of the tracery follows the pattern of that in the Worcester chapter-house, though the arches are much higher in proportion, and the cinquefoiled archlets of the lights are two-centred **103**. At Worcester **26**, true to the western regional tradition, they were trefoiled ogees. As has been mentioned, we cannot now trust the authenticity of the magnificent four-centred windows at Adderbury chancel in north Oxfordshire **120**. This was built by Richard Winchcombe in 1408–18, and enough of his authentic work is left to explain why he was later chosen as first architect of the Oxford Divinity School. He was working at Portchester Castle in 1398–99 and perhaps later on Winchester College. By 1405 he was being employed by New College and must soon have been recognised as the most distinguished architect in Oxford and its neigh-bourhood. He probably designed for New College the splendid tithe-barn (1403–) at Swalcliffe **108**. Various forms of the four-centred arch are normal in his work, which appears as an enriched development from Wynford's style

106 Broughton Castle: gatehouse 1406–

107 Caister Castle 1432–46, perhaps by William Gravour

108 Swalcliffe: tithe barn 1403–06, probably by Richard Winchcombe

109 Norwich: Guildhall from south-east 1407–11, by John Marwe

110 York: Guildhall interior 1448–60, by Robert Couper

111 Lynn: Guildhall 1421–23, probably by John Turnour

112 Lynn: St. Nicholas 1414–19, side window;
113, 114 west front; and interior looking east

115 Beverley Minster: east window 1416–(20)

109

110

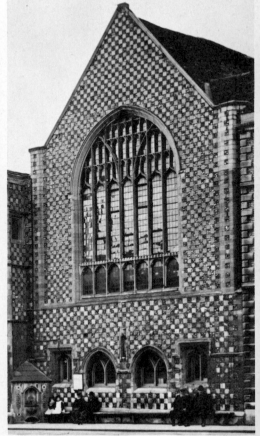

III

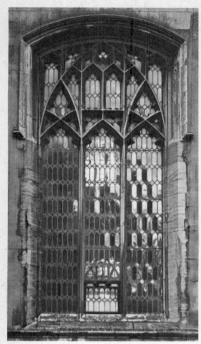

112

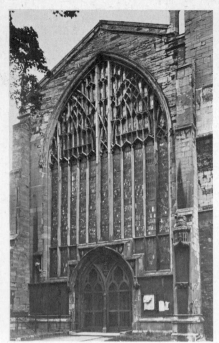

113

114

115

interpreted by a Gloucestershire man, as we must suppose from his name that Winchcombe was.

Because it is one of the very few cases where complete accounts have been preserved, Adderbury chancel is crucial as a specimen of building costs in the heyday of the later Middle Ages. The detailed study of the accounts made by T. F. Hobson fifty years ago enabled him to be precise as to the whole cost of building the new chancel, with its roofing, glazing, and pavement. The sum was £399 5s. 4d., borne by New College, Oxford, impropriators of the church, responsible as rectors for the fabric of the chancel. Mr. Hobson suggested, in the light of estimates by several historians and economists, that the figure should be multiplied by a factor of × 30 to bring it to values of building in 1926, as 'certainly not an over-estimate and it may well be an under-estimate to the extent of ten per cent. or more.' Eight years later, in 1934, the late Dr. Coulton gave sound reasons for accepting a factor of × 40 so 'that the reader can get a rough idea of the truth.' At any rate for the building trade, with subsequent adjustments for the fall in the value of sterling since 1934, Coulton's figure has stood the test of time. We cannot, for practical purposes, get much nearer than multiplying mediaeval amounts of the fourteenth century by 40 to give an idea of the cost between the two World Wars. Since then spiralling inflation has put up building costs not less than ten times, which turns Coulton's factor of × 40 into × 400, for prices of 1300–1348. The waves of inflation and deflation between 1348 and 1408 present another difficult, but relatively minor problem.

As a rough and ready approximation for our present purpose it seems reasonable to take four-fifths of the Coulton factor as representing values in the Perpendicular epoch, that is × 320 now (1977). It will be seen that this conversion is equivalent to raising Hobson's factor from × 30 to × 32 in the case of Adderbury. The agreement between his estimate, Coulton's, and subsequent investigators', is remarkably close, though it is only valid for building, and not for ascertaining the present value of any mediaeval sum of money. We are talking, then, of a parish chancel of fine quality which would cost nowadays not less than (£400 × 320) a total of £128,000, about one-eighth of a million. Labour costs show wide differentials. Labourers were paid 18d. to 20d. a week, fully skilled craftsmen mostly 3s.; after conversion this gives a minimum wage for a labourer (Thomas Gentylman!) of £24 a week, and for a skilled mason £48, exactly double. Some labourers were able to get over £26. Winchcombe did a good deal by contract, but when he was paid at a weekly rate it was 3s. 4d. (£53.33p.). He also had a yearly livery from New College in 1410–1418.

At a later stage in his career, when architect for the Divinity Schools on behalf of the University of Oxford, Winchcombe received an annual fee of £2 (£640), with a weekly rate of 4s. (£64) when actually engaged on the works, a yearly robe of the livery of gentlemen (*de liberata generosorum*) or in lieu 13s. 4d. (£213.33p.), as well as lodging for himself and his assistants and reasonable travelling expenses when on the business of the University. These fees compare with the pay and allowances given to the chief masters of the King's Works of

1s. for every day of the year, viz. £18 5s. (£5,840) and £1 (£320) for clothing allowance. Men such as Henry Yeveley, even though paid throughout the year for their official work, were none the less free to carry on a great deal of private work in addition. We have to see the wide gap between such remuneration and conditions and that of the ordinary skilled craftsman, perhaps working a 60-hour week for his 3s. (£48), as largely justified by the architectural services given by the chief masters. The creative design of the work was then, as always, rewarded at a higher rate than mere handiwork; but in the Middle Ages the differentials and the consequent incentive to acquire 'professional' skill were greater than they have generally been since.

Continuing to take the accounts for Adderbury chancel as a convenient yardstick for the period, we may consider the costs of materials and plant. Freestone, bought by the foot from the quarries at Taynton, cost from 1½d. to 2d., an extremely low price compared to those quoted by Salzman and equivalent to perhaps 2s.–3s. per ton (£32–£48). To this had to be added carriage from the quarries to Adderbury at 2s. or 2s. 6d. per cartload (£32–£40). Quicklime cost 20d. or 22d. per quarter (between £25 and £30), and a basket to carry it in was bought for 3d. (£4). Hurdles for making the staging of the scaffolds also cost nearly 3d. each. Boards for making templates and iron hammers were bought together in 1410 for 4s 11d. (just under £80). Timber brought from Wychwood by John Gylkes the carpenter cost £1 (£320) and its carriage amounted to 7s. 10d. (over £125). Wrought ironwork such as hinges and bars was usually priced at 1¾d. per lb. (about £260 per cwt.). Wax and resin were purchased for making cement, that is a waterproof mortar, for 10½d. (£14). On the other hand, the whole of the glazing of the windows was done for £10 6s. 4d. or, say, £3,300. Possibly the most interesting item of equipment was the *vernum* or hoist, which needed 4½ days' work by John Carpenter and his mates to get it into working order, and later repairs to the wheel. This altogether amounted to about £1 (£320). A cable and sling for raising stones cost 10s. 10d. in 1412–13, and next year 10s. was spent on an old cable, while in 1414–15 a new cable cost 16s. 4d. (over £260).

Adderbury is exceptionally well documented, but without considering the real total of building works at the time, we can get a statistical sample. Between 1375 and 1415, roughly the reigns of Richard II and Henry IV, some 140 different builds that are dateable can be identified. Either the year of the start is exactly known or the margin of error amounts only to a year or two. These builds include works ecclesiastical, military and civil, sometimes whole major churches or castles, though more often a specific gatehouse, or hall, chapel, cloister or chapter-house. Sometimes the work is not new, but an extensive rebuilding, such as the rehabilitation of the King's hall at Westminster, or the restoration of the chapter-house at Worcester. Out of 144 builds only one-twelfth were civil or domestic; castles, walls and towers, and gatehouses account for another 21; the vast majority were churches or colleges, monasteries and hospitals, or parts of them. There were no fewer than 21 complete churches built, or largely built, as well as 29 church towers great and small. These figures which, though they include a high proportion of builds of major quality, are all the same only a part of the architectural output, give some idea of the preponderance of religious motives in mediaeval building. In view of the often repeated view that, after the thirteenth century the age of faith had disappeared, this merely factual statistic should supply a much needed corrective. It must in any case be an understatement, for through the accidental loss of records, the total does not include any works on the many churches of friars; yet the four great mendicant orders: Dominican, Franciscan, Carmelite and Austin Friars, were throughout the latter part of the Middle Ages exceptionally favoured by gifts and bequests from the laity, largely converted into buildings, as at the Blackfriars of Norwich **205**.

From this interlude we may return to consider the remaining output of this 40 years. What has already been dealt with consisted of works which, by the use of the four-centred arch and related forms, were moving towards the new norm of Perpendicular. There was, however, a large body of work that remained relatively close to the official style of Yeveley. It was not until after about 1415 that the old canons of orthodoxy were to any large extent abandoned. It should be emphasized that in many ways the style and pattern-book of Yeveley and the details and mouldings used by him, dominated until the very end. This was most notably the case in buildings near London and Westminster, or produced officially, but it was not without effect in remote parts of the country too.

We have seen that there was within this period a move towards four-centred traceries and features of cognate type in two main areas: one in the West Midlands, moving outwards from Gloucestershire towards the north and east; and the other on the eastern side of England, between Cambridgeshire and the Scottish border. These two provincial schools or types were quite distinct, as was each from the older official Perpendicular, mainly employing the two-centred arch. If we consider some of the fundamental motives of this older official style, we shall see that within this same 40 years they were already tending to consolidate, grouped in some broad regions rather than others.

Taking first the standard two-light window with a single straightened reticulation, this had a wide general distribution over the South, but had not been accepted in the North or North-West, though found as a London export in the Neville Screen shipped to Durham **40, 42**. The closely similar three-light window with two straight reticulations, providing the basis for the whole of Alternate tracery, had a markedly distinct distribution. It was almost exclusively used to the west and south-west of London. The split version of the two-light window, though of general distribution like the first with open oculus, has a tendency to the East and South, avoiding the Midlands and the North-West. The three-light development of this, forming a window vertically panelled in the head and the basis for Supermullioned tracery, has a general distribution except in the South and the more remote South-West. Like the more fully developed tracery of gridiron form which emerged from it rather later, this was typical of the eastern side of the country.

Then, a survival from Decorated, there is the Y-tracery, generally cinquefoiled in each light and with a quatrefoil in the spandrel. This is a mark of the Court style, persisting throughout, but hardly ever found in the West, South-West or South. Another form derived from the practice of the Court masters is the three-light window with strong mullions and subarcuation of the two side-lights containing inverted daggers, far more frequent in the South-East than elsewhere, and, when found in the remoter parts of England, likely to indicate the intervention of a royal architect or fairly close contacts with London. It is an apparent paradox that the two species of tracery most obviously derived from pre-Perpendicular practice should be the most clearly indicative of Court influence. In other words, the radically new elements in Perpendicular, though extensively employed by the generation of Yeveley, were developed further by provincial artists outside official circles. The King's Works maintained an extremely conservative tradition.

When we leave the simpler motives and consider less usual tracery, a peripheral resistance to domination from London becomes evident. This resistance took different forms but tends to be more marked as we get further from the metropolis. The strong regionalism of Alternate tracery, nearly confined to the sector south-west of London, has already been remarked, as also the strongly eastern grouping of subarcuated intersecting windows **Map IX** with supertransoms. Certain other aspects of regionalism will make their appearance as we consider the residual works of the generation after *c.* 1380. Notwithstanding the firmly unifying tendency of the greater architects much in demand among courtly patrons, there was already a wide range of differentiation, despite similarities imposed by regional materials and by local schools of traditional masoncraft. In the account which follows, the main groups of counties, starting from the London area, will be dealt with in a clockwise order.

The especially noble parish church of Ashwell in the north of Hertfordshire is precisely documented by an inscription stating that the church was completed in AD 1381. Just how much earlier the work began is far from certain, but it is obvious that the start was made before any signs of the Perpendicular style had got 40 miles north of London. A good deal of what we now see is much later than 1381 and has to be subtracted. It is then clear that what was finished at that date was the top storey of the western tower, a plain unbuttressed cubical stage on top of the splendidly proportioned buttressed lower storeys. The traceries of the twin windows in the belfry stage below are of substantially earlier date, though of the same general pattern; they have now all been renewed but to the old design, of which vestiges survived; the base of the tower was built before the Black Death. The church belonged to Westminster Abbey, which may explain why so important a church was built in a remote place. So far as the work is Perpendicular, it is of the official school. The same can be said of Wymington church in the north of Bedfordshire, where the Curvilinear work in the chancel suggests a beginning around 1360, but the tower was finished shortly before the death of John Curteys who died in 1391. Also close to Wynford's version of the royal style is the church of Westbourne in Sussex, near the Hampshire border, built *c.* 1390. At Houghton Conquest in Bedfordshire is a tower built by contract in 1392–95 by William Farele of

Dunstable and Philip Lessy of Totternhoe for £40 (now, say, £13,000). Dr. Eileen Roberts has shown how this work to some extent reflects a regional style around the Totternhoe stone quarries, but the use of the double-ogee moulding and of two standard types of tracery brings the work into the official orbit. Lessy had actually worked at the manor of King's Langley in 1368, and Dr. Roberts has pointed out the close likeness of the window with strong mullions and inverted daggers to one at King's Langley church.

The collegiate church begun at Pleshey in Essex in 1393, now destroyed, would have witnessed the spread of royal style from London, on account of its foundation by the Duke of Gloucester. A contrary movement is shown by the west window at Watford, Hertfordshire, a church begun in 1399. This is practically a copy of the side windows of the north transept at Gloucester, designed in 1367. At St. Albans, however, where the Abbey were owners of Watford, the town clock tower **82** was built between 1404 and 1411 as a small-scale version of Yeveley's Westminster belfry. Thomas Wolvey was probably the designer. Moving across London to the south-east we find that the Guardroom or Great Parlour of the Archbishop's Palace at Croydon (*c.* 1400–10) is conventional London work of the time, and so is the tower at Addington, Kent, built in 1400–03. At Crayford, Kent, the tower was under construction in 1406 by a mason, John Wells. For the west window he used the two-light Y-tracery standard in the king's works.

Rather enigmatic is the Lady Chapel at Christchurch Priory, Hampshire **92**, almost certainly the 'New Chapel' in which Sir Thomas West wished to be buried when he made his will in 1405. He left £100 to the work of the church, which on stylistic grounds would seem to imply completion of the Lady Chapel and adjacent parts. The details and traceries, though related to the south-eastern supermullioned style, also include supertransoms and carry mullions up to the apex of subarcuations. There is as well a mixture of two-centred and ogee heads to lights. The unusual vault is very fine and related to the net-vaults of Sponlee in the Aerary Porch at Windsor (1353) **11** and of Wynford at New College (*c.* 1385) **12**. It was imitated in the Christchurch choir not built until *c.* 1502. The idiosyncrasies of the Lady Chapel have not so far been matched elsewhere, and may be the work of a man who either died young, or spent most of his life in the service of the Priory. We have a documented instance of a working career in one employment in the case of John Croxton, master mason to the city of London for 35 years, from 1411 to 1446 or later. His main work consisted of the Guildhall which still remains in spite of disastrous damage in the Great Fire of 1666 and in the Second World War. Enough of the original detail survives to show that he was a faithful continuator of the style of Yeveley. Towards the end of his career Croxton built the Guildhall Chapel about 1440–42, and though this has been destroyed its details are on record. They show a heavily panelled style with a great west window of seven lights with two level ranges of latticed transoms. The contrast between this somewhat pedestrian work and the Guildhall itself suggests that Croxton, when he began in 1411, may have been carrying out designs supplied from Westminster. There is a known link between Yeveley

Fig. 12 Examples of Late Perpendicular tracery

1 BRIDPORT
S. AISLE c.1397

2 BRIDGWATER
TRINITY CHAPEL
1403

3 CATTERICK
SIDE WINDOW 1412
Richard Cracall

4 WINGFIELD
MANOR 1443
Richard Kyng

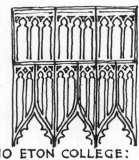

5 CHURCH
HANBOROUGH
1399

6,7 WINGFIELD: DE LA POLE CHAPEL
—1415— SIDE AND EAST WINDOWS

8 FARLEIGH
HUNGERFORD 1443

9 HEREFORD: SOUTH
CLOISTER c.1412
Thomas Denyar

10 ETON COLLEGE:
HALL ORIEL 1441—
Robert Westerley

11 LOWICK: GREENE
CHAPEL   1468

**DIAGRAMMATIC SKETCHES
NOT TO SCALE**

14 HATFIELD: OLD
PALACE c.1480

12 LYNN ST. MARGARET
AISLES 1472

13 CATTERICK: EAST
WINDOW   1412
Richard Cracall

15 WORSTEAD
CHANCEL 1484

J.H.H.

1977

and Croxton in that Walter Walton, Yeveley's deputy, left his best compass to Croxton when he died in 1418.

Details from London had reached Cheddar in Somerset by *c.* 1380. St. Mary's Chapel **fig. 6.10**, newly founded by 1382, is at the north-east angle of the church and, though much altered, has a standard Perpendicular two-light window and a three-light east window of mullioned and panelled tracery, employing trefoiled cusping to the main lights and with a pleasantly quirky little filling to the lateral spandrels. Since Cheddar was a peculiar of the dean and chapter of Wells it is likely that Wynford was concerned in this work. At Exeter Cathedral, as we know, it was Robert Lesyngham from Gloucester who had charge through most of the last quarter of the century. He designed the great east window **31** inserted in 1390–92, close to both Gloucester and Winchester, as well as the delightful little fan-vaulted north porch of the west front **32**.

At Bridgwater church the Trinity (north-east) chapel was built in 1403–15, and has three-light alternate windows with split panels in the head. This is carried out rather in the Bristol manner, but shows signs of official influence. More definitely in the south-western alternate manner is the nave aisle tracery at Bridport in Dorset, three-light Perpendicular with five-foiled cusping. The work was probably done shortly before 1399 when the church was dedicated. The tower at St. Peter's, Dorchester (Dorset), finished by 1412, has two-light windows of the strictly London style. On the other hand John Tynlegh, the master probably responsible for the new windows in the Exeter chapter-house **135**, designed *c.* 1413, was already deeply imbued with Devonian feeling. The four-light windows are subarcuated and of two different patterns. In one the alternate and through-reticulated character is stressed, with subreticulation beneath each subarcuation and inverted cusping at the base of each tracery light. The other has a supertransom in the spandrel, with the panels treated as small windows throughout, having five-foil cusping at the heads only. The main lights all have ogee heads. Here is a work pioneering in the lead of the later West-Country Perpendicular.

Moving up into the West Midlands we find a much earlier example of the subarcuated window with through reticulation and ogee heads in the chapter-house of St. Mary's, Warwick. This little building may well be of about 1390, and is not likely to be much later, as there are double-cusped trefoils to the main lights. Of 1392–93 are the very singular upper windows, two-light with an ogee hoodmould, of the upper stage of the Edgar Tower, the gatehouse to Worcester Cathedral Priory. These were designed by the Master of the Earl of Warwick on a visit, when he was presumably called in because of the death or resignation of John Clyve. Also in the diocese, though in Warwickshire, is Knowle, where the church was built in 1396–1402, being made collegiate in 1416. The nave aisle windows have three lights with trefoil cusping and simple alternate tracery **43**.

In Oxfordshire the standard Perpendicular two-light window is found in the tower of Combe church, *c.* 1395, and at Church Hanborough, begun in 1399, where there are also square-headed windows with ogee trefoiled filling **fig.**

12.5. The official style also occurs at Broughton Castle near Banbury, where the gatehouse **106** was built for Thomas Wykeham, the bishop's nephew, in 1406. The design looks, as has been suggested by Sir William Hayter, as if it might have been Wynford's last work before he died (26 July 1405), carried out posthumously. Variants of the Court style three-light window occur in the tower at Cirencester in *c.* 1402–03, with strong mullions and simple panels; in both three-light and five-light versions at Battlefield church (1406–09) in Shropshire **116**, where an oculus with quatrefoil surmounts the panels; and at Tong collegiate church **118**, founded in 1410, with inverted daggers and supertransom, as at Winchester College chapel. Since Battlefield was rebuilt by Henry IV as a chantry its detail can have come straight from the drawing boards at Westminster.

Three-light windows of a most curious design are found, differing only slightly, at St. Asaph Cathedral in Flintshire, in the tower built by Robert Fagan of Chester in 1391–92, and in the Clopton Chapel at Stratford-on-Avon (*c.* 1410–15) by John Kyrton. The main lights have trefoiled two-centred heads and these are then treated as a pair of intersecting ogees terminating in vertical supermullions. At Stratford the lateral spandrels are cusped falchions and the central oculus is a quatrefoil; at St. Asaph it has five-foil cusping at the head only. Kyrton was a mason of Winchcombe; Fagan later became master mason in Cheshire and North Wales under the Crown, from 1396 to 1413. A common training in the traditions of the diocese of Worcester might best explain this unusual coincidence. The treatment of the heads as interlacing ogees derives from the early part of the Gloucester east cloister **29** and the windows of the Hereford chapter-house recorded by Stukeley.

In the North a marked regional style was developing around Hull and York during the last years of the fourteenth century. From Patrington's handling of tracery derived the windows at Skirlaugh Chapel **105**, designed as late as 1401, with delicate falchions as fillers in the spandrels of subarcuations. In other respects this finely proportioned little building comes close to southern norms, and Somerset influence has been detected, to be accounted for by Walter Skirlaw's two years (1386–88) as bishop of Bath and Wells. This should be understood as implying personal contacts with Wynford, since no 'Somerset School' existed by that date. Other contacts with official masters are implied by details of the tower at Tickhill, dated to between 1373 and 1399 by heraldic references to John of Gaunt, Duke of Lancaster. A date of design near 1390 is to be presumed. More direct domination from Westminster is proved by Henry IV's action in sending William Colchester, the Abbey master, to take charge at York Minster after the partial collapse of the central tower in 1407. Colchester had been Yeveley's right-hand man at the Abbey by 1395 and succeeded as master on Yeveley's death. Colchester, described by the king as 'mason, expert in that art and much commended', was accompanied by William Waddeswyk his assistant. Both were murderously assaulted in York, and Waddeswyk seriously injured. He survived all the same to become the third Westminster-trained architect to rule the Minster works, from January 1426 until his death late in 1431. Colchester eventually made his peace with the city of York and

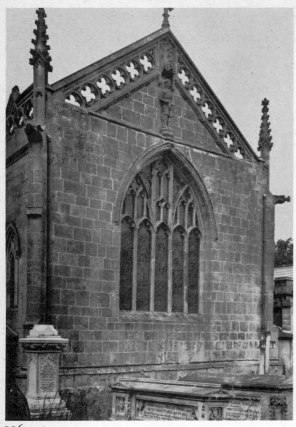

116

117

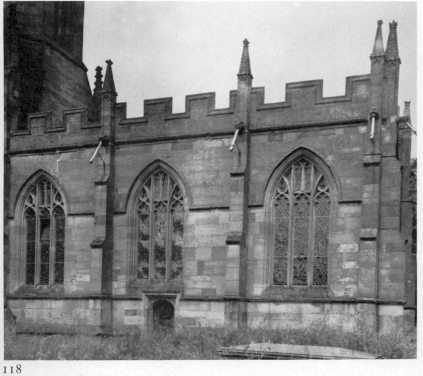

118

119

took up the freedom in 1417. On his death towards the end of 1420 he was succeeded at Westminster Abbey by his warden John Thirsk, and at York by John Long, an Abbey mason since 1394. Long became free of York in 1421 and died in 1425. Waddeswyk continued as a subordinate and took up the freedom of York only in 1427, after succeeding Long as master.

This Westminster influence upon the style of the great northern cathedral lasted from 1407 for nearly a quarter of a century and was responsible for the introduction of important features of London character, in sharp contrast to the work of Hugh Hedon, who had been in charge from *c.* 1394 and designed the choir bays and the new crossing-arches inserted beneath the tower. The 'strainer' screens introduced by Colchester across the north and south choir aisles to stiffen the eastern crossing piers **fig. 27**, and the original design for the pulpitum screen between the piers **fig. 29**, were the first-fruits of this intervention. Colchester also designed the Old Library (*c.* 1414–19) and the new central lantern **6**, intended by him to be surmounted by an upper belfry stage of the kind later seen at Durham. The actual construction of the lantern did not come until long after his death, with changed details. On the other hand, the stone altar screen (now a careful replica made after the fire of 1829) may well have been executed under Colchester **fig. 29**, since the new High Altar existed by 1416. The design of the western towers, of which the south-western was in progress by 1433, may have been made by Waddeswyk before his death **101**.

London style was carried further north into county Durham, where the octagon of the tower at Chester-le-Street (?*c.* 1400) has windows of Y-tracery of official type. A personal link was Thomas Mapilton, master at Durham Cathedral from 1408 to 1416. Mapilton is known to have gone to London from the south of Derbyshire, probably with his brother John before 1390, and most of his later career was based on London. He was the king's chief mason from 1421 to his death in 1438. Unfortunately his main work at Durham, on the cathedral cloisters, has been destroyed or altered beyond recognition. Mapilton's services were much in demand: he designed the south-west tower of Canterbury Cathedral **98** in 1423, advised on the maintenance of Rochester Bridge, built the old church of St. Stephen Walbrook in the city of London (1429), and in 1430 surveyed the dangerous western tower of the abbey church at Bury St. Edmunds. London influence appears, mingled with elements of northern design, in two churches of high quality in and near York. All Saints Pavement, in the centre of the city, belonged to Durham, though this would not necessarily have any architectural bearing upon the western tower which, with its exquisite open lantern **100**, was in course of building from 1395 to about 1425. At Bolton Percy, eight miles to the south-west, the chancel **117** was built by Thomas Parker, rector 1411–23, and dedicated in 1424. The side windows of alternate Perpendicular, doubly divided with Y-tracery and with cinquefoiled cusping throughout, look very southern but the east window comes close to the western window of All Saints Pavement. Both appear to owe something to the tracery of Great Shelford, Cambs. **76, 95** of *c.* 1396–1411, which has, however, trefoiled cusping in the tracery lights.

116 Battlefield Collegiate Church: east front of choir 1406–09

117 Bolton Percy Church: chancel from south-east (1411)–23

118 Tong Collegiate Church: choir from south 1410–

119 Fotheringhay Collegiate Church: nave 1434–(41), by William Horewode

This brings us full circle to the eastern side of England and East Anglia. We have seen that this was an area where the four-centred arch took hold early, as well as the extensive use of horizontal supertransoms producing rectilinear tracery. Rectilinear cusping, still further accentuating the impression of a grille of bars, has been noticed at Balsham, Cambs. **70**, under the rector John Sleford, and also at Sleaford, Lincs. **104**, very likely his birthplace, by about the turn of the century, and at Croyland Abbey a little later. A rather different and richer style is found at Cavendish in Suffolk **68, 69**, where the chancel was rebuilt after 1381 under the will of Sir John Cavendish. Considerable use is made in this of daggers and falchions, as in Patrington's work at York, though Cavendish is clearly by a different hand, incorporating Flowing and Geometrical elements into a pattern otherwise completely Perpendicular.

At Peterborough, where a new parish church of St. John the Baptist was built in 1402–07, most of the tracery has been destroyed, but the tower windows show the strong influence of London, presumably brought along the North Road. The upper stage of the tower, however, between slender octagonal turrets, is perhaps considerably later than the rest of the building. This could not be deduced from the tracery as it fits well into the typological pattern of the period near 1400. We are left with one more notable work near Norwich, the tower over the central crossing of Wymondham Abbey **28**, built for the monastery in 1390–1409. The details of the windows are advanced for this date, combining Y-tracery of the Court style, as well as inverted daggers and subreticulation, with ogees and with depressed four-centred heads. The tower is an octagon of two stages based on a square crossing, with the change masked by diagonal buttresses stepped back at the corners. It was probably capped by a tall spire, and the design was based on the usage of the greater friars' churches.

We have now surveyed the national style in its early maturity. While Yeveley, Wynford and a few other outstanding architects such as Lesyngham at Gloucester and Patrington at York were scoring their triumphs, many lesser men were beginning by force of imitation and the steady pressure of fashion to build up a background of varied combinations of the new elements. Well before 1400 the whole country had firmly rejected the promising beauty of Curvilinear and Flamboyant art, and this had been snapped up by eager continental architects anxious to break away from the antiquated hegemony of French Gothic. Another of the battles of North against South had been fought and lost: not even the powerful patronage of Archbishop Melton and the splendid results achieved by the new style of Ivo de Raghton at Carlisle, York, Beverley, Selby and Southwell, could win against the firmly disciplined taste of the king. Edward III, even while he was promoting the cult of his martyred father at Gloucester, was looking for something stronger, less luxurious, perhaps consciously nobler, than the lush curves and crockets breaking down into romanticism. In the 1330s the first steps had been taken, by English architects and carvers, towards the creation of Sondergotik as an international Romantic movement, reacting against the dead hand of classicism. In a broad sense they succeeded, though the new forms they created appealed more to foreign than to homebred fancy.

The reaction away from Curvilinear and the artistic licence which was its logical outcome lay in fundamental traits of English character, full of practical common-sense. Our deeply imbedded love of the line, especially the clear outline, was offended by convolutions which seemed, in the hands of some sculptors, almost to wriggle with a pulsating life of their own. England was ready to turn away in dislike, and for once found itself behind the personal taste of a great sovereign. Edward III was no ascetic; he clearly delighted in rich apparel and magnificent accoutrements. Yet in fundamentals he was a soldier, with the soldier's capacity to shear away all that is unessential to victory, or to survival. He was too a learned, or at least a very well taught man, tutored by the book-loving Richard de Bury. Bury was, among much else, the leading orientalist of his day, and hoped to see the fulfilment of the papal decree setting up professorships of Hebrew, Arabic and Aramaic at Oxford. The 'numerous astronomical treatises' in Arabic were seen by him as of transcendent importance. Another of the king's intimates, Thomas Bradwardine, was the greatest mathematician of the age. It is not unduly far-fetched to see in such contacts a predisposition towards the geometrical. The creative discipline of the well wielded compasses, derived from Arabic art and already introduced to English architecture at Canterbury, exercised a greater attraction than the unbounded variations of free fantasy.

Hence the accidental coming together of several factors in design, when the Ramseys of East Anglia interchanged ideas with the court masters of London in a climate of taste dominated by the Kentish school, yielded a style with positive appeal. From the king's appointment of William Ramsey as chief architect – for so we must term his chief master mason south of Trent – the radically new idea developed of itself. Once the germ of Perpendicular had started to grow and to take root, it acquired a life of its own. Successive masters, notably Yeveley, might tend it and prune it, shape it by topiary, but its individuality was assured. It may be no coincidence, psychologically speaking, that when Edward III appointed Ramsey he was a young king in the first flight of his victories over Mortimer and then the Scots, meditating his claim to the throne of France. He was, consciously, a national king, relying on English men-at-arms, English bowmen. As a mere side-issue, he assured the creation of an English national style of architecture.

CHAPTER SIX

Lancastrian Variations

1400–1460

The style launched by Edward III and furthered by his art-loving grandson Richard II had reached its full potential within two generations. Not all of its promise had yet been realised, but virtually the whole of its repertory was there. What remained was to use the motives in a series of variations, continually modulating, ever seeking to come closer to perfection in the individual units, door, window, pier, vault-bay, roof-truss, and to improve the general composition of all together. The volume of works was very large and though it would never again reach quite to the peak attained under Richard II, what was done in the periods 1425–50 and 1460–85 was astonishing. The troughs of low pressure, when comparatively little was achieved – or at least few new buildings were begun – were due to factors of interference. Firstly the new century opened on the discord produced by the usurpation of Henry IV and subsequent rebellions against the changeling dynasty. Then came the renewal of the war with France, Henry V's costly campaign of Agincourt, and the bitter futile struggle to maintain a footing across the sea carried on until 1453. By that time, indeed, England was entering upon its own civil war, the Wars of the Roses. The fifteenth century was, until after 1485 and the end of our period, often sad and depressing.

It would be vain to expect the very highest output and quality from a country rent by faction, burdened with debt, and in many places suffering from urban decay and impoverishment. In spite of all these adverse factors, however, the sheer bulk of building of good structural quality is daunting. Hardly a parish but did something to its own church, whether by popular effort or through private enterprise of landowner or merchant. Those parts of the country which maintained a relatively high level of prosperity, particularly Somerset and East Anglia, lavished money on fine builders' work and enrichments of every sort. We cannot here enter into detail of the fittings produced, but the screenwork, the paintings and statues, the benches – commonly in use for the first time – the stalls, the roof carvings, exist in incredible variety to tell the tale. The level of handicraft very seldom dropped below excellence: sturdy construction allied to fine finish has seldom been maintained for so long on such a high plane.

Nor was the multitude of various works confined to the churches only. An increasing body of well-to-do squires and merchants was beginning to demand greater luxury and privacy in home life. Substantial stone houses of architectural pretensions, soon followed by other interpretations in brick, began to cover the land. What had been an isolated exception in the fourteenth century: a large unfortified residence like Dartington Hall became a relatively common phenomenon in the fifteenth. Though some areas were suffering severely from poverty and decay, others were expanding mightily. It is the plenty in the midst of poverty and despair that is so striking a feature of the time. Where there was money, it was made to flow like water. After the inflation caused by the Black Death, or rather by the succession of plagues and other disasters including war and civil disturbance, the cost of living had settled down to something not very much above what it had been in 1348. Yet wages remained for the most part at a much higher level. For those in work, much of the fifteenth century was a period of prosperity, when income tended to outstrip expenditure and there was a surplus to invest. What is to our present purpose is that a large part of the investment was, quite exceptionally in English history, in works of architecture.

Once the flood of a new architectural tide had set in there was the incentive of rivalry, between squire and squire, parish and parish, to go one better in church or house, chantry chapel or tower. This is actually on record in many of the surviving building contracts, where it is a matter almost of common form to find the qualifying clause: 'as good as the ... at X or better', or more precise instructions as to where the master was to seek inspiration. At a later date, at the very end of our period, mass production had reached the stage where it was very nearly possible to buy a chantry chapel out of the catalogue. Similarly clients could visit the town shop of a mason, not merely for a family tomb or slab with engraved brass, but for a doorway, a window or an oriel. The age of ready-made rather than purpose-made was waiting just beyond the horizon of Perpendicular, but here it is unnecessary to think in terms of church furnishing and the doom of individual design.

There was, throughout the fifteenth century and especially before 1485, an abundance of individual architects and other artists competing for jobs. For the most part they were not merely kept occupied, but moving from place to place. This is not to revive the old fable of the wandering masons, travelling as an organised group with their scaffolds and plant, touting for custom. Quite normal laws of supply and demand operated, and the master who produced a design to the client's satisfaction had then either to find a contractor able to work to his drawing and specification, or undertake the work himself if he had the capital and the right basis: a town shop or yard, perhaps, or a small gang of men upon whose skill he could rely. We must remember, too, that then as now the same contractor might build to the designs of several architects but on some other occasion make his own drawings. The evidence of masons' marks is quite explicit as to the movement of individual masons in ones and twos from one major work to another. In the case of small country churches within one region a lesser master with his own little gang might indeed travel around from job to job.

It would be simply untrue to say that the middle of the fifteenth century was an age of genius in architecture. With the exception of a few outstanding buildings it was a period remarkable for quantity rather than quality. When compared with the output of the royal craftsmen under Edward III and Richard

II, the lack of inspiration is regrettably noticeable. Only after 1460 will we again see a sudden rise in standards of taste, and this was to lead to the tacit admission that foreign designers were on the whole more able than our own; and that in turn implied the end of Perpendicular. The rise of Tudor Gothic as a fresh style, largely fertilised from abroad, is another story. All the same, even the two generations of relative depression and mediocrity are sprinkled with a few startling works. Some of these, like the London Guildhall, may be the outcome of posthumous interpretation of earlier designs. This is probably true also of the west front and towers of Beverley Minster **99**, a work of very uncertain date: the best authority, Bilson, could only say that it belonged to the fifty years *c*. 1380–*c*. 1430. The west window, almost a twin of the great east window dated to 1416, probably implies that the upper parts including the free-standing towers were not begun until well into the fifteenth century and this is confirmed by the mouldings **figs. 13, 14** which are quite close to those of the south-west tower at York **101; fig. 29**, not begun until 1432 or thereabouts. The noble steeple of Rotherham **4**, designed before 1409, cannot have been completed until much later.

The wonderful church of St. Mary Redcliffe again has notoriously vague dates for its Perpendicular parts **196**, but in any case they derive from a basic design that goes well back into the fourteenth century. Except for these and other buildings in process of completion to earlier plans, or directly due to the surviving members of Yeveley's generation (both Wynford and the carpenter Herland survived until 1405), there is little of notable rank until after 1440. To this general rule there is one extraordinary exception, the magnificent choir of Sherborne Abbey in Dorset **146**. This had been largely completed as to its arcades and walls by 1437 when it was burnt in a fire which altered the colour of the masonry and so left 'fossilized' evidence, as has been said. The superb vault, probably the finest of all fan-vaults, was put up after the fire and finished by 1459. Provisionally the design of the choir may be put near 1425, though the clerestory and east windows are obviously by a second master trained in the Bristol region. They were almost certainly part of the works of repair in the choir to be done in 1445–46.

The original architect, responsible for the excellent bay design and mouldings, the beautifully proportioned shafting and admirably modulated panelling, must have been used to working on a large scale. As far as surviving buildings are concerned, the possible scope for such a master within the south-western region seems narrow, and it is tempting to advance the name of Robert Hulle, who had charge of the completion of the Winchester nave after Wynford's death. Hulle had high standing as an esquire of the prior of Winchester, and in 1418–19 was also giving advice to Winchester College. He executed an important contract for carving the roodloft at St. John's church, Glastonbury, in 1439–40, and from 1440 to 1442 was building St. John's Hospital at Sherborne **148**. By the end of May 1442 he was dead. For Winchester College he may well have designed Fromond's Chantry with its upper Library **144, 145**, begun *c*. 1425 and structurally complete by 1437. Common factors in his tracery at St. John's Hospital and that of Fromond's

Chantry and Sherborne Abbey, together with similar methods of panelling internal walls at the Abbey and the Chantry, make out a *prima facie* case for the attribution. Hulle is mentioned at Winchester as early as 1400, and his long career and distinguished position at the Cathedral make his wide practice intelligible.

We have seen that Yeveley was succeeded at Westminster Abbey by William Colchester; in the King's Works and at Canterbury Cathedral his mantle fell upon his friend and partner Stephen Lote, presumably designer of the pulpitum 41 built about 1410. At London Bridge regular work went on under Yeveley's former assistant John Clifford. Clifford died in 1417 and both Lote and Walter Walton in the next year. Colchester became the king's chief mason for two years, and at his death Thomas Mapilton succeeded him, while John Thirsk or Crowche took over at the Abbey, where he remained in charge until his death in 1452. Mapilton has left no surviving official works, but his south-west tower of Canterbury Cathedral 98 is a work of distinction, and had notable effects upon the later style of parochial towers in east Kent, such as Lydd 163, built in 1442–46 by Thomas Stanley, a senior mason from the cathedral, Tenterden (1449–61) and Ashford (*c.* 1460–90). The College and Bedehouse at Higham Ferrers 143, built for Archbishop Chichele, Mapilton's patron at Canterbury, are likely to be to his design as they are in the official style (*c.* 1425).

Most of the Crown works on which Lote, Walton and Mapilton were engaged have been destroyed, as has the chancel at Fotheringhay, which Lote probably designed for the Duke of York who died at Agincourt, about 1410. What survive there are the later nave and tower added (1434–) by William Horewode in a conservative official style 119. Diluted and, it has to be admitted, unexciting versions of Court usage were being turned out by other followers of the school of Yeveley. Probably the best of these was Henry V's Chantry in Westminster Abbey, on which John Thirsk was engaged from 1422 until 1450. Thomas Wolvey, based in St. Albans, was producing an output that was for the most part parochial, but is likely to have designed the giant nine-light west window for St. Albans Abbey (*c.* 1425) as one of his last works. This was destroyed in Lord Grimthorpe's campaign of vandalism, but had been photographed. It carries rectilinearity to its extreme logical conclusion, in five horizontal bands of 18 panels, diversifed only by vestigial subarcuations. Some other mason trained at Westminster will have been responsible for the chancel at Cheshunt, Herts., built between 1418 and 1448 in the rectorate of Nicholas Dixon, with gridiron panels beneath a segmental-pointed head.

By this time regional forms of Perpendicular were becoming well defined, and although allowance has always to be made for surprising cross-country contacts and for rogue eclecticism on the part of individuals, the distinctions were marked by the reign of Henry V. In the area dominated by the Court school the subarcuation containing an inverted dagger played a prominent part. This, along with the simpler forms of mullioned and supermullioned tracery, covered almost the whole of the eastern half of England. It is important to note that this included Oxford, in spite of the proximity of the Cotswold quarries. In the North inverted daggers were supported upon falchions or a pair

120

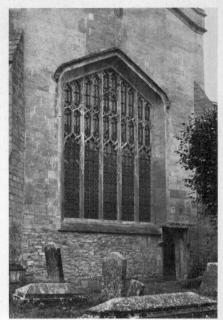

121

122

of small cusped panels, and supertransoms were usual. After 1420 the four-centred arch began to have a wide distribution in eastern England, again stretching out to include Oxford. The North on the whole remained faithful to the two-centred arch in this period. This was also the case throughout nearly all the western half of the country, but the tracery systems were quite different, being almost without exception alternate. Subreticulation and through-reticulation were also general in the West **Maps VII, VIII**. As we have seen, intersecting subarcuations belong exclusively to the East and North-East as far as Yorkshire **Map IX**; and the general use of the staggered cross-bar type of supertransom **Map V** is characteristic of the same region. In the South, but including works in East Anglia, the latticed transom is more common **Map VI**.

Two other usages affect the visual impression made by tracery and panelling. One of these is the employment of the ogee, both normal and 'four-centred', for the heads of lights; the other the retention of trefoiled cusping in such positions. For the heads of narrow tracery lights the trefoiled cusping always remained common, though cinquefoiled cusping on a small scale was introduced in some cases, especially in work of high quality. Thus we find it before 1424 in the north transept of Merton College, Oxford **124, 126**; at St. Mary, Bury St. Edmunds (1424) **136**; Higham Ferrers bedehouse (c. 1425) **143**; York, St. Martin-le-Grand (c. 1428) **132**; Louth east window (c. 1430); in the tower of Buckden church, Hunts., before 1431; York Minster south-west tower **101**; in Southwold church, Suffolk (c. 1431–); at Ewelme church, Oxon. (c. 1432); Fotheringhay church (1434–) **119**; St. Michael's chapel in Canterbury Cathedral, probably designed by Richard Beke (1437–39); and at All Souls in Oxford (1438) **141, 142**. All these belong to the eastern half of the country and were strongly influenced by the official style. But the same phenomenon occurred in the alternate traceries of the West, where the cinquefoiled cusping of narrow lights is found at North Cadbury, Somerset (c. 1415–23) **123, 125**; Ludlow church (1422) **128**; Devizes St. Mary in Wiltshire before 1436; in the choir aisle windows at Sherborne Abbey (c. 1425) **148**; the chancel of Tavistock church, Devon (1430–40); and in the stone screens made for chapels in Exeter Cathedral in 1433–34 by Denis Gabriell.

Whereas this use of cinquefoiling in work of the best quality goes back to sound precedents in the later buildings of Yeveley, Wynford, and Westminster men such as Robert Wodehirst, it is a different story with the ogee. Before the onset of Perpendicular it had been generally used, and was of course universal in reticulated windows. After that, in transitional work, it appears sporadically in different places, but was generally rejected in the first phases of the new style. Presumably the flexible curvature was felt to be incompatible with the essentially rigid and crystalline nature of Perpendicular. The ogee, banished from the Court, reappeared in precisely the same areas that fostered the four-centred arch, namely Gloucester and its region, and East Anglia. Apart from the ogees in the east window at Edington (1352) **18**, and some ogee foils at Gloucester and in arcaded transoms (e.g. the Windsor chapter-house of 1350 **16**), the motive does not occur in western dated works until the design of the southern bays of the Gloucester east cloister (?c. 1360–65)

120 Adderbury Church: chancel from south-east 1408–18, by Richard Winchcombe

121 Thame Church: north transept 1442–, built by John Beckeley, probably to designs by Richard Winchcombe

122 Oxford: Divinity School 1424–39, by Richard Winchcombe; later modified and the upper storey added 1453–72

123

124

125

126

123 North Cadbury Church (built as Collegiate): interior looking south–east (1415)–23

124 Oxford: Merton College Chapel, interior of north transept (1416)–24

125 North Cadbury Church from south (1415)–23

126 Oxford: Merton College Chapel, north transept (1416)–24

29. It was used by Lesyngham in the later cloister walks 30 and the Exeter east window (1390) 31; by John Clyve in the chapter-house at Worcester (1386) 26; at Warwick St. Mary (c. 1390) 72, 73. Then it turns up again at Exeter in Tynlegh's new windows in the chapter-house (after 1413) 135; and here and there rather infrequently, as in the Wells east cloister (c. 1420) 129; the Exeter screens of 1433; John Asser's south chapel at St. Mary-on-the-Hill, Chester (1433) 138; and at Wanborough, Wiltshire, in 1435.

In the eastern counties the recrudescence of the ogee is mainly to be connected with the splendid examples in the Ramseys' south cloister at Norwich Cathedral. It is used in the tower of Ingham church 49, very likely well after 1360, then in the Great Hospital at Norwich (c. 1380) 46, at Cavendish church, Suffolk (1381–) 68, 69, and in the central tower of Wymondham Abbey (1390–) 28. After 1400 it became a general usage in the east of the country and had reached the North Riding at Hornby and Catterick churches by 1410 and the next few years. It is at times associated with the lobed cruciform fillings of Curvilinear ancestry, as in the De la Pole chapel at Wingfield (–1415–) **figs 12.6, 12.7** and at Bardwell church before 1421. It is present in William of Croyland's work at Croyland Abbey before 1427, at John Turnour's Lynn Guildhall (1421–23) 111, and in the outstanding church of St. Mary at Bury St. Edmunds 136, begun in 1424. After this the ogee was common in the East, and used in works of distinction in Yorkshire, such as the central tower at Hedon 84 by Robert Playser (1427–37) and York Minster's south-west tower 101 of some five years later. The ogee heads of Richard Winchcombe's windows in the Divinity School at Oxford 122, 130 are more probably due to his Gloucestershire background than to East Anglian influence. If the traceries now at Adderbury 120 do represent his work of 1408, this would be confirmed.

Before leaving the subject of the ogee and of foiled heads, reference must be made to the relatively uncommon ogee head with trefoiled cusping. This is found in two different forms. In one the heads occur within a straight-headed window, alternating with inverted trefoil-cusped triangles. In the other, the trefoiled cusping stands free between mullions or between decorative ashlaring in woodwork. The first of these types was a common form of ogee tracery before the onset of Perpendicular and continued in use through the fourteenth century in work otherwise clearly of the new style, as at Yeveley's London Charterhouse of 1371–1400. Such windows occur extensively in domestic work, but also in churches, as in the chancel at Strelley, Notts. (c. 1356–90), the nave of Church Hanborough, Oxfordshire, after 1399 **fig. 12.5**, and in the new church of St. Leonard at Farleigh Hungerford, Somerset, built in 1443. In woodwork this form also appears in the spandrels of the nave roof trusses at Christ Church, Oxford, presumably of genuine form though said to have been renewed in 1816.

The second type of free-standing trefoil cusping is also developed from pre-Perpendicular use, but is rare in masonry. There is a fine window said to be of 1434 in the south aisle at Pershore Abbey, but this is much later than the instances of timber ashlaring so enriched. The crucial dated example is

127 Croyland Abbey: interior of north aisle of nave (1417–27), by William Croyland

128 Ludlow Church: interior of choir looking east 1422–(47)

129 Wells Cathedral: east cloister and library (c. 1420)–24

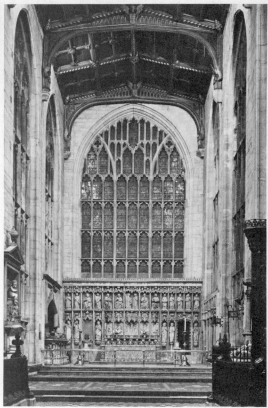

127

128

129

Westminster Hall **7**, begun in January 1394 and all but completed six years later. It is significant that some of the upper ashlaring above the main collar-beams, left unfinished, was filled in later with normal two-centred archlets, trefoil cusped. There can, therefore, be no doubt that the ogee form was Hugh Herland's own and that in his personal practice it must end with his death in 1405. This is relevant to the much disputed date of the roof of the Exeter Law Library, generally said to be a fifteenth-century copy of Westminster Hall on a reduced scale. Yet the Exeter roof has similar mouldings to Herland's at Westminster, and the same idiosyncratic cusped ashlaring, strongly reinforcing the view that associates it with journeys to Dartington in connection with the hammer-beam roof of 1389–99. Similarly, the earlier instances of this detail in woodwork are in the three great sets of stall canopies, in Lincoln Cathedral, Chester St. Werburgh's Abbey (now Cathedral) **39**, and York Minster. At Lincoln the stalls were begun by 1380 but there is no further evidence as to date; the style of armour carved on the Chester misericords and the details generally indicate a date later than Lincoln but not much after 1390; the York stalls, burnt in 1829, had been recorded by Edward Blore before 1818. The York date is quite uncertain but must have been more or less contemporary with the building of the structural choir in *c.* 1394–*c.* 1405. It needs to be added, in view of doubts expressed as to Herland's responsibility for the design of these stall canopies, that the architectural details also include substantial use of the standard two-light Perpendicular tracery, of ranges of tangential quatrefoils, and battlementings, all clear marks of the Court style within the relevant period.

We must now return to the chief builds of the earlier fifteenth century outside the orbit of the royal works. The most remarkable is the north transept of Merton College Chapel in Oxford **124, 126, 149**. This is known to have been transformed in a few years ending in 1424, probably beginning about 1416. The traceries are very closely based on Yeveley's great windows in Westminster Hall and, like them, employ Geometrical quatrefoils in circles and latticed transoms. What is astonishing at this date is the extensive use of double cusping, to the heads of the lights and also to the oculus of the seven-light north window, provided as well with a brattished transom supported on double-cusped archlets. Beneath this window is a doorway with two-centred arch inside a square surround, in Court style, and with a four-centred rear-arch to the chapel, between ranges of two-centred panels with cinquefoil cusping. The gable of the transept is flanked by pinnacles set square, with panelled sides, rather in the style of those of the nave aisles at Winchester.

On the periphery of the official style were several developing schools represented by builds of good second-rate quality. Following Robert Wodehirst at Norwich was the important master James Woderofe, responsible for the Erpingham Gate (1416–25) **fig. 21** and for the vaults of the north and west cloisters; probably also for the inserted windows in the west front of the cathedral, since he remained in charge until 1451. He must have been regarded as one of the leading architects in the country by the end of his career, as he was summoned by Henry VI to give advice at Eton College in 1449 and 1450. In the

130 Oxford Divinity School: interior 1424–39, by Richard Winchcombe; modified 1439–49, by Thomas Elkyn; vault 1479–83, by William Orchard

North the towers of Beverley **99** were, as we have seen, probably going up after 1420; the central tower at Hedon **84**, by Robert Playser, followed in 1427–37; then came the south-west tower at York **101**, and Thirsk church after *c.* 1431 **140**. All these had been strongly influenced by Perpendicular Court style and by the York succession of Westminster masters from 1407 to 1431. The tower of St. Lawrence at Ipswich (1420–31 and later) is an East Anglian semi-official work, to judge from its tracery, faithfully rebuilt in 1882. Nearer to London was the collegiate church at Lingfield, Surrey **97**, refounded by Sir Reginald Cobham in 1431 and in a modest and conservative form of metropolitan style.

Not far removed from the Lingfield pattern, or for that matter from John Croxton's Guildhall Chapel, was the undemonstrative All Souls College at Oxford **141, 142**, built in 1438–44 under Richard Chevynton, master mason of Abingdon Abbey. The timberwork was carried out by John Branche, apparently the Abingdon master carpenter. The charge of work on the site seems normally to have been in the hands of Robert Janyns senior, a mason later notable for the tower at Merton College **149**, while Chevynton spent time at the quarries by Burford. All Souls was built for Archbishop Chichele who had previously employed Thomas Mapilton for his architectural work; Mapilton's death in 1438, perhaps after he had produced sketches for All Souls, would account for the somewhat unsatisfactory feeling of the design, redeemed by the magnificent sculptures of John Massingham. Also with a general foundation of more or less official style, combined with an East Anglian flavour, is the complex of church, almshouse and school at Ewelme in Oxfordshire. The connection, through the De la Pole family, is with Wingfield in Suffolk **figs. 12.6, 12.7**, and much of the building was done between 1432 and 1440.

A supertransomed version of the large gridiron windows of the semi-official style became current in the Midlands and the North. Examples are found in John Turnour's Guildhall at Lynn, Norfolk (1421) **111**; the chancel of Luton church, Beds. (*c.* 1430–40); and the east window of the old parish church of Halifax in the West Riding (*c.* 1430–35). A great deal more interesting is William Croyland's north aisle – the parish church – of the nave of Croyland Abbey (*c.* 1417–27) **127**. Master William had been in charge of the abbey works since 1392 and had fully matured his ideas by the time he designed the aisle. His simple tierceron vault is yet unusual for its subtlety, in that though it has a ridge-rib and cross-ribs at the centre of each bay, it has no cross-arches between the bays: from the boss at the centre of one bay to the next, the ridge-rib is divided into three equal parts, providing nodes for the abutment of pairs of tiercerons. There are no capitals, and the refined continuous mouldings and absence of enrichment attain almost to the logical conclusion of the style.

As a precisely dated work, the tower of Walberswick in Suffolk **131** has considerable importance. It was contracted for by Richard Russell of Dunwich, a prominent local mason and M.P. for the town, in 1426, and probably complete except for the parapet when Russell died in 1441. On the evidence of style he seems also to have designed the later, larger and finer tower at Kessingland, of which only the bottom 30 feet are carried out to his detail, but which was ready for the bells in 1454. In a notably different and more sturdily

131 Walberswick Church: tower 1426–(41), by Richard Russell

132 York: St. Martin Coney Street, tower (1428)–37

133 St. Columb Major: church tower 1433–

134 Mawgan-in-Pyder: church tower –1433–

131

132

133

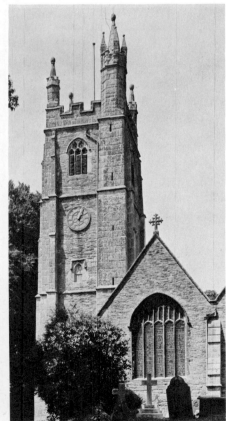

134

buttressed style is the roughly contemporary Suffolk tower of Stoke-by-Nayland (*c.* 1439–62) **160**. The origins of this kind of tower with heavy diagonal buttresses which stop before the top stringcourse is suggested by a humbler example at Wyberton, Lincs., built in 1419–21 by Roger Denys, a mason contractor. Denys had already, in 1418, undertaken the chancel of Surfleet, a few miles away. To judge from his west doorway at Wyberton and what is left of his tracery at both churches, Denys had come from London. He certainly moved there or returned there, and held the freedom when he died in January 1431/2.

There was during the first half of the fifteenth century a vogue for building libraries, generally on upper floors. We have seen that even earlier Humberville had completed Mob Quad at Merton College with library blocks; Wynford incorporated a first-floor library on the east side of the New College quadrangle; at York Colchester designed a separate two-storey building for a library completed in 1419. Lincoln Minster at once followed suit with a library of 1420–22, while at Wells the east cloister was started, with a library range above it, the first bays being built *c.* 1420–24 **129**. The chantry chapel in Winchester College, built for John Fromond's executors, was also designed with a superimposed library **145**, as was the new Guildhall Library of 1423–25 in London. At Canterbury, about 1420, Chichele had had a library built above an existing chapel, and later, in 1443, a library was begun over the north chapel of All Saints, Bristol, to house the books of the Kalendars.

This national concern over the building of libraries was to have important results at Oxford in connection with the great project, already in hand, for building the Divinity School. Designs had probably been commissioned from Richard Winchcombe by 1424 for the School building as originally envisaged. It was to have been a large hall of a single storey and as such a great deal of it was built, in Winchcombe's highly enriched personal style. In 1439, when most of the north side, both ends, and the base of the south wall had been erected, Winchcombe was dismissed on the ground of the unnecessary frivolity of his work. The new master, Thomas Elkin, had to work in a much simplified, and of course less costly, manner, but after four more years the radical decision was taken to amend the design to allow of an upper storey being made to house a library, the famous collection of manuscripts of Duke Humphrey of Gloucester. Elkin died in 1449 and the building was only structurally complete and roofed by 1466; the stone vault of the lower storey was not inserted until 1479–83 by William Orchard **130**.

The decision of 1439 to simplify the design of the Oxford Schools marks an epoch in taste, as we shall see shortly in discussing Henry VI's scheme for King's College, Cambridge, undertaken in 1443. Before reaching that point, brief mention must be made of the few other major buildings already in course of erection by 1440. Chief of the church works was the new choir for the college founded at Manchester in 1422, now Manchester Cathedral **184**. Some of the window traceries which belong to the earlier period are eclectic mixtures of alternate and supermullioned, having a central mullioned section with panels divided by a supertransom, and lateral subarcuations each essentially an alternate window with split Y-tracery, the inner super-mullions carried up in through-reticulation fashion. The blend of West and North is evenly balanced and the overall result a fine one. In the East the new clerestory windows in the nave of Wymondham Abbey (1432–45) are strangely old-fashioned, harking back in impression to Sponlee's time almost a century earlier and on the other side of the country **28**. Also in East Anglia was the unusual castle of Caister, Norfolk **107**, built for Sir John Fastolf in 1432–46. Caister is of brick, made on the spot, and has a foreign flavour probably accounted for by Fastolf's long career in the wars. Its importance is technical rather than architectural, though the surviving slender tower is a noteworthy sight.

The design of church towers of substantial scale was by now not confined to a few areas only. In furthest Cornwall two very notable towers were begun in 1433, at St. Columb Major **133** and at Mawgan-in-Pyder **134** a few miles off. In Devon another in rather similar style was built at Bradninch from 1437 onwards. In proportion to the low West Country churches to which they are attached, these towers are tall, well supported by pairs of buttresses set back from the angle, allowing the corners to show. A wave of tower building was to sweep over the greater part of the country during the last century of the Middle Ages, and it was at this time that most of the local 'schools' were taking shape. The turreted tower was well exemplified at St. Lawrence, Reading, begun in 1440 and finished in 1458; in the London area Fulham church tower was started in 1441 by Richard Garald; in the next year the central tower of the priory (now parish) church at Dunster in Somerset **164** was begun by John Marys, a local mason contractor, to the design of Richard Pope, freemason. The Kentish towers influenced by Canterbury have already been mentioned. In Norfolk a parochial west tower was built at Wymondham Abbey (1445–78) to rival the central monastic tower; it is a grandiose affair of flint with turreted buttresses **28**; also turreted but of dressed ashlar throughout is the western tower added in a similar way to Wimborne Minster, Dorset (1448–64). Another tower in Devon was that of Plympton St. Maurice (1447–), while a tower of greater influence in the West was that of St. Stephen's in Bristol **168**, begun c. 1453, but not finished until after 1480 when it had bells in the fourth stage.

The Bristol tower follows the usual West Country pattern in having paired buttresses set back from the angles. This method of buttressing was not confined to the South-West; it occurs, for example, on the north-west tower of St. Margaret's, Lynn, in Norfolk, also begun in 1453. Still in the same year was the start of the fine turreted tower of Ludlow, Shropshire, finished about 1471 **167**. The turreted design was used in Suffolk at Laxfield (c. 1450–60) and at Stoke-by-Nayland **160**, of roughly the same dates, but the latter most unusually adds diagonal buttresses projecting from the octagonal turrets. Another experimental design was tried at the sturdy tower of St. Margaret's, Leicester **165**, in progress in 1448, where there are paired buttresses below surmounted by diagonals at the top stage. Towers of good design but minor scale were begun in 1450 at St. Mary Lowgate, Hull, Yorks. **166**; and in the following year at Ryarsh in Kent. It is impossible to detail the many varieties of design, but before proceeding to the greater towers we may say something of

135 Exeter Cathedral: chapter-house 1413–39, by John Tynlegh

136 Bury St. Edmunds: St. Mary's Church, aisle window 1424–33, possibly by William Layer

137 Thirsk Church: nave windows c. 1431–

138 Chester: St. Mary-on-the-Hill, interior of south-east chapel 1433–35, built by Thomas Bates, to designs by John Asser junior

139 Louth Church from north-east: chancel and tower c. 1430–, probably by John Porter; north (Trinity) chapel c. 1460–65; spire added 1501–15, by John Cole and Christopher Scune

140 Thirsk Church from south c. 1431–60

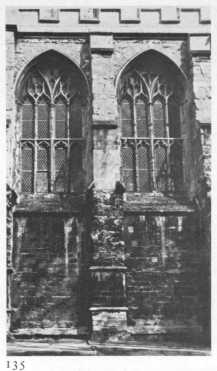

135

136

137

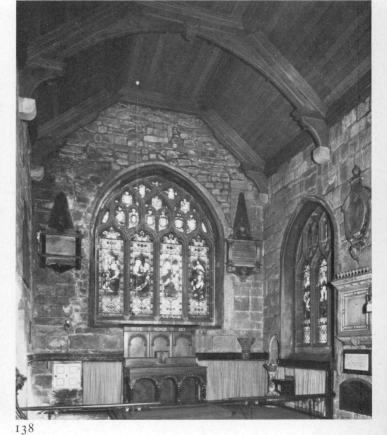

138

139

140

141

142

the methods adopted to produce one of the finest at the parish church of Totnes in Devon **161**. Early in 1449 the corporation of the borough appointed Roger Growdon as master mason to build a new belfry; overseers of the work were nominated and went to see the already famous steeples at Callington in Cornwall, Buckland (?Monachorum), Tavistock and Ashburton, with a view to selecting the best as a model. Stone was collected during 1451 and by the next year work was going ahead. Totnes has in fact one of the finest of towers, actually based on Ashburton, but outdoing the model in richness of ornament and in splendour of effect.

This background of eager rivalry between parish and parish to produce a steeple yet nobler than any to be seen in the district casts light on the degree of interest, and often also of aesthetic taste, to be found in England in the fifteenth century. Architecture was not then an overlooked or misunderstood subject; on the contrary, it was the main art accessible to the ordinary man and woman. To those who could not even visit, or only visit infrequently, the cathedral city of their diocese, the parish church was the principal work of art with which their life was endowed. At a higher level, it was the cathedral, abbey or minster tower that set the standards of design. Of major towers of the Perpendicular period there are very few. Just before the first signs of the new style made their appearance, several great towers had been designed: Lincoln Cathedral (1306); Wells and Hereford, both c. 1315; Salisbury (c. 1320); Worcester (1357) **26**. There are only four outstanding towers of the cathedral category begun before 1485: Howden **83; fig. 20**, designed c. 1390 or soon after; York, 1408 but detailed much later and not finished until 1472 **6; fig. 29**; Gloucester, c. 1450 **201**; and Durham (1465) **202; fig. 16**. We should add Southwark (Cathedral), where the lower stage (c. 1380–90) was probably by Yeveley.

Howden was well imitated at Cottingham **36**. The York tower, which must have existed as a drawing on a great skin of parchment, clearly underlay the new design for Durham made by Thomas Barton, and probably also the wonderful central tower of Doncaster parish church, destroyed by fire in 1853. Playser's central tower at Hedon may have owed a good deal to the York design, too. In the West, the slightly pre-Perpendicular Worcester derived largely from Salisbury, and Gloucester was quite strictly based upon Worcester but converted its turreted outline to diagonal buttressing, finishing with the famous 'Gloucester coronet' of filigree openwork pinnacles and battlements, so largely copied on a reduced scale for parochial towers.

One of the features most noticeable about the towers is the tendency in many cases to rich elaboration of niches, panelling, mouldings and shafts, pinnacles and battlements. They had either been designed before the puritan dismissal of Winchcombe in 1439, or disregarded the return towards simplicity urged at the highest levels. The first wave of Perpendicular towers had been nobly simple, particularly in the Somerset examples designed by or under the influence of William Wynford: Yeovil (c. 1380) **5**, Shepton Mallet, or Wells St. Cuthbert, built c. 1410–30. Far away in the North, Howden and Cottingham are likewise extremely simple, depending for their effect upon mastery of proportion and composition. After 1400 there had been a pronounced swing towards

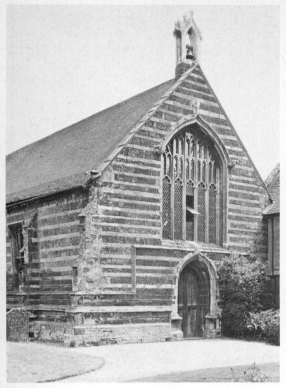

143

144

145

146

147

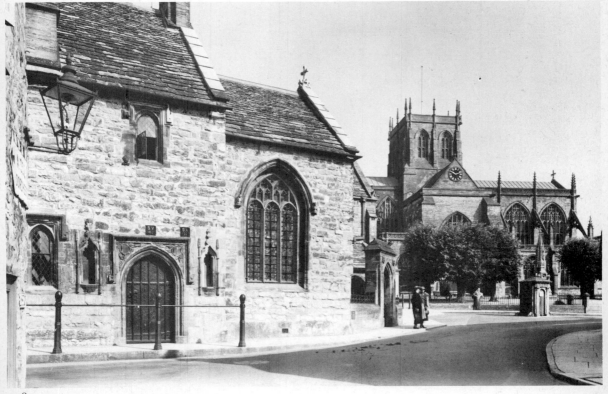

148

149

decorative enrichment as a substitute for the bold play of windows and surfaces which had been achieved by the earlier masters and most notably by Yeveley himself.

The revulsion from this heavily adorned style very probably started at the top, with the personal taste of Henry VI himself. Admitted to a share in the government at the age of 16 in 1437 he rapidly asserted himself, and in spite of his pacific nature took a strong line when he felt that circumstances required it. We must go back to Winchcombe's dismissal, implied in the terms of Elkin's appointment on 16 January 1439–40, which states that 'numerous magnates of the realm and other knowledgeable men do not approve, but reprehend, the over curiosity of the ... work already begun, therefore the ... University wishes the said Thomas ... to restrain the superfluous curiosity of the ... work, as in niches for statues, bowtels, casements and fillets, and other foolish curiosities.' We know that between 1441 and 1448 the king repeatedly visited Winchester College; in 1443 he sent his mason and in 1445 his carpenter Robert Whetely there, obtaining drawings of the buildings to study. He was undoubtedly impressed by the simplicity of Wynford's style, for when in 1447 he set out his 'intent' for King's College, Cambridge, he included the general specification: 'I will that the edification of my same college proceed in large form, clean and substantial, setting apart superfluity of too great curious works of entail (carving) and busy moulding.'

Here then, both in the reported view of the magnates of 1439 and in the king's own words eight years later, is a clearly enunciated programme of aesthetic reform for English architecture. It had become too 'busy' and needed pruning. For one generation in the middle of the century there was an ascetic movement away from the curiosity of what had been current. Outside the circles of Court and University a quiet struggle went on between the new simplicity and the rearguard action of those whose interest lay in inflating expenses and fees. On the side of the king lay the obvious need for economy, and this was helped by the introduction on a large scale of the relatively new material, brick. Following Caister came Herstmonceux Castle in Sussex (1441–46), a brick mansion on a grand scale **150**, much royal work, Tattershall Castle (c. 1445–55) **151**, and a spate of later buildings. It was not only in brickwork that the new simplicity was expressed. In the masonry on Tattershall collegiate church **170**, begun about 1440 for Ralph Lord Cromwell, who was lord high treasurer 1433–43, even cusping is altogether abolished and the impression is stark in the extreme.

There was, however, not merely a party of extravagance but one that actively preferred adornment for its own sake. Ironically enough, it was the executors of the king's own former tutor, Richard Beauchamp Earl of Warwick, who put into effect the most gorgeous project of the mid-century, the Beauchamp Chapel **71, 72**, attached to St. Mary's, Warwick (1441–52), at the very same time that Henry VI was launching Eton College **178, 179**, largely built of brick. The Beauchamp Chapel, perhaps designed by Thomas Kerver, has alternate tracery with through-reticulation and the east window goes so far in subreticulation as to have lights only one-quarter the width of a main light.

149 Oxford: Merton College, north transept (1416)–24; and tower 1448–52, by Robert Janyns senior

150

151

152

153

The vaulting is of a rare type in which bosses are replaced by open concave-sided stars. This had been foreshadowed in the vault of the choir alongside (?c. 1381–91) **73**, but formed a school of only a few examples in the mid-fifteenth century, including the vault of the Hereford cloister, probably after 1418; parts of the Wells cloisters and gates, where quadrilaterals are substituted for eight-foils and six-foils; and the cloister vaults at Lacock Abbey, Wiltshire. The earliest of the Wells cloister vaults, in the east walk, are almost certainly to be dated before 1436 for completion, which, added to the Hereford evidence, renders it improbable that the Warwick choir vault is as late as that of the Beauchamp Chapel, as Francis Bond suggested.

So much has been written of Henry VI's noble colleges that only brief consideration can be given to them here. Both at Eton and at King's College completion was so long delayed that it is hard to appreciate what the king originally intended. The same applies, incidentally, to the Oxford Schools, but in that case the florid vault **130** by Orchard, put up in 1480, must to some degree give the impression envisaged by Winchcombe. The austere concept of Henry VI and his architect Reginald Ely of the kind of building King's College Chapel should be, has been signally falsified by the rich adornment of John Wastell's completion (1508–15), magnificent as it is. We can get some idea of what was meant from the easternmost chapels **154**, where the window tracery goes back to the lobed pattern of Curvilinear origin, and the lierne vaults, partly of net pattern, spring from capless shafts with continuous mouldings as in the north aisle at Croyland **127**. It was long ago shown by George Gilbert Scott the younger that the high vault too was to have been of lierne type, and not a fan-vault as built by Wastell. The extreme simplicity, verging upon domesticity, of which Ely was capable can be much better judged from Queens' College (1448), where the main material is brick **153**.

At King's College the succession of building periods and superimposed styles is at least fairly clear when studied in detail. This is hardly the case at Eton, where the king's changed intentions, as well as subsequent alterations in execution, make it extremely difficult to obtain a clear visual or historical picture. So far as concerns the Chapel, its essential quality has been largely falsified by the mock fan-vault inserted in 1958, and by the obscure tone of the new glazing for the east window, originally intended to represent the divine *claritas* or illumination. The royal saint's expense both here and at Cambridge seems, in regard to his own expressed intentions, indeed destined to have been vain. Historically we know that work began at Eton in 1441, and upon the present Chapel in 1448; the east window **178**, an alteration in the course of the works, was built about 1459 shortly before King Henry's downfall. The succession of masters is also perfectly clear, *pace* Pevsner who obscures the issue in pursuit of the theory of the 'essential anonymity' of mediaeval design. In the early stages the King's Master Mason, Robert Westerley, was in charge and responsible for the original plan and the building of the Hall and chambers **fig. 12.10**. By 1446 John Smyth from Canterbury Cathedral, who had been warden of the Eton masons from the start, took over from Westerley, and is explicitly named as master when Henry VI required a fresh scheme for the Chapel. The

150 Herstmonceux Castle: gatehouse 1441–(48)

151 Tattershall Castle c. 1445

152 Wye College –1447

153 Cambridge: Queens' College 1448–49, by Reginald Ely

new Chapel, with its nave that remained unbuilt, was initially the work of Smyth and continued by him until 1453 when he became master at Westminster Abbey and was replaced at Eton by Simon Clerk. It has been pointed out by Mr. Arthur Oswald that the tracery of the Eton side windows **179** corresponds to Clerk's later east window in King's College Chapel (1477). The east window at Eton, however, built in 1459 and with tracery inserted only in 1460, goes back to the austere style ordered by the Founder. That this plain work is to Smyth's design is confirmed by the rich details of Westerley's oriel in the Hall **fig. 12.10**. Far from the designs for Eton indicating anonymity, they demonstrate even within the King's Works the existence of three distinct personal styles within 20 years.

It remains to cast an eye swiftly over the kaleidoscopic scene of English building in this time of contrasting ideals. There was, as always, a wide variety of extravagant and economical work, even within the field of parish churches. For some noble patrons extremely plain buildings might be put up, such as the new church of St. Leonard at Farleigh Hungerford, Somerset (1443) **fig. 12.8** and the unspoilt chapel at Rycote in Oxfordshire (1449) **162**. At the other end of the spectrum Burwell in Cambridgeshire **156, 157**, paid for by ordinary parishioners, could employ the king's architect Reginald Ely and indulge in panelling and florid Curvilinear traceries on a grand scale (*c.* 1454–67). The austere fashion approved by the king held sway at Canterbury under Richard Beke, master from 1435 to his death in 1458, and responsible for the great window of the north transept. This consists simply of ranges of narrow lights divided by latticed transoms and with trefoil cusping at head and base. Similar tracery, but enriched by cinquefoil cusping, had been used by Chevynton at All Souls **141, 142**, and in 1442 by John Beckeley in the north transept at Thame, Oxfordshire **121**. At Chipping Norton in the same county the trefoiled type was used in the gridiron, and largely square-headed, windows of the nave in progress in 1447–48. The fact, pointed out by Professor R. H. C. Davis, that the arcade design is based on the nave of Canterbury Cathedral, very strongly suggests that John Smyth was the designer after his move to Eton.

A somewhat warmer version of this style was produced by Robert Janyns senior, who had been warden under Chevynton at All Souls, and later under Smyth at Eton College. He was employed by Merton College as architect for their central tower **149**, built in 1448–52, and this finely proportioned work ensures his fame. The deeply stilted four-centred twin windows with good drop tracery set in moulded reveals are framed by buttresses of double projection and a notable coronet of battlementing and tall pinnacles. Outside the cathedral towers this was one of the principal achievements of the century, and inspired Orchard's later and larger tower at Magdalen **208**. Other collegiate and domestic buildings of the middle century are South Wingfield Manor in Derbyshire, begun in 1440 and built by Richard Kyng for Ralph Lord Cromwell **fig. 12.4**; the Hall of the Archbishop's Palace at Croydon (*c.* 1443–52); Wye College in Kent (1447–) **152**; and the cloister of the Great Hospital at Norwich, a simple work of 1448–57 by Robert Bucham **159**.

The principal civic work was the Guildhall at York **110**, built under Robert

Couper, chief mason to the corporation, in 1448–60. Couper died in 1459, shortly before the hall was finished. He was probably born at Bubwith in the East Riding and, to judge from the maturity of his design for the Guildhall and the fact that he did not take up the freedom of York until 1443, he had travelled widely in earlier life. The tracery of the side windows, simple three-light Perpendicular, could be regarded as distinctively Western, and in fact is almost identical with that of the contemporary St. George's chapel at Probus parish church in Cornwall (1447–). The five-light west window too is basically of alternate character, but the east window has split and panelled tracery with a supertransom, as typically supermullioned and originating on the eastern side of England. Couper also employed a singular two-light window with double Y-tracery under a flat 'three-centred' head, comparable to the three-centred type at Thornton Abbey **74** designed over sixty years before (1382). At York the modest parish church of St. Cuthbert should also be noticed, partly because it was built simultaneously as chancel and nave forming a single cell and differentiated only by the separate framing of the trussed roofs with a pair of end trusses in close contact at the line of junction. On a grander scale work was in hand on the chancel of Wakefield parish church, now Cathedral, by 1458.

By this time motives which had belonged exclusively to the Court style had achieved a wide distribution. This is noticeable in the case of Y-tracery, found over much of the country, though usually in buildings for noble patrons. It was used by Reginald Ely extensively at Queens' College, Cambridge **153**; at South Wingfield Manor for Lord Cromwell; at Wye College for Archbishop Kempe **152**; as well as for townsmen contributors to the tower of Ludlow **167**. In various shapes, four-centred, segmental, triangular-headed, it occurs in Norfolk in the north porch at Pulham Market (*c.* 1456) and about the same time in the top stage of the west tower at Wimborne, Dorset; in the middle windows of Stoke-by-Nayland tower in Suffolk (*c.* 1450–60) **160**; and in the side windows of Rycote Chapel in Oxfordshire (1449–) **162**. The three-light window with subarcuated sidelights containing inverted daggers, originally confined to the South-East and gradually spreading through eastern England, reached the side windows of Winchcombe church in Gloucestershire (*c.* 1455–60) **169**. The east window, four-centred and of seven lights, seems to be a development of the five-light pattern found in the Lady Chapel at Chippenham in north Wiltshire (1442–), and was later to be adapted for the east window at Stratford-on-Avon (*c.* 1466–) **187**.

Fine parish churches were going up in a wide diversity of styles: Blythburgh in Suffolk, begun about 1442 (chancel), with a north chapel some ten years later; Sudbury All Saints, with aisles built in the late 1450s and early '60s; St. George's, Stamford, in course of building in 1449. Chapels, for chantry or guild purposes were added, as the outer south aisle at Tavistock in Devon (–1445). A simple Lady Chapel, north of the chancel, was building at Woodchurch, Kent, in 1458. These slight but very numerous works contribute a great deal to the total impression of English Perpendicular. They also provide arguments for those convinced of the mediocrity of the style as a whole, but this cannot be applied to several truly outstanding designs on a grander scale.

154

155

156

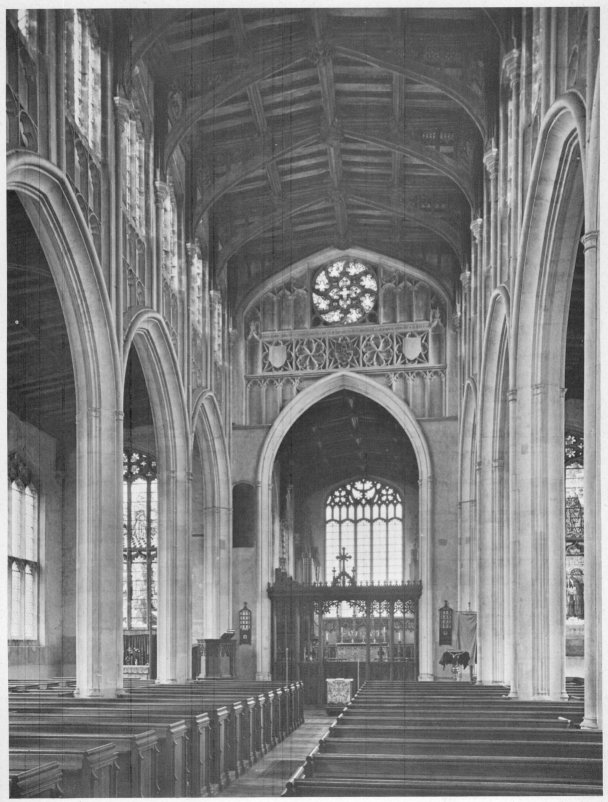

158

158 Norwich
Cathedral: north walk
of cloisters 1385–1415,
by Robert Wodehirst;
vaults 1416–30, by James
Woderofe

159 Norwich: Great
Hospital, cloister
1448–57, by Robert
Bucham

159

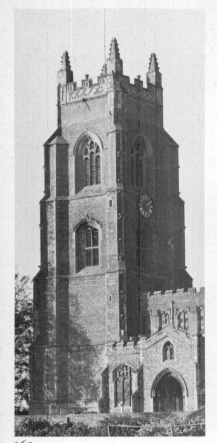

160

161

160 Stoke-by-Nayland
Church: tower
c. 1439–62

161 Totnes Church:
tower 1449–(52), by
Roger Growdon

162 Rycote Chapel
from south-west 1449–

162

163

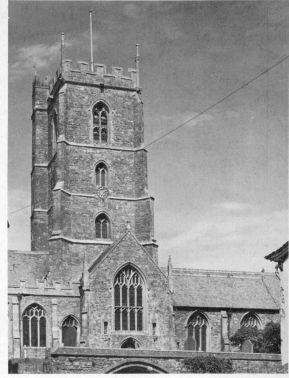

164

163 Lydd Church:
tower 1442–46, by
Thomas Stanley

164 Dunster Priory:
tower 1442–45, built by
John Marys, to the de-
sign of Richard Pope

165 Leicester: St.
Margaret's Church,
tower –1448–

166 Hull: St. Mary
Lowgate, tower 1450–

167 Ludlow Church:
tower 1453–71, prob-
ably by Clement Mason

168 Bristol: St.
Stephen's Church, tower
1453–(80), the top stage
probably by William
Hart

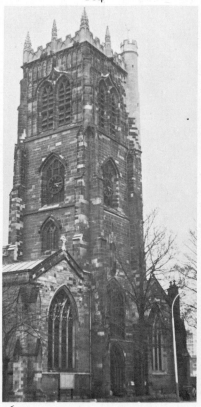

165

166

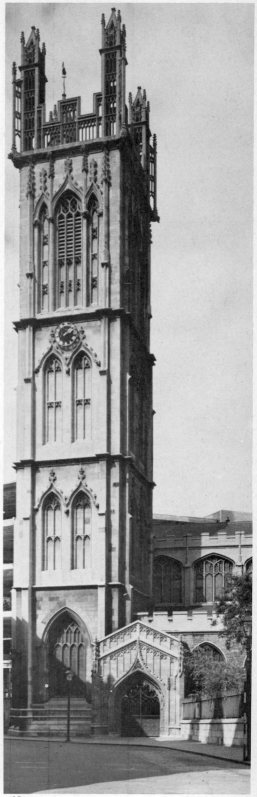

167

168

169

170

First and foremost is the renewed work at Sherborne Abbey after the fire of 1437 and apparently not undertaken until about 1445. This included the unusual fan-vault, really a combination of fan and lierne patterns **146**. The most aesthetically successful of all vaults of its type, it comes at the time least expected, when the country in decay and torn by factions was drifting towards civil war. Roughly contemporary was the reconstruction of Great Malvern priory **177, 199, 206** in Worcestershire (*c.* 1430–60), nearly related to work at Gloucester, yet enjoying a broader and happier treatment than the Gloucester Lady Chapel and central tower, with their almost metallic appearance: the Gloucester work adhered extraordinarily closely to the mouldings and traceries of the previous century. Also in Gloucestershire are the wonderful churches of Chipping Campden and Northleach **171**. The two naves, as all authorities agree, are so unusual and resemble each other so closely with their concave-octagonal piers that they must be by the same master. Yet we soon run into difficulties. The one firm fact is that John Fortey, who died in 1458/59, paid for much of the work of the Northleach nave. Mr. David Verey attributes the clerestory to Fortey, the arcades possibly to his father Thomas Fortey (who died 1447), but calls the Chipping Campden nave 'late C 15 or early C 16'. The windows of the aisles and clerestories of the two churches are very different, it is true. As regards the arcades, however, Professor Davis has shown that an unusual mason's mark occurs on those of Campden and also in the antechapel of All Souls at Oxford (1438–43), while two marks connect the Northleach arcades with Winchcombe church (*c.* 1455–60), and another with the nave arcades of Chipping Norton, which we have seen was in building in 1447–48. Furthermore, Mr. Verey points to a mark with a graffito 'Henrie Winchcombe' on the base of the south-east pier at Northleach.

We must then accept the traditional view and regard both the Campden and Northleach arcades as well as the Northleach clerestory and roof as belonging to the middle years of the century. If the literate mason who scratched his name, Henry Winchcombe, was indeed the master, then it follows that he would be the 'unknown genius' postulated by Mr. Verey. Further, there would be a strong presumptive connection either with the powerful Benedictine abbey at Winchcombe, or with Richard Winchcombe, or for that matter with both. The relationship of son/pupil to Richard could answer the question of what happened to the style of extravagance and enrichment after it was turned down by Oxford University. The University comes back into the picture with the choir of the church of St. Mary the Virgin **172, 173**. This was the responsibility of the rectors, Oriel College, and was rebuilt by Walter Lyhert, provost of Oriel and then bishop of Norwich, in 1459–65. A man called Chambyr was probably the master, but nothing more of him is known. The two-centred supermullioned windows, the east window having a supertransom and cinquefoiled lights, and the form of the heads to the main lights suggest that the designer came from East Anglia, explicable as the bishop's residence. The choir, of notable quality and excellent composition, brings to a fitting close the reign and educational idealism of King Henry VI.

169 Winchcombe Church from south-east 1455–(61)

170 Tattershall Collegiate Church from north-east (1440)–55–; tower –1482–, by John Cowper

171

172

171 Northleach Church: nave interior –1458–, possibly by Henry Winchcombe

172, 173 Oxford, St. Mary the Virgin: choir 1459–65, by ————Chambyr, interior looking east; and exterior from south-east; the nave added 1487–1503

173

CHAPTER SEVEN

Yorkist Prosperity

1460–1485

The political revolution at the end of the Wars of the Roses had a much sharper effect upon the royal works establishment than had the usurpation of 1399. Henry IV had continued all the master craftsmen in office, and dealt severely only with a few highly placed opponents. In the course of the long series of faction fights which had followed one another through the reign of Henry VI for nearly 40 years, tempers had become embittered and everything was seen as a matter of party. For years the new king, Edward IV, revolted by the cruel death of his father the Duke of York, had no patience with Lancastrians or even their servants. He surrounded himself with new men, and as far as lay with him, caused work to be stopped upon the colleges of Henry VI and Queen Margaret of Anjou. Naturally this political upset had relatively slight effect upon ordinary work in town and village, but it brought to an abrupt close the Court fashion of austere or puritan design. Edward IV was a brilliant young man, loving luxurious appointments, and his own taste was very different from that of his saintly predecessor.

When Edward IV came to be a patron of architecture, as he would in full measure, the wheel swung full circle in the direction of magnificence and enrichment. Even through the period dominated by a contrary view, we have seen that not all masters could be restrained. There were still designers who believed in adornment, carvers and painters who could provide decoration of very high quality. The first measures of the new Yorkist government were of retrenchment, and the fees of craftsmen were cut, but within a few years prosperity returned and it was once more possible to spend lavishly. So at the highest level little was done for some time, yet outside official circles the return of peace meant that building could proceed. There was a trough of relatively slight activity for several years, but from 1465 the number of new works quickly doubled.

After the long doldrums the signs of returning life came suddenly, even a little before the Yorkist victory. It was as though coming events had cast a ray of light before them. So we find that it was precisely in 1459–60 that the Chain Gate at Wells was built, one of the most remarkable single works of the whole period, and unlike all other surviving buildings in detail **174**. The same master may have designed the Newton chapel in Yatton church, as suggested by the late Kenneth Wickham, but that is all. The purpose of the gateway was to provide a covered passage between the Cathedral and the Vicars' Hall on the other side of the road. It was in any case a piece of ingenious planning and design, with a high wagon-way in the centre and lower arches for pedestrians at

174

175

176

each side. Above the archway is a covered gallery communicating at one end with the top of the chapter-house stairs, and at the other, by a few steps, with the first-floor hall of the Vicars' Choral. The purpose is purely utilitarian, but the building was made the excuse for a display of virtuosity in architecture. Ample light was provided for the two narrow footways by building the main vault on an arcade on each side of the road. The lower level of the gatehouse is panelled above the smaller arches of the footways, between shafting which is carried up in front of the gallery, past the pierced battlements to end in pinnacles set diagonally. All the arches are four-centred, the windows are either of two or of three lights. In the two-light windows is Y-tracery enriched with lower four-centred heads to the lights and vertical linking bars; the windows of three lights have strong mullions and a central light similarly treated or a central niche instead of a light, holding a statue.

The mouldings **fig. 23** are fine but not unduly 'busy', yet the whole impression is of a luxury rather than a merely functional necessity. The vault over the carriageway is like those of the Cloisters in having a quadrilateral instead of a normal boss, but the work otherwise does not resemble the Cloister nor anything elsewhere about Wells, except in the nearby house called The Rib. Even the likeness of the tracery in the Newton Chapel at Yatton is puzzling, since its date should be *c.* 1488 or nearly a generation later. If the vault provides any clue it suggests that there may be some connection with the West Midlands – certainly well beyond Bristol – and in a general way the Chain Gate has more kinship with the Beauchamp Chapel **71, 72** than with any other major building. It is natural to go on to the chancel of the collegiate church at Stratford-on-Avon **187**, built for Thomas Balsall, warden of the college 1466–91. The design, judged stylistically, may be early in this period, as it seems close to that of the west tower of Sheldon near Birmingham, begun in 1461. Southern Warwickshire, in fact, is an area where a rather rich style has a continuous history through the middle of the century, making few concessions to the cult of austerity.

We cannot, of course, mark any sharp division between the generations at 1460 or anywhere near it. Over much of England what may be described as good, sound building went on and produced a large volume of churches piecemeal, a tower here, a chapel there, sometimes rebuilding a chancel or adding a clerestory to a low nave. The bulk is formidable but comparatively few individual builds call for comment in a general history of the style. The main divisions were still those of the regions and counties, though as time went on and single masters travelled over wider fields, some motives tended to cross boundaries with greater frequency. It remained true that alternate patterns were of the West, supermullioned and gridiron traceries of the East. Alternate tracery, however, surprisingly combined with a crested supertransom, appears in the Trinity (north) chapel of Louth church, Lincs. **139**, in *c.* 1460–65. In the opposite direction, supertransoms were incorporated in western windows: the west window of the Temple church, Bristol (*c.* 1460–); the east window of Bodmin church in Cornwall **183**, built in 1469–72 by Richard Richowe; and the east window of High Ham church, Somerset **191**, completed in 1476.

174 Wells: the Chain Gate 1459–60, from east

175 Wells: the Deanery, windows (1473)–83, probably by William Smyth

176 Oxford: Magdalen College Chapel, cloisters and Founder's Tower 1474–90, by William Orchard

Three-light gridiron windows of the plainest kind, two-centred, were used in the clerestory of the large town church at Trowbridge, Wilts. (c. 1475–83). The west window in the tower at Charing, Kent, a work begun in 1468, of four lights with subarcuation, has a supertransom immediately above the heads of the lights and looks like a hybrid between the West Country and East Anglia.

This tendency to cross boundaries is, among other things, a mark of growing sophistication. Even if there were fewer architects of genius than there had been a century before, probably there was a higher percentage of literacy among the whole body of masons – and carpenters – concerned with design. Craftsmen were not yet able to obtain printed textbooks or engraved copies of detail, and those developments were not to come until after the end of our period. It is likely, all the same, that there was an increase of activity with sketchbook and album: strange ideas were noted down because of their very strangeness, rather than instinctively, xenophobically, rejected. This new attitude naturally had a great deal to do with the acceptance, by 1475, of detail that was definitely foreign in immediate origin even if ultimately English. Such receptiveness of foreign details was much more marked in timberwork than in stone masonry. It is possible that immigrant Flemings and others found it easier to obtain work as specialist joiners and carvers than to break into the ranks of the freemasons.

There are curiosities of distribution, even within a single region of England. The side windows of Richowe's church at Bodmin **183**, begun in 1469, are of four lights, subarcuated and with through-reticulation, four-centred heads to the main lights and cinquefoil cusping. Almost identical windows are found, but with markedly ogee heads to the lights, in St. Andrew's at Plymouth by John Daw, in progress in 1481–82; and exactly the same pattern but with two-centred heads to the main lights was employed by Thomas Lovell for the nave of Steeple Ashton in Wiltshire **192**, begun about 1480. Reverting to St. Andrew's, Plymouth, we find that at the same time that it used the four-centred ogee curve it was also employing two-centred lights with both Geometrical quatrefoils in circles and falchions as spandrel-fillers. In such cases it seems that the designer was not concerned to adhere to one consistent group of patterns, but simply created a tracery on the drawing-board, filling space with motives that happened to be convenient for his purpose. Another, six-light, version of the alternate window, subarcuated and with through reticulation, is found at Wells and at Little Malvern in Worcestershire. At Wells this is the normal tracery of the Cloisters **129**, adopted in or soon after 1420; at Little Malvern Priory it has been, by about 1476, depressed into a four-centred shape but remains otherwise almost identical.

The four-light alternate window, subarcuated, as used in the West but with each reticulation split by a Y-supermullion, was adopted for the School at Wainfleet, Lincs., completed in 1484. It is uncusped, and belongs to the same school of simplified detail as Tattershall church **170**, where the tower was being built by John Cowper in 1482. Uncusped tracery of this time occurs also in the tower of Silkstone church in the West Riding, begun in 1479; in the elaborately supertransomed west window of Hawton church, Nottinghamshire, c. 1482; and in the unusual five-light lancet design of 1475 at St. Helen Bishopsgate, in

177 Great Malvern Priory Church: interior of choir looking east c. 1430–60

178, 179 Eton College Chapel 1448–60: east window 1459–60, by John Smyth; north side, windows c. 1460–, by Simon Clerk

177

178

179

the city of London. It was becoming normal also in domestic buildings: at West Wickham Court, Kent (*c.* 1469–); Kirby Muxloe Castle, another work of John Cowper (1480–84); and at the Old Palace of the Bishop of Ely at Hatfield (*c.* 1480–86) **fig. 12.14**, both in square-headed Perpendicular windows and in three-light 'triple lancets' under a four-centred head. It is also unexpectedly associated with an enriched fan-vault in the Red Mount Chapel, Lynn (1483–85), built by Robert Curraunt but possibly designed by Simon Clerk (died 1489), as Mr. Oswald suggests. Cusped heads were still in use in square-headed windows at the Bishop of Lincoln's Palace at Buckden, Hunts., built between 1472 and 1494, and in untraceried three-light windows in the north nave clerestory of *c.* 1474 at Glemsford in Suffolk. In spite of the trend towards enrichment and a luxury style, there was certainly a counter-current of simplistic building, perhaps encouraged by necessary economy.

Another survival, perhaps because it was in tune with what was once more coming into fashion, was the cruciform lobed tracery **Map X** of purely Curvilinear type which had been used at King's College Chapel by Reginald Ely. It occurs in the south aisle of Cavendish church, Suffolk **155**, built in 1471, the year of Ely's death. A different version, with the lobes placed X-wise, formed the filling to a window of Y-tracery in the Greene Chapel of Lowick church, Northamptonshire, in progress in 1468–70 **fig. 12.11**. Along with such survivals, and by now revivals, of Curvilinear character, the trend to ogee heads became more pronounced. Two-centred heads were the normal official practice, but in provincial buildings they were tending to be superseded by the ogee about 1470 in many areas where they had formerly resisted. The Greene Chapel at Lowick, just mentioned, preserved the two-centred head, and so did the windows in the tower of the same date, with strong mullions, intersecting subarcuation and inverted daggers. But in the tower of Westwick, Norfolk **180**, built 1460–73, both types of archlet are used, the ogee predominating. At Manchester by *c.* 1480 the windows have taken on a stilted segmental-pointed form and have ogee heads **184**. The aisle windows at Trowbridge, Wilts., built between 1460 and 1480, still have two-centred archlets, but in the nave of St. Augustine the Less, Bristol (now demolished), the subreticulated windows of 1480 had ogees.

At William Orchard's Magdalen College, Oxford **176**, there are three-light supermullioned windows with two-centred arches, some with two-centred archlets to the main lights, others with ogee heads. The nave aisle windows at Sherborne Abbey have lights with two-centred heads, those of the clerestory ogees; but it is not likely that there was any very long gap between the dates of design (*c.* 1475). The clerestory windows with strong mullions and uncommon tracery of generically Bristol type, are by the same hand as the surviving blind tracery of the west wall of the demolished Cloister Lady Chapel at Wells (1477–88). Similarly the fan-vaults of the Bow Chapel and the north transept of Sherborne closely resemble the fragments of the fan-vault of the destroyed chapel, and the vault in the crossing of the Cathedral. The Wells master of the period from 1475 or earlier was William Smyth, who died in 1490. To him can be attributed not only these works at Wells and Sherborne, but also the crossing

180 Westwick Church: tower (1460–73)

181 Croyland Abbey: tower (1460–69)

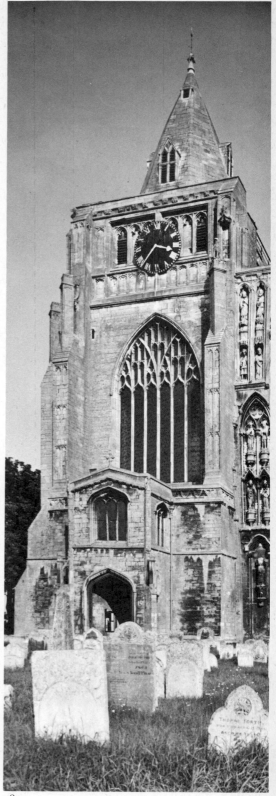

180

181

vault at Milton Abbey, Dorset, and the nave and west front of Crewkerne church, another work of *c.* 1475–90. All that part of Crewkerne church which is manifestly in Smyth's style has ogee archlets, contrasting with the rest of the nave, which cannot have been built many years earlier.

William Smyth, probably the man of that name who, without specifying his trade, took up the freedom of Wells in 1475, was the chief figure in the West of England at the last stage of the Perpendicular style. He is named as having carried out works at St. John's, Glastonbury, in an undated account of the middle or later part of the century, along with other men, apparently taking on contract work as a group, perhaps after the fall of pinnacles from the tower in 1465. At Wells Smyth received a yearly fee of £1 6*s.* 8*d.* and had a house rent free, apart from pay when at work. He must have been the architect for Dean Gunthorpe's alterations (*c.* 1473–83) at the Deanery **175**, where the great oriel in the hall has a fan-vault resembling the crossing vault and the fan-vaults of the period at Sherborne. Diminutive fan-vaulting of the same type is used in Sugar's (died 1489) chantry chapel in the Cathedral. Whatever may have been the circumstances of Smyth's life we must salute him as the last great architect of western Perpendicular.

In the other regions it is hard to find any parallel personality. Robert Everard of Norwich, master at the Cathedral from 1451 to 1485, was the builder of the great stone spire after the lightning stroke of 1463, and apparently also of the very fine lierne vaults of the nave (*c.* 1464–72) and presbytery (*c.* 1472–99) **204, 33**. In spite of his long career, little else is known of Everard's practice and no other major work can be assigned to him. Not much more can be said of Thomas Barton, designer of the central tower at Durham Cathedral **202**. From the general likeness of the scheme to that intended for York Minster it is probable that he was son of the John Barton who worked there between 1415 and 1447, taking up the freedom of York in 1427, and eventually became master from 1444 to *c.* 1450. Thomas Barton took up the freedom of York in 1447 and later presumably migrated to Durham, where he was in charge of the new tower from its inception. The old central tower had been burnt in 1429 and repaired by 1437, but was regarded as unsafe in 1456. It was seriously damaged by lightning in 1459, and complete rebuilding had been decided upon by 1465. The whole work was built by *c.* 1488, during the last five years under John Bell junior, who was probably responsible only for detailing of the top stage. Thomas Barton, able to get access to the York plans while his father was master there, produced a noble adaptation which, on its rather smaller scale, was capable of completion, as the York tower was not.

Until we come to the royal works of Edward IV, what is left of large-scale design consists of torsos and fragments. At Croyland Abbey **181** there is much of a grand north-west tower including a fine six-light window and admirably managed paired buttresses at the outer angle (*c.* 1460–69). At Ripon Minster are remains of an ambitious proposal to rebuild the crossing and the central tower which had been in a dangerous state from 1450 to 1465. What was done seems to date from 1466 and the next ten or fifteen years. It was decided to case the older piers of the crossing with a thick skin of new masonry, worked into shafts, and to replace each of the original semicircular arches with a new steeply pointed arch. These give almost a parabolic impression but are stilted two-centred arches. The shafts are made of a continuous deep roll moulding on plan, uninterrupted by fillets, a virtually unique solution. Only half of this underpinning was completed, so that both old and new designs co-exist and provide an impressive example of mediaeval methods of conservation in practice.

Among the greater parochial towers that are closely dateable that of Eye in Suffolk is outstanding **182**. It is of the turreted type, carried out in elaborately panelled flintwork, with a panelled ashlar parapet carrying stepped battlements. The tower at Eye, being built from about 1470 to 1485 – it was in progress in 1479 and the bells had been hung by 1488 – is of particular interest for the forms of arch used simultaneously, or nearly so. The west doorway has a normal two-centred arch framed in a square; the great west window has a very slightly pointed segmental arch, deeply stilted to provide drop tracery; and the twin belfry windows have more sharply pointed segmental heads. At Clare church, also in Suffolk, the chancel was built in 1478 and rebuilt in 1617; the east window now has an unpointed segmental head, though the tracery seems to be reused original masonry. It is possible that a slight point at the apex was smoothed out in the rebuilding. At St. Margaret's at Lynn in Norfolk, however, in the reconstruction of the aisles in 1472–83, the windows have three-centred arches with no trace of a point, trefoiled ogee heads to the main lights, and a curvilinear oculus **fig. 12.12**. Somewhat similar, but bluntly four-centred tracery was used (?c. 1481) in the tower of Coton, Cambs., but the lights have cinquefoiled two-centred archlets. At Wetherden in Suffolk the work of the porch and south aisle begun in 1483 is uniformly provided with ogee curves and with curvilinear oculi. In the porch the heads are trefoiled, but cinquefoiled in the aisle, which has two-centred arches with basically Perpendicular tracery, though the porch has a segmental-pointed arch.

The architects of the time, especially in East Anglia, were quite deliberately seeking for variety and moving away from the regularity and uniformity of parts which had been essential components of the style as formulated in the previous century. This is seen not only in the medley of arches of different shapes, sometimes introducing what look like deliberate discords, but also reviving the use of the falchion and of asymmetry. Thus at Ash-by-Wrotham in Kent, in the chapel of St. Thomas added between 1462 and 1467, the windows are of two lights with a central mullion; the arches are segmental-pointed, and there is drop tracery with ogee trefoiled heads to the lights and a pair of 'affronted' falchions leaning towards each other beneath a four-centred subarcuation over each light. The tower at Prestbury, Cheshire, in course of construction in 1480, has two-centred windows with Y-tracery; but the Y is managed asymmetrically so as to produce averted trefoil heads, leaning away from each other to the jambs of the window. At Worstead church in Norfolk **fig. 12.15** there are four-centred mullioned windows in the chancel clerestory of 1484–85. The two side lights have normal archlets with cinquefoil cusping, but the central light is given an ogee form and a pair of uncusped falchions 'affronted' above.

182

183

184

Quite orthodox patterns continued to be used elsewhere, and it is in this generalised mixture of old and new methods that the difficulty of dating undocumented works resides. At the very end of his long career Reginald Ely was still using plain Y-tracery at the Cambridge Schools, in the South Room of 1466–71. Simple cinquefoiled heads in Y-tracery were likewise provided for the Vestry at Lavenham church in Suffolk (1470–86); the unusual feature of these windows is the steepness of their four-centred arches, comparable to fourteenth-century work in the West Midlands. Conventional windows with two-centred arches and lights, and plain supermullioned tracery were used in the south chapel of Broxbourne church, Herts., in 1476. This is hardly surprising, since the mason was Robert Stowell, who had been master at Windsor Castle from 1452 until the fall of Henry VI and thereafter worked at Westminster Abbey, being appointed master in 1471. The south aisle and western part of the nave at Long Melford in Suffolk (c. 1480–84) continue the use of two-centred window-arches, though with ogee cinquefoiled heads. At Ashby-de-la-Zouch Castle (1474) the Chapel has the remains of windows which can be reconstructed with the help of the Bucks' view taken in the eighteenth century. They were of two-centred form with trefoil-headed lights and rectilinear tracery of supermullions and an arcaded supertransom.

We have seen that by the reign of Edward IV several things at once were happening to architectural style in England. The King's Works tended to maintain a rigid conservatism, and had been expressly warned against innovations by the aesthetic puritanism of the magnates and the king himself enunciated in the 1440s. The official style provided a backbone of continuity or, one might say, a ground bass against which the rest of the performers might execute variations. These were abundantly forthcoming, at any rate on the eastern side of the country and especially in East Anglia. Conservatism in detail still reigned over much of the North, influenced largely by the generation of Westminster men who had had charge at York Minster, the greatest lodge of mason's work north of Trent. On the contrary, at least one architect of genius was at work by the 1460s at Ripon, where the pier mouldings and crossing arches indicate a striking breakaway towards functionalism. Outstanding mastery of brick building came with John Cowper, trained as an apprentice at Eton College (c. 1452–59) and later the favourite architect of Bishop Waynflete of Winchester, for whom he worked at Esher, perhaps at Farnham and on the School at Wainfleet, and also on the tower at Tattershall church 170. His planning and design had a free field at Kirby Muxloe Castle in Leicestershire, the masterpiece which he was building for William, Lord Hastings, in 1480–84. Simplicity, the use of a well proportioned four-centred arch, and avoidance of cusping are marks of Cowper's style.

Although there were signs, at Ripon, Tattershall and elsewhere, of a precocious simplification looking a long way ahead to the end of Tudor Gothic, a stronger tide was setting in. The cult of simplicity had for the time being had its day, and once money was forthcoming, England entered upon an age of rich and even overloaded adornment. It could at times be said that architecture was no longer the Mistress Art, but rather that it had become a

182 Eye Church: tower (1470)–85

183 Bodmin Church from south-east 1469–72, by Richard Richowe

184 Manchester Cathedral from south, c. 1465–

mere framework on which to hang carving, and a background for the extravagant laying on of colour and gold. By no means all building was reduced to this and the ensuing Tudor Gothic style produced splendid masterpieces of composition that owed little to enrichment. This new style was, however, distinct from Perpendicular, in that it decisively moved away from the rigid norms of orthodox treatment which had ruled for a hundred years or more. In a broad sense this movement could be described as caused by the Renaissance, though it had little if anything at all to do with the renewed interest in Roman remains and in classical Latin literature. In English architecture the Perpendicular style had been created by crystallization, a stiffening of the relationships between the fluid motives of late Decorated art. What was happening in the reign of Edward IV was a return to fluidity. Whereas the onset of the specifically Perpendicular complex of motives had been distinguished by the fact that, in Willis's phrase, the mullion was carried up – to cut the arch; now it once again became normal in traceries that looked superficially like Perpendicular, to avoid carrying the mullion up, rounding it off into the arch.

A transition was beginning, but inasmuch as its first works belong to the old rather than to the emergent style, it is right to treat of them here as the natural culmination towards which the efforts of one hundred and fifty years had been tending. We can divide the transition itself, the quarter-century of the reigns of Edward IV and V and Richard III, into two parts approximately divided at 1475. In the first 15 years not much of first-class importance was built. The few outstanding builds were mostly provincial and have been discussed: the vaults and spire at Norwich, the tower of Durham, and William Smyth's transformation of the nave of Sherborne Abbey. The last can in some sense be considered the final achievement of pure Perpendicular. The other great works, built within the region of London, were mostly designed in or after 1474 and principally for the king himself. Before discussing the royal works there are several peripheral buildings to be considered.

Chronologically the first is Crosby Hall **188**, the chief part of Crosby Place in the city of London, begun in 1468 for the rich merchant and alderman Sir John Crosby. Crosby died in 1475 after the mansion had been finished, and by 1483 the Duke of Gloucester, soon to be King Richard III, was living there. The house was thus recognised as of the highest rank outside royal palaces, and this can still be seen in the fine design and superb craftsmanship of the hall, removed and re-erected at Chelsea in 1910. The first thing to be noticed is that, though in no way explicitly departing from the received norm of official Perpendicular, there is not a single example in the stonework of the hall of the crucial detail of the style. Every window, every section of blind wall-panelling, has cinquefoiled Y-tracery. The exquisite little oriel has a tierceron-and-lierne vault of eight-foiled star-pattern with carved bosses. The panels are not cusped and there is no influence from fan-vaulting, in fact nothing positively Perpendicular in detail. Even the mouldings, bowtells and hollow chamfers linked by fillets, are not distinctive in the way that the ogee, double-ogee and casement had been. The carpenter's work of the timber roof is again a radical departure from the open timber trussed roofs which had been usual. Trusses there were, of course, entirely hidden by a boarded ceiling as in some church roofs. But here the span is not simply divided into ranges of square panels grouped between beams, purlins and ribs. It is divided into four longitudinally, yielding an unresolved duality, with pendants along the centre-line, towards the walls, and at the walls as wall- or pendant-posts. Between the pendants, both longitudinally and crosswise, are arches of pierced wooden ashlaring only vaguely Perpendicular. Above the windows at wallplate level runs a band of framed quatrefoils with a battlemented cresting above it, as much late Decorated as anything.

The building of Magdalen College, Oxford, has already been mentioned, but something more must be said. We know that the architect was William Orchard, who lived on until 1504, and this was an early work. None the less it was the first real advance in planning since Wynford's New College laid out nearly a century before. At last the quadrangle of the college was integrated with the cloister **176**, and the buildings became a palace rather than a mansion. Battlements were provided from the start, not added as in earlier colleges; and there were remarkable enrichments such as the skeleton arch and panelled niche-work around the Chapel doorway. In a design of *c.* 1475 it is notable that the mouldings have been reduced, as at Crosby Hall, to bowtells, hollow chamfers, and linking fillets. The arches of the niche-canopies are more or less segmental, with seven-foil cusping. After completion of the main collegiate ranges the great tower **208**, a showpiece, was built on the street frontage. It is the nearest English counterpart to Giotto's campanile, a detached shaft from the ground up, turreted, with a most carefully thought out system of fenestration gathering force as it mounts to the tall twin three-light windows of the belfry stage. These are essentially a borrowing from Janyns' tower at Merton College **149**, and the open battlements and pinnacles owe much to him. The tall spired turrets at the four corners thrust their ranges of crockets to the sky with the abandon of a firework display.

So to King's College, Cambridge, where a period of dereliction had been succeeded by the second work, of 1476–85. Simon Clerk, who had been Ely's junior partner, was in charge, and provided a filling for the east window: idiosyncratic tracery compounded of official forms, such as the super-mullioned scheme and inverted daggers of the London school, and eclectic use of trefoiled cusping for the main lights and intersecting subarcuations. What was done, with help tardily given by Edward IV was but an intermediate stage; the finish had to wait for another 30 years. This retarded completion of King's College Chapel followed at a long interval the comparable phenomenon of the finishing of the Oxford Divinity School **130**. At Oxford the magnificent vault, again by Orchard, was at last inserted beneath the floor of the Library in 1479–83. Another unfinished building was the Chapel at Eton College **178, 179**, intended to have a very large nave. The fall of Henry VI led to a minimal fulfilment only, when a lower antechapel was built to west of the collegiate chapel, also a work of William Orchard in 1476–83.

At length we come to the buildings put up at the command of Edward IV himself. The king had considerable work done to the residential quarters of Dover Castle, and something at Windsor, as well as at Nottingham, one of the few mediaeval royal residences remote from London. Nothing of architectural significance now survives from these builds. What have come down to us are two major buildings: the great Hall of Eltham Palace in Kent **189, 190**, and St. George's Chapel in the Lower Ward at Windsor **185, 186**. For Eltham we have the dates, 1475–80, in which it was erected and, upon very strong presumptive evidence the fact that the designs must be attributed to the King's Mason, Thomas Jurdan, and Carpenter, Edmund Graveley. Jurdan had been a working mason at Eton College from 1444 and by 1461 was chief mason of London Bridge. A few months later he was appointed Serjeant of the King's Masonry to Edward IV, and held both offices until his death in 1482, a year before the king's. The likeness of the masonry work of Eltham to that of Crosby Hall is marked, and it is all but certain that Jurdan must previously have been responsible for that private building. The Y-tracery, tierceron-and-lierne vaults over the oriels, and the mouldings, are all much the same. For the king, Jurdan enriched the windows with peculiar 'horned' double cinquefoil cusping, but otherwise the effect of the two halls is very similar. Eltham is much bigger, 101 by 36 feet against Crosby Hall's 69 by 27 feet.

Although Crosby Hall and Eltham almost certainly shared an architect, their timber roofs are very different. The ceiling at Crosby Hall is *sui generis* and in its own off-beat manner a great success. This cannot be said of Graveley's oddly unfunctional imitation of a hammer-beam roof at Eltham. Instead of using the hammer-beam as a means of balancing the thrusts and bringing them down to the level of the internal corbels, Graveley's roof consists structurally of pairs of principal rafters linked high up by a pegged and strutted collar, with pendants and purely ornamental arch-braces hanging from this real truss above. Even more difficult to understand, from a man who had been a warden of the London Carpenters' Company, is the omission of trussed purlins lengthwise along the line of the false hammer-posts. The actual side-purlins are both visually and constructionally a most inadequate substitute. What has to be said about the hall at Eltham, as concerning Crosby Hall, is that it well exemplifies the approaching breakdown of the English method in architecture, which was not merely a style but an organic system.

Though first planned rather before Eltham, St. George's Chapel remained unfinished at the death of Edward IV and was not completed until 1528. The new chapel was already in contemplation by 1473 and certainly planned by 1474–75. Henry Janyns, shown by documents to have been the master mason in charge from 1478 to 1484, was assuredly the designer. He came from the same family as the two Robert Janyns, senior and junior, associated with the quarries at Burford in Oxfordshire. It is very likely that he was the elder Robert's son, engaged on carving for the gateway of Merton College, Oxford, in 1463–64. The plan is in many ways revolutionary. It provided from the start for a choir and nave of the same width throughout and a transept terminating in semi-octagonal apses. Choir and nave were to be of wide span, but the transept was relatively narrow. The resulting oblong crossing was, nevertheless, to have

185, 186 Windsor: St. George's Chapel 1474–, by Henry Janyns; vault of north aisle of choir 1480; and interior looking east; vault 1506–08, by John Aylmer and William Vertue

187 Stratford-on-Avon Collegiate Church: interior of choir (1466–90), possibly by Thomas Dowland

185

186

187

188

189

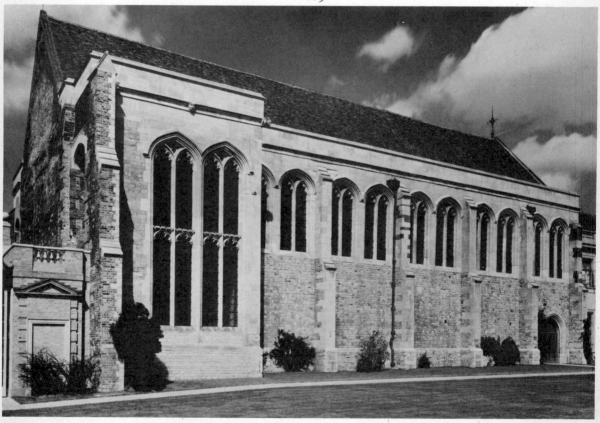

190

carried a tower, not in fact built. It would have been like the later tower of Bath Abbey, certainly based upon the St. George's scheme. As eventually finished, St. George's is extraordinary in presenting an almost symmetrical show-front to the south, with the polygonal transept in the centre, and smaller polygonal turrets to east and west. At the west end the turrets are an integral part of a second build not originally contemplated, though it is not certain that a permanent west front was to have stood on the foundations discovered one bay to the east. At the east end the polygonal turret, John Schorn's Tower, is probably a later rebuilding of a ground level chapel. It is now impossible to say, therefore, if the appearance of Renaissance symmetry goes back earlier than the revised designs made by William Vertue about 1500.

The design of St. George's shows a remarkably wide acquaintance with English precedents, at any rate back to St. Stephen's Chapel, as well as some knowledge of foreign examples of the polygonal transept. The vaults of the choir aisles 185, the only ones belonging to the work done under Janyns, are excellent fan-vaults of the West-of-England type found in Smyth's work at Sherborne. They were not built until 1480, and it is reasonably certain that their design was later in date than the earliest of Smyth's vaults at Sherborne and his design for the Wells Cloister Chapel begun in 1477. Janyns did, however, introduce a feature now unique: an octagonal spandrel-piece between the fans instead of the usual circular panel; this was apparently inspired by the vault of the Warwick choir. The bay design is superb, with excellently moulded piers and main shafts in advance of the panelled walls above the four-centred arcade arches 186. Ultimately derived from St. Mary Redcliffe, this is the finest of all Perpendicular interiors of the fifteenth century with the possible exception of the Sherborne choir. It is, all the same, slightly stretching the facts to call it Perpendicular, for the traceries and wall panelling already show the determination to round off the intersections at the vital point. Four-light windows of double Y-tracery in the aisles have very flat four-centred arches, practically what was to be called 'Tudor'. In the clerestory are steeply four-centred arches like those used in the West Midlands a century before.

These clerestory windows, with their spandrels filled by Geometrical quatrefoils in circles, may possibly echo the design of the older chapel to the East, what is now the Albert Memorial Chapel. This had been altered for Edward III in c. 1352, and its windows would have had the standard two-light detail with a straight reticulation here making its reappearance. The present altered state of the Memorial Chapel is due to works done for Henry VII soon after 1500, and is irrelevant to Janyns' designs. It is noteworthy that Janyns' mouldings, unlike Jurdan's, make extensive use of the double-ogee and are still consistently Perpendicular. He and his royal master both lived to see the seven bays of the choir completed and roofed, though not vaulted in the main span, and the wooden stalls erected. The lower stage of the transepts too had been built before the death of Edward IV, and the foundations laid for six bays of the nave. Unfinished as it was, and verging upon the coming change, we may still acclaim Henry Janyns' Chapel of St. George in Windsor Castle as the last great building of the Perpendicular style.

188 London: interior of Crosby Hall 1468–(72), probably by Thomas Jurdan

189, 190 Eltham Palace: Great Hall, interior 1475–80, by Thomas Jurdan, the timber roof by Edmund Graveley; and exterior view from south

191

192

CHAPTER EIGHT

Prospect and Retrospect

In following the progress of the Perpendicular style through the vicissitudes of a century and a half, it has not always been easy to see the wood for the trees. At the end of our period, too, we are left gazing into a future which, however distinct from true Perpendicular, was none the less bound to it by many links, as it had itself been to the Decorated style from which it sprang. From the very first Gothic in England in the twelfth century on to the last sporadic survivals in the eighteenth there was a continuous thread. While it is not our present business to follow this throughout its course, it is necessary to look where that course was leading when Bosworth Field was lost and won in 1485. At the same time we can consider the main achievements of Perpendicular itself and their relationship to the future of English architecture.

What then were the achievements of Perpendicular? They may be summed up in the word Unity. Starting from the plan and working through all the members of the building, the parts became subordinated to the whole, and that transcended the sum of its individual parts. It is true that, long before the fourteenth century, the model for the integrated square plan had existed in the monastic cloister. Yet the surrounding buildings had not, in the claustral plan, been more than artificially linked to one another as a matter of convenience. Out of this merely accidental and functional connection was to grow the philosophical and aesthetic union found in the collegiate plan as it was developed in England after 1350. The way had been pointed out by William Ramsey when he set the new chapter-house of St. Paul's, not on the periphery of the cloister, but actually within it, organically a part of it, a major stroke of genius. In a different way, the later colleges from Windsor to the integrally cloistered Magdalen College at Oxford and, in Tudor times, Cardinal College as Wolsey would have had it, were not composed of separate pieces strung like beads on a necklace, but dovetailed or jigsawed together.

Following Ramsey, indeed perhaps carrying out plans made by him before his death, John Sponlee produced in the new quadrilateral at Windsor a first attempt at a collegiate establishment clamped rather than tied together by its cloister. The second renewal of the old chapel of Henry III, carried out in the reign of Henry VII, has obscured the refashioning done by Sponlee. Within little more than five years from 1350 he had produced out of disparate buildings of various ages a single college. In another 20 years Yeveley was to plan such a work *de novo* on a clear site at Cobham in Kent; in less than 30 Wynford was laying out New College as the pioneer of a new way of life for the universities. In a strictly architectural sense he was able to profit from his experience at

191 High Ham Church 1476, from south-east

192 Steeple Ashton Church: nave from north-east (1480)–1501, by Thomas Lovell

215

Oxford to develop an even more closely integrated, yet more complex, group of buildings at Winchester. It is striking that these projects of the fourteenth century were brought to fruition. The programme, whether devised by Edward III or by Wykeham, and its formal expression designed by Sponlee or Wynford, was in scale not merely with its human users but with the resources available for its completion. The far more ambitious schemes of Henry VI in the fifteenth and of Wolsey in the sixteenth century were ineffective in that they had to be greatly cut down in execution.

From plans we turn to elevations, and here the story is of the same kind. The disposition of wall, window, buttress, plinth, stringcourse and parapet was so calculated as to concentrate attention rather upon the total composition than upon the beauties of individual sections. There was no attitudinising but a display of team spirit by the whole cast acting as one. Technically this was achieved by the application of systems of proportion and by the overriding principle of simplicity of massing. Not only outside but also in the interior of the building this rule can be seen at work. Each bay of piers, arcade, windows, vault; each truss of a timber roof such as Westminster Hall, is finely proportioned in itself, and *can* be viewed as a thing of beauty on its own; but this requires an effort. The overall beauty of shape and volume of space, the mesh of light and shade portrayed by the mouldings, concentrate interest upon the total nexus rather than upon the things combined. This achievement is the more remarkable in that the illusion is created almost in the full light of day. The windows, large and relatively clear, admit a brilliant illumination which can be religious but is rarely dim. The success of Perpendicular architecture owes nothing to darkness; with the ability to concentrate on any detail at will, successively, we are nevertheless struck by all at once.

Internal bay design, though subordinated in this way to the overall effect, was carefully cultivated. Long before the fourteenth century the tendency to unify the upper stages: triforium and clerestory, had set in, and in the greater churches including the most notable parish churches this was carried further still. The most difficult problem was the linking of the upper stage to the main arcades, which in most pre-Perpendicular work had been cut off beneath a horizontal string-course as a separate layer of the building. This effect was minimized by emphasis on strong vertical shafting standing in front of the string-course, with great success in the western nave at Llandaff Cathedral soon after 1200, and at York in Master Simon's nave of 1291. In neither case was there any serious attempt to break up the staring triangular spandrels above the arcades, though this had been achieved by William FitzThomas in the nave of Lichfield (*c.* 1265–93), where cinquefoiled circles were placed to fill the double spandrel, and the vertical shafts superimposed across them. Yeveley at Canterbury **85** improved upon this by recessing the panelled wall surface of the clerestory and reducing the horizontal string-course, while giving to the vertical shafts greater prominence and providing them with a background of wall shafts and arches which unified the whole of the bay from floor to vault. Wynford at Winchester **193** adopted a form of panelling in the spandrels, surmounted by a heavy cornice and pierced parapet. Owing to the rather low vault, steeply pitched and so with a very low springing, this parapet gives the impression of being a high-level gallery from end to end.

The number of Perpendicular, and for that matter Tudor, interiors of greater churches is very small, even when the outstandingly important parish churches are included. Where there was a serious attempt at architectural treatment of the bay, four main types can be discerned. Of these the first is the aisleless chapel panelled throughout, based on the presbytery and choir of Gloucester **203**, and seen on its own merits in the Lady Chapel **194** there, built between 1457 and 1483 but with extraordinary conservatism of style and detail. King's College Chapel at Cambridge is, of course, the other main instance of this type. Secondly we have derivatives from Yeveley's Canterbury nave, of which the most important is the nave of Chipping Norton; Chipping Campden and Northleach belong to this family, and all three are of the middle of the fifteenth century. Though only remotely derived, one may mention here the late nave of Cirencester church, built in 1515–30. In third place there is a development of the enriched spandrels with a substantial horizontal 'frieze' above them, owing something to Wynford's nave treatment at Winchester. Although the dates are rather vague, it seems certain that the first major instance of this type is in the choir of Manchester collegiate church (now Cathedral). This was begun in 1422 but the arcade design **195**, followed in the nave also, may be as late as the works of 1465–80. It therefore substantially precedes the outburst of this pattern in East Anglia. There it was taken up by John Wastell, to whom all the major examples are attributed upon very strong evidence by Mr. Oswald: Great St. Mary's at Cambridge (1491), Lavenham (1495), and Saffron Walden (1497).

Lastly comes the most satisfactory solution, where the vertical panelling formed by the window mullions and wall tracery is carried down to the extrados of the arch. In principle this goes back to St. Paul's chapter-house by way of the presbyteries of Wells Cathedral and Gloucester, and the earlier use of it is typically West-Country. The important instances were: Sherborne choir (c. 1425) **146**; Coventry St. Michael's (1434) now destroyed, followed by Holy Trinity; the choir of Great Malvern Priory (c. 1440) **177**; and the main vessel at St. Mary Redcliffe **196** as Perpendicularised by William Canynges c. 1446–70. The Redcliffe panelling is exceptionally well managed and was probably by the Bristol freemason John Norton. The idea was then taken up at Burwell, Cambs. **157**, where the arcade design must have been prepared by 1455, by Reginald Ely according to Mr. Oswald. As we have seen, it was adopted by Henry Janyns at St. George's, Windsor **186**, in or soon after 1474. The later examples of this pattern of bay again move eastward, to Shelton in Norfolk, in progress in 1487, and to the fine town church of St. Stephen, Norwich, by 1501.

One of the curiosities of Perpendicular is that as a style it made relatively slight use of the stone vault, but raised the design of timbered roofs to a fine art. Something must all the same be said about such vaulting as was erected. Like so much else, vaulting is divided into an eastern and a western form. These are not mutually exclusive, but at their most typical appear entirely distinct, though they share a common origin in the tierceron-and-lierne vault in the crypt of St. Stephen's, Westminster. Long before our period English vaulting systems had

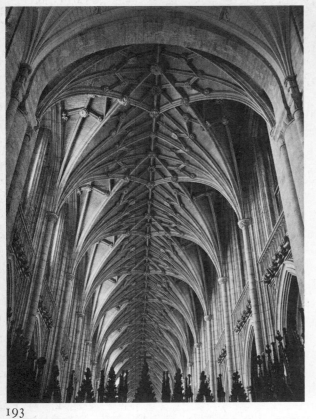

193

194

195

196

become sharply differentiated from those of France in two ways. The essential distinction was the almost universal adoption of the ridge-rib, running along the crown of the vault, and at the apex of the cross-vaults of the bays. This usage probably began at Lincoln choir (1192–1210), where the staggered asymmetrical system of cross-ribs required a ridge-rib for abutment. In the vaults of the nave at Lincoln (c. 1225–53) by Master Alexander, not only were longitudinal ridge-ribs employed, but also sections of ridge-rib running across and abutting the upper ends of a pair of intermediate ribs or tiercerons. From these simple beginnings English vault patterns arose.

At St. Stephen's Chapel, in the vault design for the crypt, a further development of pattern for its own sake appeared. Besides ridge-ribs along the vault and across the whole span of each bay there were the usual cross-arches and diagonal ribs; at each side a pair of tiercerons like those at Lincoln, but also in each of the four inner compartments of the vault, abutting on the longitudinal ridge-rib, a triangle of ribs meeting at a central point. Seen from beneath this produces a series of lozenge shapes spanning the central ridge-rib and supporting it from end to end. This invention was taken up and developed in two distinct manners. In the King's Works, and generally in eastern England, the ridge-ribs were preserved and additional tiercerons and linking ribs (liernes) were added to yield a complete circuit of lozenges surrounding the central boss of each bay. As far as is known, this was first done in the new vault of the rebuilt choir at Ely begun by John (? Ramsey) about 1325. A star of six points was produced in each bay of vaulting. In the meantime, however, the possibilities were being explored in a different way at Bristol. In the high vault over the unique hall-church choir of St. Augustine's Abbey (the Cathedral), the architect took the St. Stephen's pattern and, instead of adding to it, unpicked it. By removing the longitudinal ridge-rib altogether, he left a line of lozenges along the crown of the vault. Then on each side he placed a similar lozenge next the arcade, but still leaving a length of ridge-rib running across at the centre of each bay. Whereas the Ely vault looks very like its model at St. Stephen's, this Bristol version appears to be totally distinct. The date of design is not likely to be earlier than 1311, and completion was by 1332; at Ely the more orthodox scheme was complete by 1336. The two widely different children of Westminster were therefore very nearly contemporary.

It will have been noticed that these two radically different kinds of vault, both yielding attractive patterns, made their appearance at the very same time that William Ramsey was creating the first Perpendicular details at St. Paul's. Edward III and other patrons of architecture had before them a choice between the two forms: the star-vault of Ely, and the net-vault of Bristol. Both were to contribute largely to the more complex patterns of later Perpendicular and Tudor art, as well as to continental Sondergotik. We need not here recount the stages of development, but must note that Sponlee at Windsor II by 1353 had produced an early Perpendicular vault in which an eight-pointed star at the centre of the bay was surrounded by eight open squares, breaking the lines both of diagonal and ridge-ribs, an attempt to make the best of both worlds. The net-vault was carried further by William Joy at Wells in the presbytery during the

193 Winchester Cathedral: interior of nave 1394–(1405), by William Wynford

194 Gloucester Cathedral: interior of Lady Chapel (1457–83), possibly by John Hobbs

195 Manchester Cathedral: interior of choir c. 1465–80

196 Bristol: St. Mary Redcliffe, bay of nave looking north-west c. 1446–70, probably by John Norton

197

198

199

200

1330s, and by him and other masters of the Bristol school at St. Mary Redcliffe and, with curving ribs, at Ottery St. Mary *c.* 1337–42. With the added interest of pendants forming a sort of false springing, but with continuous ridges and diagonals, this kind of pattern was used for the Lady Chapel of Christchurch Priory **92** in 1395–1406.

The highest flight of the vault of official type was attained by Yeveley in the nave of Canterbury **85**, designed *c.* 1390. There the groups of liernes form a symmetrical series of four hexagons about each central boss, producing a series of cruciform flowers along the ridge. There is the additional subtlety that the subordinate ribs are relatively slender and so give the impression that the vault is further away, and higher from the ground than it really is: 80 feet, barely over half the height of Beauvais or Cologne. A very different method was employed by Wynford in his high vault at Winchester **193**. At New College about 1385 he had used a pure net-vault over the staircase to the hall **12**, and we must remember his probable origin at Winford in Somerset, less than ten miles from Bristol, and his association with Sponlee at Windsor. For Wykeham's chantry in the Winchester nave he designed a miniature vault of lozenges and triangles with a central hexagon of open sixfoil cusping in place of a boss. In this he made some use of ridge-ribs, and there is adherence to the old motives of Westminster in the double-cusped archlets, cinquefoil fillings to Perpendicular traceries, and wall-panelling with Y-tracery. Here the shaped panels were mostly cusped in the Bristol manner, but not so those of the high vault, possibly for reasons of economy. There was a level ridge-rib running the whole length from east to west, but no continuous cross-ribs. Cross arches, not specially emphasized, but of steep section, divided the bays, but there were no diagonal arches. Instead, the ribs which started as diagonals from each pair of wall-shafts crossed each other some way from the ridge and formed a large lozenge in the centre of the bay, subdivided by the ridge-rib and by a mesh of minor ribs radiating from a central boss. The subordination of this mesh behind the plane of the main ribs is handled in masterly fashion, so as to convey the illusion of diminishing branches and twigs derived from the great boughs as they in their turn from the massive trunks of the piers.

It cannot be claimed that the Perpendicular vault ever surpassed these twin peaks: Yeveley's orthodoxy, the eccentric fantasy of Wynford. Yet within the framework of the English vault of traditional ribs some magnificent work remained to be done. Further variety was possible by the introduction of more tiercerons and by different arrangements of liernes. Yeveley and his junior, Lote, showed the way in the handsome vaulting of the Canterbury cloisters **198**, with an eight-petalled rosette finely cusped in each bay, and a multitude of heraldic shields instead of bosses. Within this orthodox school the peak of achievement was reached by Robert Everard with his vaults at Norwich **204, 33**. First the nave, a design of about 1464, then the presbytery some eight years later, stamped with the approval of starlike forms amid graceful sheaves of ribs the solid Norman arcades of the cathedral. In the West, the nearly contemporary high vaults of St. Mary Redcliffe similarly put the finishing touch upon the school of Bristol. At Gloucester too, in the Lady Chapel **194**, the

197 Gloucester Cathedral: interior of east walk of cloisters *c.* 1360–, probably by Thomas Cambridge

198 Canterbury Cathedral: interior of north walk of cloisters 1397–1414, by Henry Yeveley, completed by Stephen Lote

199 Great Malvern Priory Church: vault of crossing *c.* 1440–60

200 Warwick, St. Mary's Collegiate Church: chantry chapel off the Beauchamp Chapel 1441–52, perhaps by Thomas Kerver

fourteenth-century choir vault was echoed on a smaller scale. Here and at Great Malvern Priory **199** the independent school of vaulting that had begun with the nave of Tewkesbury in the mid-fourteenth century retained its individuality to the end, preserving as its hall-mark a pair of subsidiary longitudinal ribs on each side of the main ridge. The Salisbury crossing vault of 1479 continued the Bristol style of the previous century, as at Redcliffe.

Tewkesbury, which as far as we know originated the later type of vault employed at Gloucester and generally considered the 'Gloucester' school, has to its credit also the very earliest model for the fan-vault. The monument to Sir Hugh Despenser, who died 1349, has an imitation vault carved out of a solid block in conoids. In form it is a perfect fan-vault on a small scale, and was originally painted with ribs to look like vaulting. The design is more likely to belong to the years after the Black Death than to Despenser's lifetime. Yet as we have seen the real fan-vault was in existence on a large scale at Hereford by 1364 and in the Gloucester east cloister **197** quite possibly sooner. Springers of fan-vaulting type existed in the nave of Hereford Cathedral before the collapse of the western tower in 1786, but the vault itself was of a simple tierceron kind, and that over the south transept, built shortly before 1404 and associated with an advanced Perpendicular window, is also tierceron. The implication seems to be that, after completion of the fan-vaulted chapter-house *c*. 1370, it was intended to use fan-vaults on a large scale but that the idea was given up within a few years. Together with the failure to use the fan-vault at Gloucester for anything more than the cloister, this suggests that the invention of the fan system is not to be referred to Gloucester. Either it stems from Tewkesbury or from Hereford, or else from one of the great western abbey churches now altogether lost, such as Cirencester, Evesham or Winchcombe.

After Hereford, the first adoption of the fan as an aesthetically desirable solution on a large scale was in the wooden vault of Winchester College Chapel **89**, designed about 1390 by Hugh Herland. Even this use at a building of influential standing seems to have failed to produce any serious emulation until the second quarter of the fifteenth century. Chantry chapels and the like, on a small scale, were provided with fan-vaulting, but there is no evidence of a major structural design before that for the Sherborne choir **146** of about 1425. The wall-shafts, already built before the fire of 1437, prove that a fan-vault was intended from the first. This in turn strengthens the attribution to Robert Hulle, who knew Herland's timber fans at Winchester. The Sherborne choir vault most ingeniously avoids the structural weakness of the flat spandrel between the cones by inserting a central section of lierne vaulting made to extend in a natural way to a conventional ridge-rib. The later fan-vaults at Sherborne **147**, Wells, and the crossing at Milton Abbey were produced by William Smyth in the final years of Perpendicular. With these exceptions the whole output of major fan-vaults belongs to the succeeding Tudor style.

Like the fan, the pendant was slow to develop as a feature of vault design. What is meant here is not the isolated pendant, simply a boss extended downwards, that hangs from the centre of some vaults, but the systematic use of a pair of pendants, set in from the side walls, and forming the springers of the central vault. In such cases the structural arch from which the pendants hang is so managed as to suggest that the visible vault is flying in air, supported upon the pendants. This most attractive scheme, lending itself to extremely beautiful variants, was seldom used. What appears to be the earliest example is that mentioned as forming the vault of the Lady Chapel at Christchurch Priory **92**, designed about 1395. It was suggested by Francis Bond that the internal treatment of the presbytery clerestory at Norwich **33** gives a visual suggestion of this kind of pendant. Since the construction of Everard's vault after 1472 this has been the case, but it is not clear that there was any earlier vault carried upon the tall shafts of Wodehirst's inner transparency, though one may have been designed. While it is possible that the capitals of these shafts, attached by elegant little arches to the outer traceried plane of the apse, might have suggested the idea of the pendant to the Christchurch master, the thesis is likely to remain beyond proof.

The pendant vault at Christchurch is not a fan-vault but a net-vault closely based upon Sponlee's vault beneath the Windsor Aerary of 1353–54 **11**. The Christchurch section is, however, two-centred instead of four-centred as at Windsor. The next occurrence of the motive is in the miniature vault of the chantry chapel squeezed between the Beauchamp Chapel and the choir of St. Mary's, Warwick **200**. It is of the date of the Beauchamp Chapel (1441–52) but ingeniously incorporates partial fans springing from the side walls with conoids generated by the axes of the pendants, not vertical but normal to the slope of a flattened four-centred cross-section. Though only a beautiful toy it would seem that this must have given Orchard his inspiration for the vault inserted in the Oxford Divinity School in 1479–83 **130**. The choir vault at St. Frideswide's (now Christ Church Cathedral) is also to be attributed to Orchard, and was finished by 1503 at the latest, shortly before his death. Both these Oxford vaults are alike in that they are pendant lierne-vaults, not fan-vaults. So is the presbytery vault at Christchurch Priory, built between 1502 and 1530, a copy of the earlier vault in the Lady Chapel. It was left to the royal masters to combine the pendant and the fan in a structural and aesthetic masterpiece at Henry VII's Chapel at Westminster, designed in 1503.

Both the fan-vault and the pendant-vault were creations of the Perpendicular style, and were carried over into Tudor. The lierne vault, in its star and net forms, effectively ended with our period. The great majority of important vaults carried out between 1330 and 1485 are in fact of lierne type, and we have to consider just how far they were independent of Perpendicular. The lierne, in English usage, is a rib which does not start from the springing and is not a ridge-rib: Francis Bond long ago disposed of the fallacy that the decagon of ridge-ribs in the Lincoln chapter-house was composed of liernes, pointing to St. Stephen's crypt as the first known example. That is not very likely to have been designed before 1319 when work was resumed after a long interval, and therefore by Michael of Canterbury in old age, or by his son Thomas. They were, it is true, working in a pre-Perpendicular manner, but equally they had moved away from Decorated usage. Just as other individual features, notably the four-centred arch, existed before the Perpendicular style

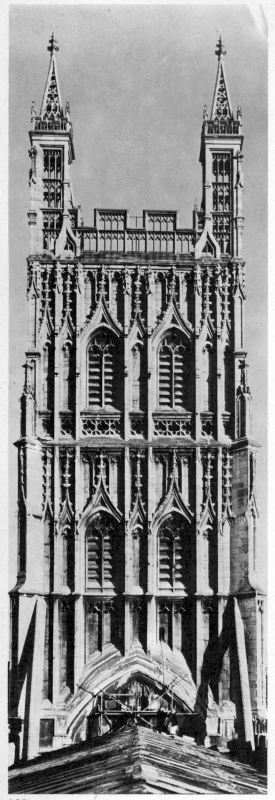

201

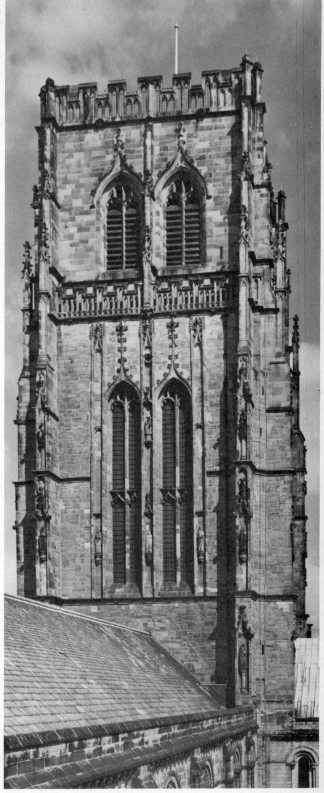

202

yet typically belong to it, it may be contended that the lierne vault is essentially a part of the Perpendicular movement and expresses the same spirit.

At this point we digress in order to discuss the date of the high vault of the choir of Bristol St. Augustine's, the present Cathedral. It has become fashionable to date it as early as 1298 on the ground that the known builder was Edmund Knowle, then treasurer and from 1306 abbot. He died in 1332 but the major campaign of works was finished only in the time of his successor John Snow, abbot until 1341. The dates of construction are then contained within a total period of 43 years, ending after the start of Perpendicular. Now it was pointed out by Rushforth, and stressed by Dr. Joan Evans, that the heraldic evidence of the glass in the east window tends to limit this glazing to the ten years 1313–22, which proves only that the choir must have been roofed by about 1320. High vaults were commonly the last works to be done in large buildings, and the design with its use of liernes to form a net pattern, utterly unlike the curious system of the earlier aisle vaults, probably did not form part of the original plans, whenever they were made. Secondly, the vault is necessarily subsequent to that of the crypt of St. Stephen's, for while the eccentric Bristol design can be derived simply from the orthodox development at Westminster, the converse is unimaginable, on geometrical as well as historical grounds. The vault at St. Stephen's *might* have been designed during the first phase of work in 1292–98, but this would run counter to the weight of evidence. It is in all respects simpler to accept that the Bristol design is a good deal later than is generally supposed, and belongs between 1320 and 1335, bringing it into a closer relationship with the vaults at Wells and at Ottery St. Mary.

This tentative conclusion in respect to the date of the Bristol vault leads to consideration of another discrepancy. At such a date as 1320 or later, the Bristol design invites direct comparison with that of other West Country vaults. Those at St. Mary Redcliffe, at Wells and at Ottery belong quite clearly to the same school and there is good reason to associate some of this work – the presbytery vaults at Wells on documentary evidence – with the important master William Joy, known to have become architect to Wells in 1329 and to have been still alive in 1347. The links with Bristol tend in a southerly direction, as is borne out by later events and the migration of tracery designs into Somerset and Dorset. In the opposite direction the next great building lodge was that at Gloucester, with which at this time Pevsner would associate Bristol. Yet in contradistinction to the parallels with Bristol usage, which are evident at Wells, there is a wide difference between it and any of the successive builds at Gloucester from 1331 onwards. None of the traceries at Bristol resemble either those of the side or south windows in the Gloucester transept; still less are they like those of the presbytery or the immense and wiry great east window at Gloucester **203**. The Bristol mouldings are extremely unlike any of those at Gloucester; richly carved capitals contrast with simple turned bells. The awkward mitred vault of the Gloucester south transept is as unlike the superbly modulated Bristol example with its carved bosses and sharply cusped panels as any contemporary work could well be. Finally, the Gloucester high vault built

201 Gloucester Cathedral: central tower (1450–60), by John Gower (?)

202 Durham Cathedral: central tower 1465–75, by Thomas Barton; the top stage (1483)–88, built by John Bell junior

after 1337, along with that over the nave at Tewkesbury, initiates a highly distinctive pattern stressing the function of the ridge-rib which is, in complete opposition, totally omitted at Bristol.

Both Bristol and Gloucester made use of hexagons but so did Canterbury in the early years of the fourteenth century. Canterbury motives are actually echoed at Gloucester, with the use of unusual forms of cusp and the pierced trefoil lobing which might have come by way of Westminster. In so far as the style used at Gloucester is regional it contrasts sharply with Bristol but is closely related to Tewkesbury and, quite possibly, to what we may reconstruct as the usage of Winchcombe. At other times, both in the ball-flower work of the south nave aisle (1318–29) and later in the fan-vaulted work of the east cloister, there seems to be a very near link to Hereford. At a later date Gloucester style moves in exactly the opposite direction: whereas Bristol masons 'colonized' Somerset, Dorset and the South-West, those from Gloucester either went eastwards to London or northwards into the West Midlands. We may also mention the almost universal employment of the diagonal buttress on Gloucestershire church towers, including St. Nicholas in Gloucester and the Cathedral **201**, in contrast with the general Bristol use (including St. Augustine's) of paired buttresses set back from the angle **207**, as in Somerset and the West of England. The tower at Arlingham, Glos. **37**, built by the Gloucester mason Nicholas Wyshongre in 1372–75, though only marginally Perpendicular by the top stage, has the county's typical buttresses.

This brings us to the important question of towers as a principal element in style, and the immense emphasis laid on the building of church towers throughout our period and on until 1540 and the breakdown of the Middle Ages. We have seen that in some cases, such as Walberswick **131** and Totnes **161**, towers were built in direct imitation of others, and this is evidenced also from the Continent, in Spain and in Germany, where drawings survive showing successive stages in the adaptation of steeples. Clearly there were in England also many drawings preserved on sheets of parchment as long as any part of the work still remained to finish, and then scraped for re-use or discarded. We have seen that there is circumstantial evidence that the design for the central tower of York Minster **6**, intended to have an upper belfry stage, was used as a basis for the tower at Durham **202** actually completed. The main storey or lantern at York was indeed built; but in another case, that of the tower intended by Henry VI to have been built at Cambridge, nothing was erected on that site; yet, as Mr. Gerald Cobb has pointed out, a version was made from the surviving drawing as the tower of the London church of St. Mary Aldermary, begun in 1510. As mentioned above, there are distinctive characteristics of towers in different counties or regions, as well as variations due to other causes.

Apart from local variations there are other factors which differentiate towers one from another. The chief of these is their position: central, standing on top of the crossing of a church, astride its roofs; terminal, often in pairs, to dignify a west front or transept; and free-standing or attached only on one side. Each of these main kinds of tower gave rise to distinct problems in design. The central tower or towers placed on a front already had a base provided for them. Their

203 Gloucester Cathedral: interior of presbytery 1337–67, probably based on designs by William Ramsey

204 Norwich Cathedral: nave vault 1464–72, by Robert Everard

205 Norwich: Blackfriars' Church, nave (St. Andrew's Hall) c. 1450

203

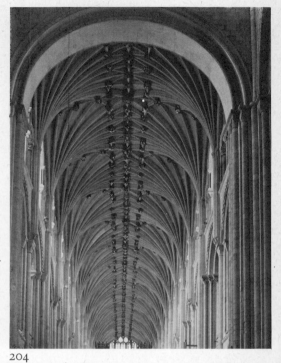

204

205

composition had to be considered in relation to a pre-existing building. The free-standing belfry or a western or lateral tower attached only at one side was a separate work of art allowing relatively free rein to the imagination. Certain main types of structural treatment were applicable to all towers. They might have no angle-buttresses at all, like the original central tower of Old St. Paul's before flying buttresses had to be added, or the central tower at Wells, or Yeveley's Westminster Clock Tower. Secondly, there might be a single buttress placed diagonally at each angle, the prevalent method in Gloucestershire and generally throughout the old diocese of Worcester except Bristol, as we have seen. The diagonal buttress was also commonly used for the less distinguished towers of the Home Counties and sporadically in East Anglia. Then there is the clasping buttress, a projecting mass folded around the angles as in some early towers (St. Albans Abbey, lower stage), and a few fine parochial towers of our period such as Elton in Huntingdonshire and others mostly in the South Midlands. A visual development of the clasping buttress is the turret, more or less polygonal and usually finished with upstanding shafts and pinnacles. A large proportion of the greater towers belongs to this category, regardless of district except that it is virtually unknown in the North and the South-West.

There remains the most important type, that with a pair of buttresses placed at right-angles to the corners. The great majority of important parochial towers belongs in this class, but divided into two groups: either the buttresses are placed so as to let the angle of the tower show between them, as is almost universal in Somerset, Devon and Cornwall; or the re-entrant angle between the buttresses conceals the tower, as is usual in Yorkshire and Lincolnshire. There are exceptional towers of highly individual design which cannot be placed firmly in any one category but these are rare exceptions and not often of high quality. Certain substantial groups, however, involve a degree of mixture or hybridization, as it were, between the characters of main classes. This is true of many of the finest towers in Somerset, which follow the practice of Wynford at Wells (derived from earlier work there) in placing a pair of diagonal buttresses at the top stage, standing on the square buttresses. In other examples, generally of less importance, these are reduced to a single diagonal buttress. A variation of this is to sink the diagonal buttresses of the upper stage into the wall so that only a triangular section, or little more, projects: the tower of Sherborne Abbey is a notable instance.

The subject of church towers has often been studied, notably by Dr. Allen in his great book with its extensive series of fine illustrations. There has been considerable emphasis on classification, but it is evident from the discrepancies between the results achieved that no 'natural' arrangement has yet been discovered. A completely satisfactory classification would be by designer and by date, but it is only in a minority of cases that these facts can be discovered. Study of towers of known date suggests that even close general resemblances in design may not indicate more than careful imitation. On the other hand, a single designer, William Wynford, within the same few years produced the unbuttressed tower at New College, Oxford **81**, and the elaborate buttressing system of the south-west tower at Wells **20**. Rice Merrick, in his *Book of Glamorganshire Antiquities* written in 1578 towards the end of his life, stated that the tower of the church of St. John the Baptist at Cardiff was made by one 'Hart, a Mason, who made the tower of Wrexham and of St. Stephen's in Bristow.' Merrick, who as clerk of the peace was well placed to obtain local information, is not likely to have been altogether wrong in this statement though Hart could not both have produced the original design for St. Stephen's *c.* 1453, and have built the tower at Wrexham in 1505–25. Even the top stages of the three towers differ very widely, though there is some kinship between the turreted crowns of Cardiff and Wrexham.

To consider briefly the greater Perpendicular towers, those of cathedrals, monasteries and the grander collegiate churches, we must deal first with the turreted class, going back to much earlier times, but codified by Richard of Stow's work on the central tower at Lincoln in 1306–11. By *c.* 1320 this had led on to the design for Salisbury, probably in the first instance by Master Robert, but mostly carried out by Richard Farleigh after 1334. This type was incorporated with a great deal else in the eclectic design for Worcester **26**, but also gave rise to the smaller version (?*c.* 1335) at Pershore. For the tower at Worcester we have exact dates of construction, 1357–74. The lower stage is quite pre-Perpendicular in detail, yet affected by the vogue for vertical panelling; it has paired buttresses. The same structural methods internally continue up through both stages **fig. 25**, and it cannot be deduced that the architect was not the same throughout: for the latter part of the work he was John Clyve, a mason from the works of Windsor Castle where he was occupied in 1362–65 under Wynford. This may account for the adroit transformation to a pair of diagonal buttresses, later modulating to turrets. The mouldings, though not the tracery, of the upper stage are Perpendicular; those below are transitional but make use of the wide and shallow casement moulding. Altogether Worcester is the most subtly proportioned and consequently the most aesthetically satisfactory of all cathedral towers of the period.

The turreted tower only reappeared at Canterbury (1493–1505), by John Wastell, and at Bath Abbey (1501–39), by the brothers Robert and William Vertue, in the Tudor age, but among parochial towers it had had a widespread vogue and was taken up in the great Cambridge design of about 1450. The earliest of the turreted towers seem to be those in Wiltshire, presumably inspired by Salisbury: Mere and Marlborough St. Peter. Within the same diocese are dateable towers of this kind at Reading St. Lawrence (1440–58) and Wimborne (1448–64). It is less easy to account for the contemporary outburst of turreted towers in East Anglia, where a half-dozen fine examples are accurately or approximately dated. These are, in order: Stoke-by-Nayland (*c.* 1439–62) **160**; Bungay (*c.* 1441–74); Wymondham west tower (1445–78) **28**; Laxfield (1452–60); Redenhall (*c.* 1460 onwards); and Eye (before 1470 to before 1488) **182**. The Tudor example of *c.* 1494–1512 at Dedham in Essex was by John Wastell. Deriving from Mapilton's pinnacles on the south-west tower at Canterbury are the towers at Lydd **163** and Tenterden already referred to, but these are only turreted at the top stage. The central tower at Ashford, however, is turreted throughout. The most splendid tower of the whole class, apart from cathedral towers, is undoubtedly that of Magdalen College, Oxford **208**. Though not built until 1490–1509, its design, presumably inspired by the Cambridge drawing, had no doubt been made earlier by Orchard, largely influenced by the tower at Merton **149**. The tower of the parish church at Connington, Hunts., probably built about 1500, is another to be linked to the unexecuted Cambridge design.

The plain towers without buttresses have an ancient ancestry which becomes Gothic with the central steeple of Old St. Paul's (*c.* 1200), and was adapted later for the noble church at Witney, Oxfordshire, a manor of the bishop of Winchester and probable origin of Thomas Witney. His intervention explains the appearance of the same type, with three windows on each face, in the central tower of Wells in 1315–22. A reduced version with twin windows was adopted, almost certainly by Yeveley, for the tower of St. Mary Overy in Southwark (lower stage). This was part of the works undertaken in 1380–90 and was finished before 1424. Its influence is obviously strong on the design of the buttressed central towers of Howden **83** and Cottingham **36** in East Yorkshire, and underlies Colchester's scheme for York **6** and thus the central tower at Durham **202** also. All of this group, along with the western towers of Beverley Minster **99** and York **101** and the central towers of Hedon **84** and of Doncaster (destroyed), had paired buttresses, apart from the central tower of York, where they were set back from the angles with excellent effect.

At Westminster Abbey, where the west front was designed by Yeveley but only in small measure built in his lifetime, the western towers were meant to have clasping buttresses above the roof, as can be seen from Hollar's engraving of the unfinished works. We can get some idea of Yeveley's intentions from the completed front and towers of St. Gudule in Brussels, one of the few instances where strong Perpendicular influence upon a continental design is evident. There is probably also some influence from the Westminster design upon the late tower of Lavenham in Suffolk (*c.* 1486–1525), attributed by Mr. Oswald to Simon Clerk. The Lavenham tower has panelled clasping buttresses against which are applied pairs of set-back buttresses in the same manner as the buttresses on each side of the west porch at Westminster Abbey. It seems significant that when John Thirsk, at that time master mason of Westminster Abbey, carved a statue for the Lollards' Tower of Lambeth Palace in 1434, he was assisted in making the niche for it by the young Simon Clerk.

The towers of Gloucester (*c.* 1450–60) and of Great Malvern Priory, roughly contemporary, are so much alike that they have to be attributed to a single designer **201, 206**. Both have diagonal buttresses and rather fussy panelling suggestive of metal strips. Of splendid massing when seen at a distance they are disappointing at close quarters if they are considered as logical developments from the Worcester tower. At St. Augustine's (Cathedral), Bristol **207**, the tower (?*c.* 1466–71) has paired buttresses which higher up give way to a diagonal at each corner. The remaining cathedral towers of importance have already been discussed: the south-west tower of Wells **20**, by Wynford, and that of Canterbury **98** by Mapilton. Both were highly influential in forming

206 Great Malvern Priory Church: view from north-east *c.* 1430–60

207 Bristol Cathedral from south-east: central tower *c.* 1466–71; battlements of choir (1474–80)

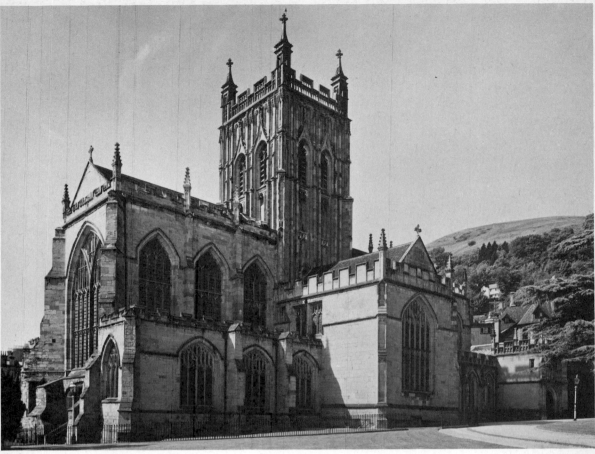

206

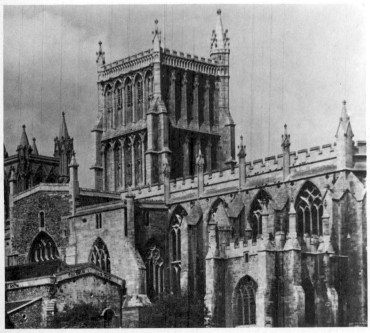

207

schools of parochial design. Both have pairs of set-back buttresses, which at Canterbury lead to turreted pinnacles; at Wells to a pair of diagonal buttresses and a crested parapet struck off on a level line.

We cannot here follow out in detail the complicated development of the western towers influenced by Wells, but attention needs to be drawn to the two early Perpendicular west towers at Shepton Mallet and at Yeovil **5**. Though very different in detail they both owe a great deal to Wynford. Shepton Mallet, with its characteristic twist from square to diagonal paired buttresses, cannot be divorced from consideration of the cathedral south-west tower only five miles away. The work at Shepton is not likely to have begun before *c.* 1375, and Wynford had been engaged as master to Wells Cathedral ten years before that. Yeovil is strikingly like Winchester College in the handling of its buttresses and string courses, and this agrees well with the presumptive date of design in the 1380s. Most of the aesthetically famous Somerset parochial towers are Tudor in date, but several of the grander and simpler designs are truly Perpendicular: Wells St. Cuthbert (*c.* 1410–30); and Mells, begun before 1446 although finished much later. The great west tower of Bruton had been begun by 1456 and perhaps earlier. Glastonbury St. John was built within the period 1456–93; its 'Gloucester coronet' of battlements and pinnacles may well be Tudor, but the design is Perpendicular and, to judge from the handsome square-headed wall-panels filled with Y-traceries, influenced from Westminster to a degree most unusual in the West.

Two of the most remarkable of all the parochial steeples are in Lincolnshire, at Boston and at Louth **139**. Both started as thoroughly Perpendicular designs with paired buttresses, Boston *c.* 1425–30, and Louth rather later, *c.* 1440–45. Both ended with Tudor turrets: Boston with an octagonal lantern of *c.* 1510–20 which never had a spire (hence 'Boston Stump'), Louth with the superb spire built in 1501–15 under John Cole, followed by Christopher Scune who also worked at Durham and Ripon. Louth is a prebendal church of Lincoln Cathedral, and the original design for the tower was probably made by the Lincoln mason John Porter who flourished there from 1423, was called to York Minster to advise in 1450 and became master from 1454 to his death in 1466. Last of all we may mention the western tower of Manchester Cathedral **184** which, in spite of rebuilding in the 1860s, preserves the original design seen in Britton's plate of 1810. With set-back buttresses and a deep coronet of traceried battlements and grouped pinnacles it remains one of the quiet triumphs of the last days of Perpendicular.

208 Oxford, Magdalen College: bell-tower, designed *c.* 1480 by William Orchard and built 1492–1509 by William Reynold senior

Epilogue

The end of the course has been reached. Perpendicular architecture, which began at the same time as the personal rule of Edward III, was already passing away when the royal coronet fell into a thornbush from the helm of Richard III on 22 August 1485. Perpendicular was the artistic style of the later Plantagenets and reflected their personalities and their manner of exercising a national sovereignty. Leadership in style lay with their officers of the royal works, though the regions and counties of England were free to cherish their own particular traditions and there was considerable scope for the exercise of personal individuality. From royal palaces down to small private houses, from cathedrals to remote chapels, a system of unity in diversity reigned. Perpendicular was at the same time a royal, an aristocratic, and a popular architecture.

Here was a form of art which expressed the identity of purpose which, despite the setbacks of civil wars and internecine quarrels, on the whole united the Crown to the whole of the English nation. The style, with its capacity for peaks of grandeur seen against a background of commonsense, was an aesthetic as well as a structural and technical reflection of the political purpose which was in the same period engaged in fighting the Hundred Years War. The parallelism between political and artistic developments is very close. The occasion of the War lay in the death of Charles IV of France in 1328; the war itself began at Cadsand in 1337. Between these two dates the first Perpendicular details were cut at Old St. Paul's. What was to be seen in retrospect as the end of the War, the defeat of the English in 1453, was not so accepted at the time. In reality for those then living the conclusion of hostilities came with the Truce of Hesdin in 1463, finally ratified after a further English invasion in 1475 at the Peace of Picquigny. Again, it was between those two dates that we have seen the angularity of Perpendicular first softening and becoming as it were liquefied by the returning Curvilinear forms.

In these circumstances it is less surprising that Perpendicular won no acceptance abroad. There were a few instances of influence, it is true, but they amount to very little and can hardly be claimed as demonstrating any English domination over continental art. Within the town and pale of Calais there were certainly English Perpendicular buildings on continental soil, but they gave rise to no school of anglophile work across the frontier. We have seen English style implanted in Scotland in the new presbytery of Melrose, but this was but honourable amends for damage done by our army there. Quite late in the period, *c.* 1468, a window of reticulated tracery with some supermullions rising to cut the arch was built in a chapel of Orense Cathedral. One can suppose that this was due to an individual English mason who stayed on in Galicia after a pilgrimage to Santiago de Compostela. Later still, between 1500 and 1533 the church (later cathedral) of Barbastro in Aragon, designed by the Spanish master Juan de Segura, was covered with fan-vaults – of a kind! Here there is not the slightest suggestion of anything more than a sketch in an album at most; Segura may have had some contact with England, direct or indirect, when Aragonese ambassadors travelled to arrange the royal marriage between the Princess Catherine and Prince Arthur Tudor.

There certainly was a more general influence through the Low Countries and as far as the Rhineland. Dr. Joan Evans has pointed out that there is panelling of Perpendicular inspiration on the Cologne Rathaus of 1407–14. We have seen that the west front of St. Gudule at Brussels, contemporary with that of Westminster Abbey as designed but never completed, has an English look and an English treatment – though no English detail. There is even a good deal of English massing and composition about the west front and towers of St. Wulfran at Abbeville, not begun until 1488 or more than ten years after the final seizure of the town by Louis XI. But Abbeville, under the dukes of Burgundy since 1435, had been the capital of the politically English county of Ponthieu since the time of Edward I: if English artistic influence was to penetrate France at all, it would be there.

So far as English art had captivated continental artists or their patrons, it was the older Curvilinear pattern taken to Catalonia by an Englishman about 1325, and rejected by Court circles after reaching its peak in the 1330s. Not only the flowing line of traceries but types of moulding current at the transition to Perpendicular were taken up in Germany by the family and school of Peter Parler. The great lodge of Strassburg Cathedral had founded its jurisdiction upon the English fashion as far back as 1275 and the atmosphere, political and commercial, of the next fifty years or so was congenial. English influence there certainly was, and within the area bounded by the Channel coast from Calais to Holland, the old French frontier and the Rhine, a wedge of English architectural motives pushed on towards central Europe. After a century-and-a-half the tide turned and, by way of Flanders and the Burgundian Court, our details were returned with interest to form the basis of the Florid Gothic of late Yorkist and Tudor times.

The return of Curvilinear detail from Greater Flanders in the 1470s is an observed fact; but why should this have happened at all, and why at that particular time? Close political and cultural links had bound the fortunes of England to those of the Burgundian realm over a very long period, and there was no obviously new factor either in the political or the economic field. The fundamental reason probably lay in the weakening of English cultural life in the Wars of the Roses after 1455 and in the disillusionment that followed the catastrophe of the last phase of the wars with France. National confidence must have been severely shaken by these blows coming on top of a deep-seated economic depression. Edward IV's dismissal of Lancastrian servants of the Crown broke an ancient continuity, and the stringency of his early economies gave little encouragement to the arts. This caution had its reward in the increased prosperity of the latter years of Edward's reign, once he had recovered the ground lost by his overthrow and exile in 1470–71. It is only after his return from Flanders that the transition to Florid Gothic can be detected in detail.

The evidence is thus very strongly in favour of the king's personal taste as the deciding factor: Edward IV was, like other European sovereigns, moving towards enlightened despotism. A country tired of internal and external conflict and anxious to be rescued from trade recession was ready to accept an absolutism which looked forward to that of the Tudors. The monarch was once again in control, as he had been in the late thirteenth and through most of the fourteenth century. Perpendicular became the accepted national style by the choice of Edward III, and was raised to a higher power by the exercise of Richard II's exquisite discrimination. Even in the less propitious atmosphere after 1399, Henry IV's action in sending William Colchester to take charge of the works of York Minster profoundly affected the future of the style outside the metropolitan area. After a phase of uncertainty a new personal lead had been given by Henry VI, directing fashion towards 'clean' line and 'substantial' form, the qualities he saw in the great colleges built for Wykeham and the other works of their time. Now his opponent, determined to be done with the long Lancastrian usurpation, along with it effectually rejected the English Perpendicular style.

The chief influence upon English architecture was then that of the king himself. He was usually supported by the taste of the small compact body of the higher nobility, much intermarried and immensely wealthy. There is little or no evidence to suggest that independent lines of architectural development were fostered by particular individuals or families, and the known careers of architects show that they worked for the Crown, for noble, ecclesiastical, mercantile and parochial interests without distinction. The money available dictated scale and to some extent the amount of enrichment, though that was also controlled by the express personal preferences of the patron. There is no sign of any stylistic differentiation, other than that implied by relative simplicity or by the better or worse quality of workmanship, between works done for clients of different categories. Hence it would be out of place, in regard to Perpendicular, to discuss it as an art dominated by class: it was not distinctively a Court art, nor aristocratic, ecclesiastical, monastic or burgher, but all by turns throughout the period of its development. The marked distinctions were, as we have seen, mainly those between several regional traditions. The personalities of the leading architects, as individual artists, counted for a great deal more than the social background of their clients.

It is as though the aesthetic unity which was the dominant feature of the style imposed upon it also this unity of impression. Modulating with the landscape of different regions, coloured by the geology of the local or available stone, the buildings within one district give out an air of family relationship, embracing cathedral and wayside chapel, castle, mansion, and market town. At a given date there is a much closer resemblance between the various kinds of building within a single area than between buildings of the same kind in different places. The controlling factor is less client than climate, rather county than caste. As the late T. D. Atkinson showed, England is divided into a multiplicity of local styles, mainly following the lines of the shires. Yet it is in spite of these local patriotisms that Perpendicular rises above them, distinguishable as a national form of art.

It has already been noticed that mass-production was not a major feature of strictly Perpendicular architecture, though it was to play a large part very soon afterwards. The standardized details, and even whole chantry chapels to an identical design, sent out from town shops throughout a district, were to be a function of Florid or Tudor Gothic but are not our concern. It may be asked, however, whether quarries were not centres of regional style. At first sight it seems likely that the distribution of stones ready cut, or even carved, from the quarry would tend to the dispersal of a particular version of style. Yet this does not normally seem to have been the case. There are obvious reasons. In the first place, quarries and quarrymen have no more inherent control over architectural style than firms of building contractors. It is only in the case where a quarry-owner is at the same time an architect that similar details spread out from a single quarrying centre to his separate jobs, and this would be exclusively in virtue of his function as designer, not that of quarryman. Secondly, we know that long before the Perpendicular period it had become normal to send patterns – 'false moulds' – to quarries at a distance or even abroad, as at Caen. The details were designed by the master and merely made by the stonecutters at the quarry, to save transport charges by lightening the load. No independent design was in such cases carried out by the quarryman.

Where a quarrying district did influence surrounding style it was an indirect rather than a direct effect. The concentration of stoneworkers in the area undoubtedly gave rise to families of masons, some of whose members became masters of design, i.e. architects. These masters went away and followed their art, practising in the traditional style of their place of origin, perhaps overlaid with experience gained in the King's Works. While such local influences cannot be dismissed they should not be overrated. In any case we must remember the many buildings where the source of stone changed from time to time, sometimes with curious results on appearance, but without alteration of style as such. Very occasionally the ownership of quarries of different sorts or colours of stone by the same patron, for example a monastery or the chapter of a cathedral, might result in experimental polychromy. In such cases the effect upon architectural style was determined by the master at his tracing-board, deciding how to use the various stones, not by the quarries themselves.

Such considerations bring us to the question of aesthetic effect: how far is the impression made by our mediaeval buildings due to deliberate intention? We have seen that it was commonplace for clients and their architects to visit existing buildings in order to find models to copy or surpass. At the parochial level this was a main factor in design, and chapels, naves and especially towers are direct witnesses to the positive taste of the moderately well-to-do man in the street. Where the services of a distinguished master were obtained, the buildings are also evidence of the aesthetic intentions of the architect. Both on the part of the patrons and of the designers there was explicit and conscious emulation; the attempt to go one better than the admired model was a main reason for the widespread success of Perpendicular art. For we must make no mistake about this: subjective as such judgments may be, there is no possible doubt that the Victorian critics were wrong. Their adverse view was the outcome, not of a positive taste, but of an artificial preconception based on an *a priori* philosophy of religion.

Perpendicular, on the contrary, is a pragmatic architecture. It was developed and flourished mightily, first because it pleased King Edward III, and later because it became a national second nature. The sum total of the many individual expressions of artistic creativity in the style constituted a national idiom and the natural flowering of the period. Nothing really comparable appeared elsewhere during the Middle Ages. In no European country is there an architectural countenance of equivalent and recognizable individuality. This could not be expected in fragmented Germany or Italy, any more than among the kingdoms of the Peninsula. England's counterpart in monarchical nationalism, Hungary, had even a similar shire division, yet its Gothic remained an import derived from French, German and Bohemian masters and was eventually dominated from outside by the Vienna lodge of masons. The nationalism of France, invoked late in the day to counter the English invaders, was unable in the Middle Ages to overcome the centrifugal forces of the great provinces of Gaul. In so far as French Gothic was ever a national style it was at a much earlier period and was the expression of a minuscule 'nation' comprising little more than the Ile de France. It is only in the sister island, Ireland, that something comparable took place at the same time. In spite of the lack of any Irish political cohesion there arose a distinctive form of Curvilinear art, owing little to Perpendicular, and of virtually national extension.

Very different was the case in Wales, to which few references have been made. The reason is lack of evidence for dating rather than any deficiency in architecture of Perpendicular character. Several points, however, must be emphasized. The first is the small scale of almost all Welsh mediaeval building. Secondly, the work is in only a few instances outstanding in quality: the towers of Gresford and Wrexham, the churches of Brecon, Cardiff, Haverfordwest or Tenby are exceptional. In third place, most of the Welsh Perpendicular that can be dated in fact belongs to the Tudor period. It is belated Perpendicular when set against the normal English standards of typology. Hence it has little or no place in a history of the development of the style. The few outstanding buildings for which evidence is available turn out to be due to Englishmen: the tower at St. Asaph to a Chester mason, those at Cardiff and Wrexham to one from Bristol.

The chronology and the topography of Perpendicular have been described, and its association with the national outlook of the time. Not much can be said of any special relationship to building materials, beyond the regional impact of quarries of good building stone on the one hand, and on the other the lack of it which profoundly affected the areas largely dependent upon flint. Brickwork existed in earlier times and was to be used far more extensively after 1485, though it is true that buildings of great importance were first built of brick in this country during the Perpendicular period. Possibly of more real significance is the lowering of the pitch of roofs during the fourteenth century. Associated as this is with the saving of timber and lead, we may suspect that economy had something to do with the elimination of the spire and the new aesthetic of horizontals complementing, though subordinate to, verticals. May we assume, too, that the building masters had become more aware, empirically rather than scientifically, of the dangers from tempest and lightning stroke which might be reduced by adopting the new architecture?

Certainly craftsmanship had advanced by the middle of the fourteenth century and continued to advance during the period. Bands of hidden wrought-iron reinforcement were laid in the transom of the great south window at Gloucester about 1335, and around the same time were in use under Richard Farleigh in the thickness of the walls of the great tower at Salisbury. Improved hoisting plant enabled the very large blocks of stone, typical of Perpendicular ashlar, to be lifted into position. Conservation too was making strides: we have noticed the restoration of the Norman chapter-house at Worcester in 1386–92, and the underpinning of the Ripon tower in 1466–80. Major repairs were done at Fountains Abbey in 1483 to save the Chapel of the Nine Altars from ruin. Wooden roofs were substituted for vaults to eliminate thrust, and buttresses were added, with carvings recording the date and the abbot responsible, John Darnton. Respect for ancient work was shown at Malmesbury in the 1330s, when the architect of the Decorated alterations – probably Thomas Witney – encased the splendid Norman carved porch to assimilate the old to the new. The nave of Beverley Minster was continued according to the older Early English design, and much the same thing was done at Westminster Abbey under Yeveley.

Less than five centuries have gone by since Bosworth Field, yet a great gulf of transacted history separates us from the age of the Perpendicular style. Notwithstanding what has happened, the destruction, the burden of progress and of change, we may still feel kinship to the men who commanded, who paid for, who devised, who wrought this laden harvest of churches, houses, furniture and enrichments. Many of their problems are still our own: disease, tempest, financial inflation and the need for economy and the conservation of materials. There is food for thought in the mere fact that they built to last: in spite of time and weather and human vandalism, many hundreds of the churches they built – each the centre of human lives and aspirations within one small area – still remain to serve our needs today. Other buildings too survive, but it is this great crowd of churches built partly or wholly in our most English way, that bears the most eloquent witness to the faith and the works of our forefathers. Might it not be a worthy ambition, that what we do in our own lives should last as well and carry down to generations unborn a like and satisfying garner of use and beauty?

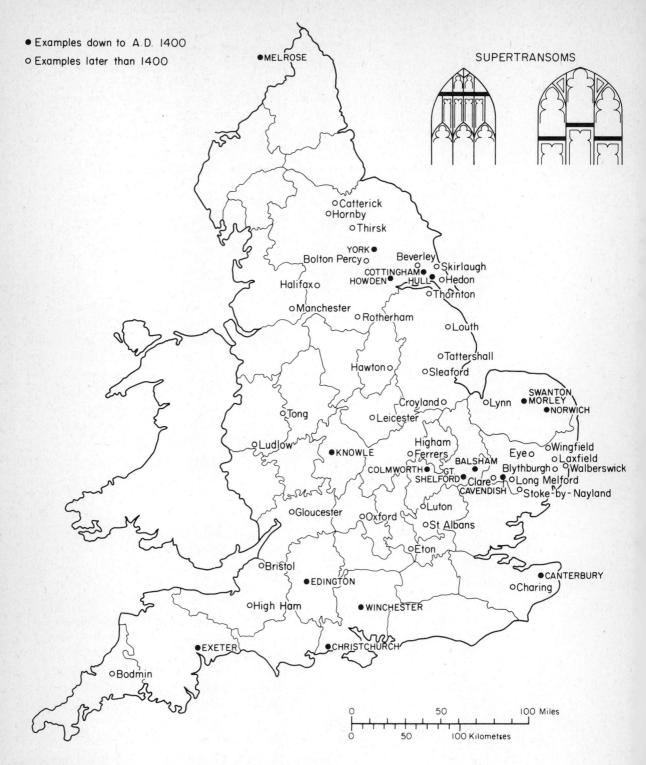

Map V Distribution of dated examples of Supertransoms

Map labels:

- Examples down to A.D. 1400
- Examples later than 1400

SUPERTRANSOMS

MELROSE

Catterick
Hornby
Thirsk
YORK
Bolton Percy
Beverley
Skirlaugh
COTTINGHAM
HOWDEN
HULL
Hedon
Halifax
Thornton
Manchester
Rotherham
Louth
Tattershall
Hawton
Sleaford
SWANTON
MORLEY
Croyland
Lynn
NORWICH
Tong
Leicester
Ludlow
Higham
Wingfield
Ferrers
Eye
Laxfield
KNOWLE
COLMWORTH
BALSHAM
Blythburgh
Walberswick
GT.
Clare
Long Melford
SHELFORD
CAVENDISH
Stoke-by-Nayland
Gloucester
Luton
Oxford
St. Albans
Bristol
Eton
CANTERBURY
EDINGTON
Charing
High Ham
WINCHESTER
EXETER
CHRISTCHURCH
Bodmin

0   50   100 Miles
0   50   100 Kilometres

- Examples down to A.D. 1400
- Examples later than 1400

LATTICED TRANSOMS

Manchester

Lynn

Stratford-on-Avon

Cambridge

Bury

Southwold

HEREFORD

CAMPDEN

GLOUCESTER

Winchcombe

OXFORD

Thame

WESTMINSTER

Bristol

Chippenham

MAIDSTONE

Canterbury

Lingfield

WINCHESTER

ARUNDEL

Tavistock

Plymouth

0   50   100 Miles

0   50   100 Kilometres

Map VI Distribution of dated Latticed Transoms

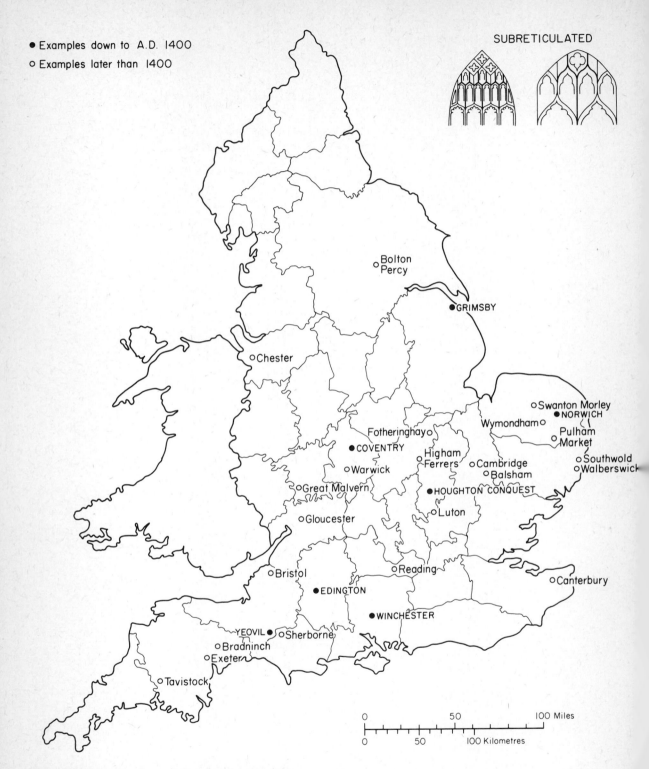

● Examples down to A.D. 1400
○ Examples later than 1400

Bolton Percy ○

● GRIMSBY

○ Chester

○ Swanton Morley
● NORWICH
Wymondham ○
Pulham Market ○

Fotheringhay ○

● COVENTRY

Higham Ferrers ○
Cambridge ○
Balsham ○

○ Southwold
○ Walberswick

○ Warwick

○ Great Malvern

● HOUGHTON CONQUEST
Luton ○

○ Gloucester

● Bristol

○ Reading

○ Canterbury

● EDINGTON

● WINCHESTER

YEOVIL ● ○ Sherborne
○ Bradninch
○ Exeter

○ Tavistock

0   50   100 Miles

0   50   100 Kilometres

Map VII Distribution of dated Subreticulation

Examples down to A.D. 1400
Examples later than 1400

THROUGH RETICULATION

Nottingham

Ludlow
WARWICK
WORCESTER Stratford-on-Avon
Great Malvern
Hereford Little Malvern
GLOUCESTER Northleach
OXFORD WATFORD
Steeple Ashton CANTERBURY
Cheddar EDINGTON Charing
Wells
High Ham Lydd
Wimborne
Exeter
Bodmin
Plymouth

0   50   100 Miles
0   50   100 Kilometres

Map VIII Distribution of dated Through Reticulation

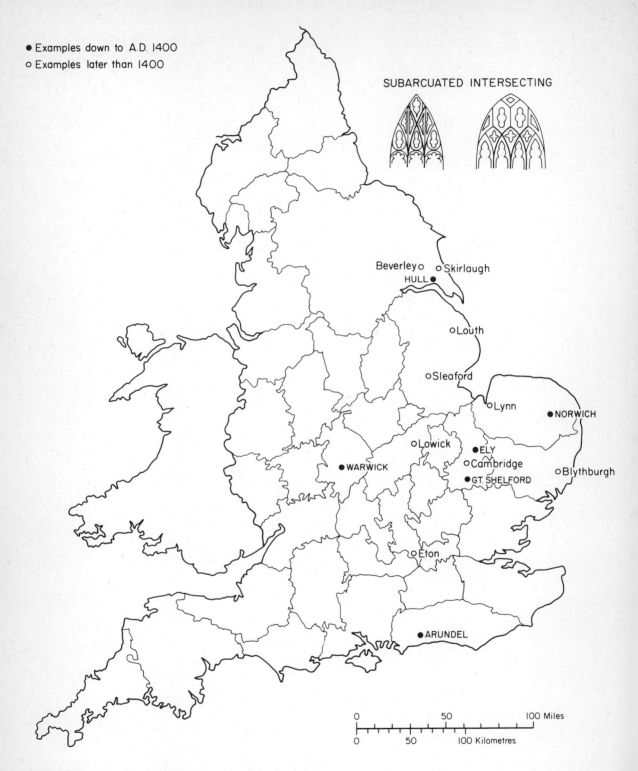

Examples down to A.D. 1400
Examples later than 1400

SUBARCUATED INTERSECTING

Beverley ○ ○ Skirlaugh
HULL ●

○ Louth

○ Sleaford

○ Lynn   ● NORWICH

○ Lowick   ● ELY
● WARWICK   ○ Cambridge   ○ Blythburgh
● GT. SHELFORD

○ Eton

● ARUNDEL

0   50   100 Miles

0   50   100 Kilometres

Map IX Distribution of dated Subarcuated Intersection

CRUCIFORM LOBING

INGHAM ●

NORWICH ●

Lowick ○   Bardwell
                        ● ELY   ○ ● Wingfield
              Cambridge ○ ○ Burwell
         GREAT SHELFORD ●
○ Hereford   Cavendish   ○ ○ Long Melford

                        ● WESTMINSTER

● EDINGTON

                        ● ETCHINGHAM

0 ─── 50 ─── 100 Miles

0 ─── 50 ─── 100 Kilometres

Map X Distribution of dated Cruciform Lobing

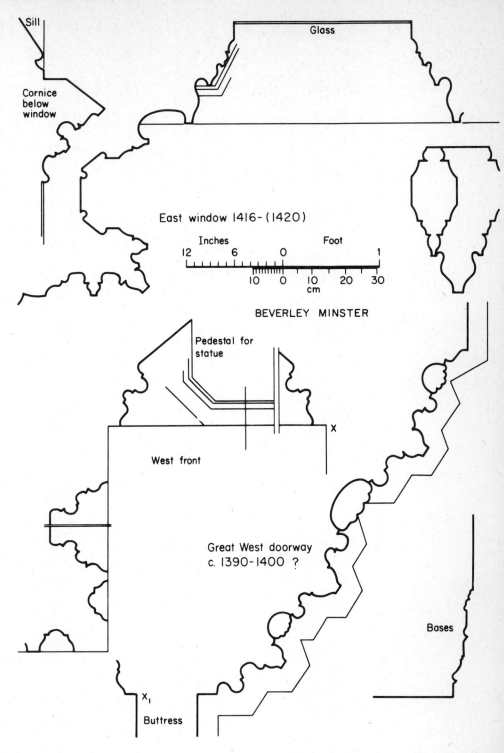

Fig. 13 Moulding profiles at Beverley Minster *c.* 1390–1420

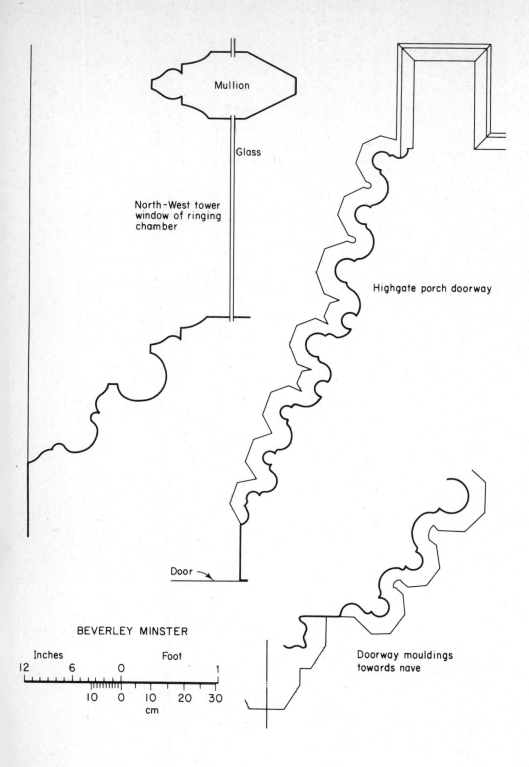

Mullion

Glass

North-West tower
window of ringing
chamber

Highgate porch doorway

Door →

BEVERLEY MINSTER

Inches   Foot
12   6   0   1

10   0   10   20   30
cm

Doorway mouldings
towards nave

Fig. 14 Moulding profiles at Beverley Minster *c.* 1380–1430

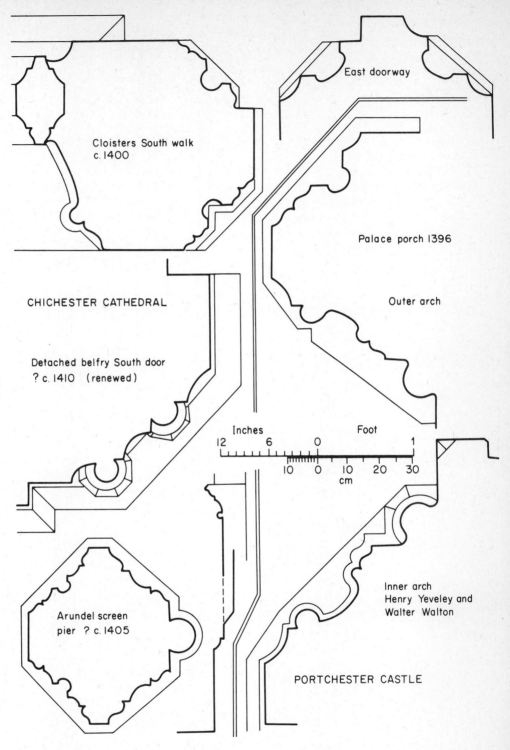

East doorway

Cloisters South walk
c.1400

CHICHESTER CATHEDRAL

Palace porch 1396

Outer arch

Detached belfry South door
? c.1410 (renewed)

Inches   Foot
12   6   0   1

10   0   10   20   30
cm

Inner arch
Henry Yeveley and
Walter Walton

Arundel screen
pier ? c.1405

PORTCHESTER CASTLE

Fig. 15 Moulding profiles at Chichester Cathedral *c.* 1400–10; and at Portchester Castle 1396

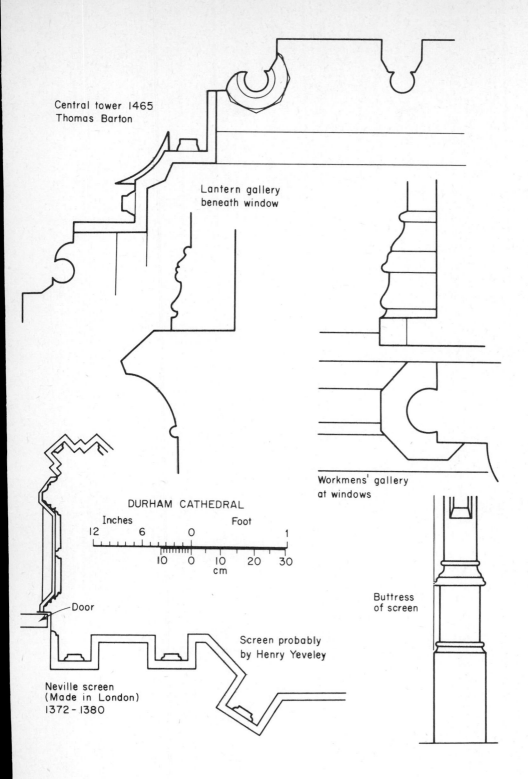

Central tower 1465
Thomas Barton

Lantern gallery
beneath window

Workmens' gallery
at windows

DURHAM CATHEDRAL

Inches   Foot
12   6   0   1
10   0   10   20   30
cm

Door

Buttress
of screen

Screen probably
by Henry Yeveley

Neville screen
(Made in London)
1372-1380

Fig. 16 Moulding profiles at Durham Cathedral 1372 and 1465

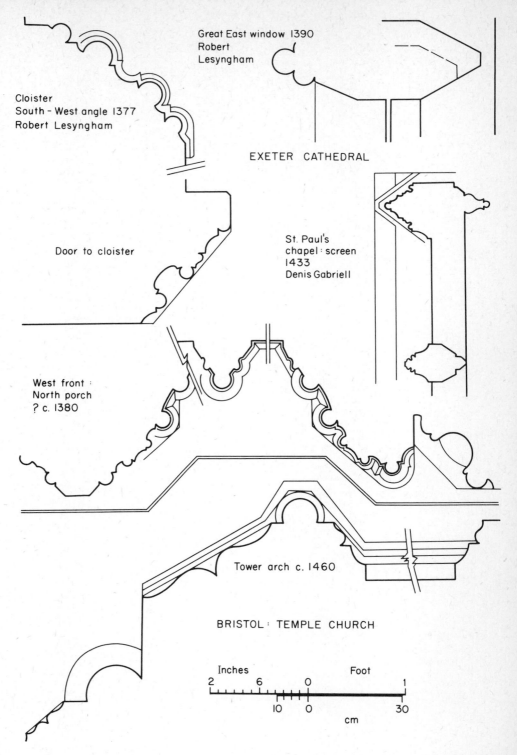

Cloister
South - West angle 1377
Robert Lesyngham

Great East window 1390
Robert
Lesyngham

EXETER CATHEDRAL

Door to cloister

St. Paul's
chapel : screen
1433
Denis Gabriell

West front :
North porch
? c. 1380

Tower arch c. 1460

BRISTOL : TEMPLE CHURCH

Inches   Foot

Fig. 17 Moulding profiles at Exeter Cathedral 1377–1433; and at the Temple Church, Bristol *c.* 1460

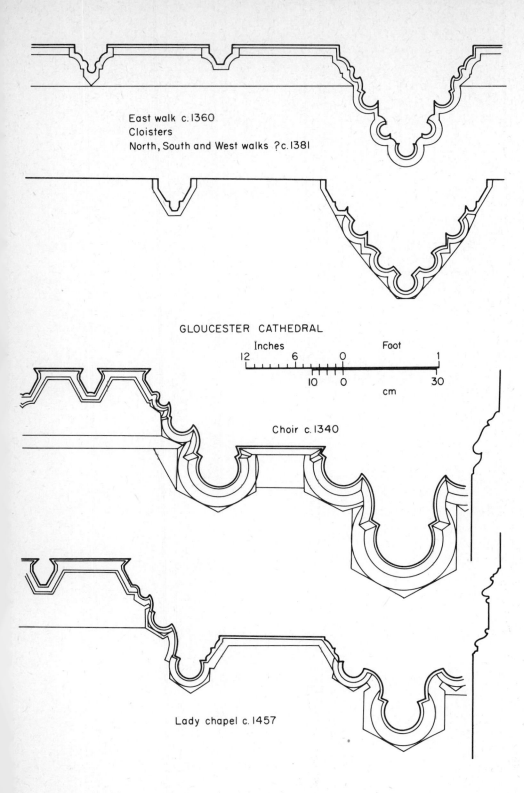

East walk c.1360
Cloisters
North, South and West walks ?c.1381

GLOUCESTER CATHEDRAL

Inches   Foot
12   6   0   1
            10   0   30
                      cm

Choir c.1340

Lady chapel c.1457

Fig. 18 Moulding profiles at Gloucester Cathedral *c.* 1340– *c.* 1457

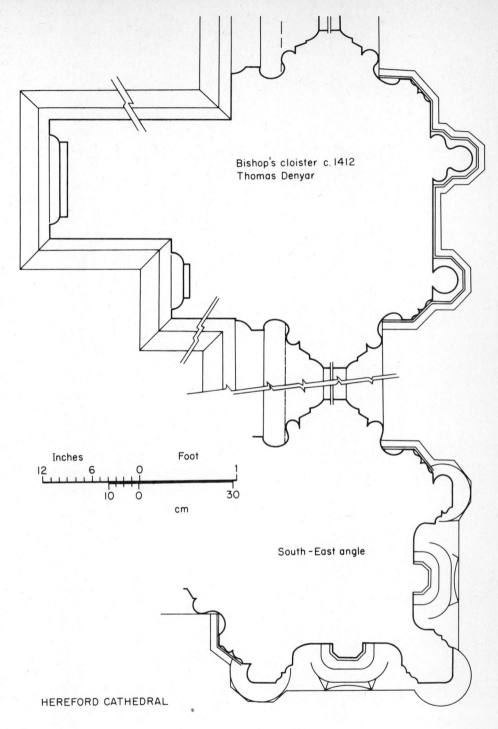

Bishop's cloister c.1412
Thomas Denyar

Inches   Foot
12   6   0   1

10   0   30
cm

South-East angle

HEREFORD CATHEDRAL

Fig. 19 Moulding profiles at Hereford Cathedral *c.* 1412

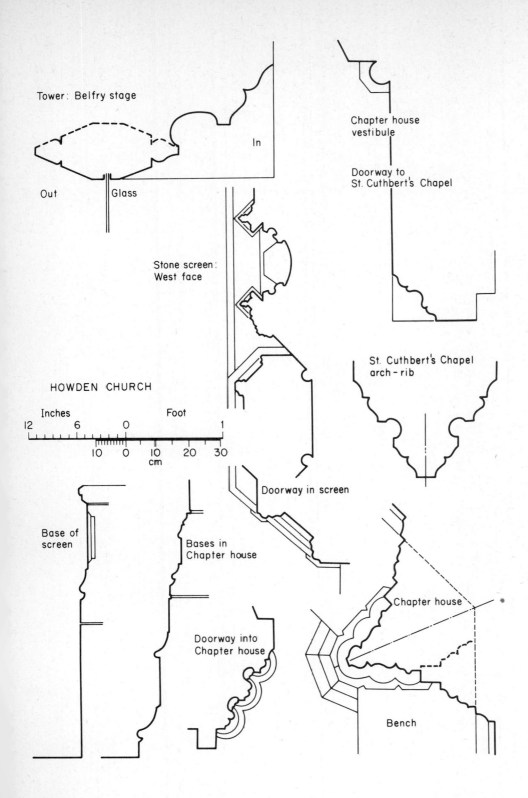

Fig. 20 Moulding profiles at Howden Collegiate Church 1380–(1400)

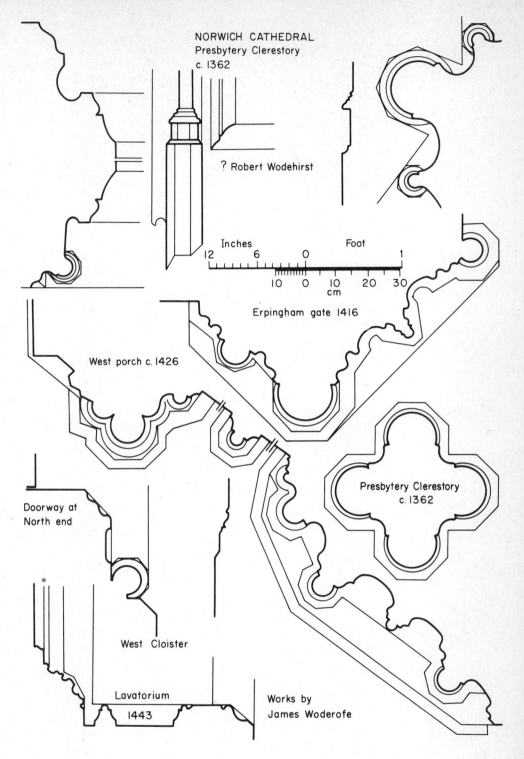

NORWICH CATHEDRAL
Presbytery Clerestory
c. 1362

? Robert Wodehirst

Inches   Foot
12   6   0   1

10   0   10   20   30
cm

Erpingham gate 1416

West porch c. 1426

Presbytery Clerestory
c. 1362

Doorway at
North end

West Cloister

Lavatorium
1443

Works by
James Woderofe

Fig. 21 Moulding profiles at Norwich Cathedral *c.* 1362–1443

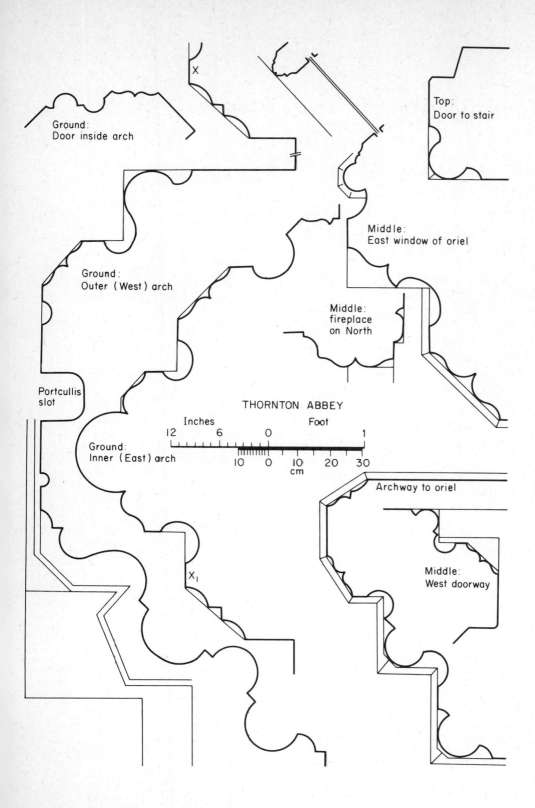

Ground:
Door inside arch

Top:
Door to stair

Middle:
East window of oriel

Ground:
Outer (West) arch

Middle:
fireplace
on North

Portcullis
slot

THORNTON ABBEY

Inches   Foot
12   6   0   1

10   0   10   20   30
cm

Ground:
Inner (East) arch

Archway to oriel

Middle:
West doorway

Fig. 22 Moulding profiles at Thornton Abbey 1382–89

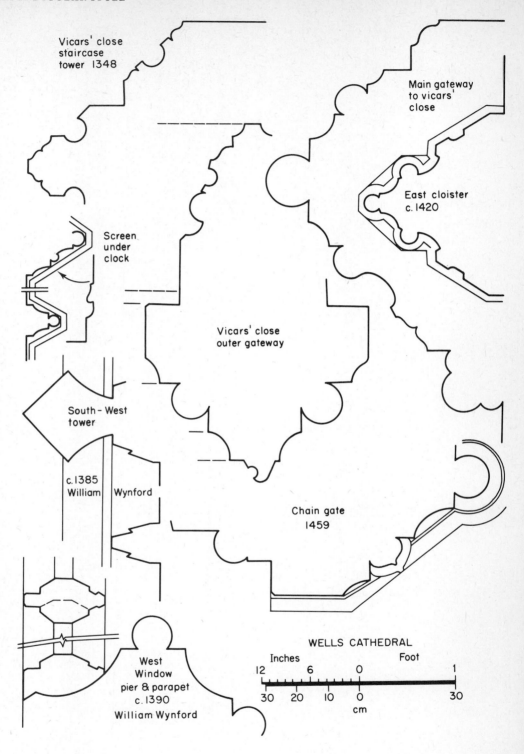

Vicars' close
staircase
tower 1348

Main gateway
to vicars'
close

East cloister
c. 1420

Screen
under
clock

Vicars' close
outer gateway

South-West
tower

c. 1385
William Wynford

Chain gate
1459

West
Window
pier & parapet
c. 1390
William Wynford

WELLS CATHEDRAL

Inches   Foot
12   6   0   1
30   20   10   0   30
cm

Fig. 23 Moulding profiles at Wells Cathedral 1348–1459

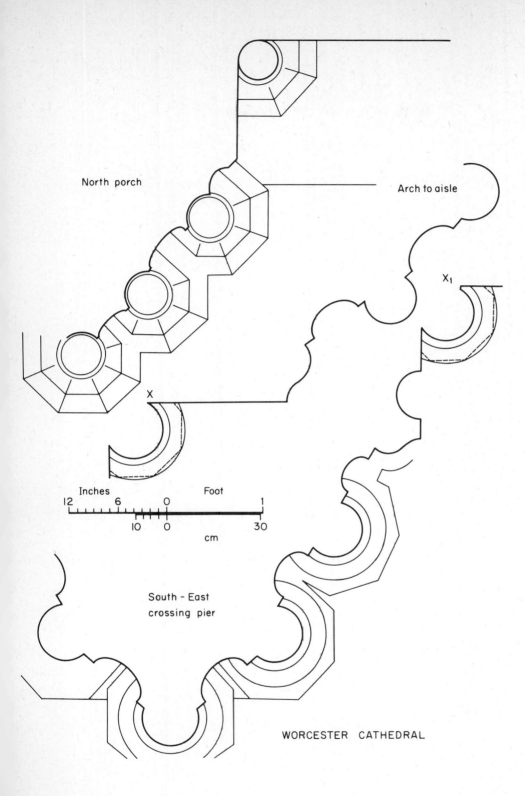

North porch

Arch to aisle

X₁

X

Inches　　　Foot
12　6　　0　　　1
10　0　　　30
cm

South - East
crossing pier

WORCESTER CATHEDRAL

Fig. 24 Moulding profiles at Worcester Cathedral 1357–86

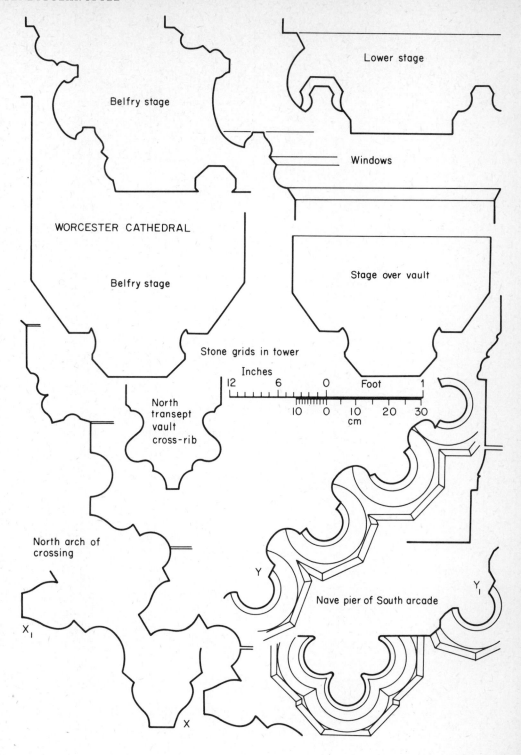

Fig. 25 Moulding profiles at Worcester Cathedral 1357–76

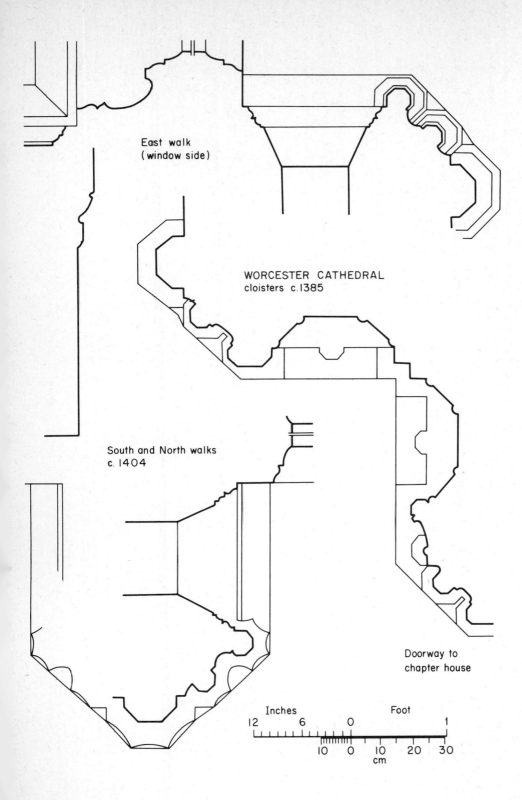

East walk
(window side)

WORCESTER CATHEDRAL
cloisters c.1385

South and North walks
c. 1404

Doorway to
chapter house

Inches   Foot
12   6   0   1

10   0   10   20   30
cm

Fig. 26 Moulding profiles at Worcester Cathedral *c.* 1385–1404

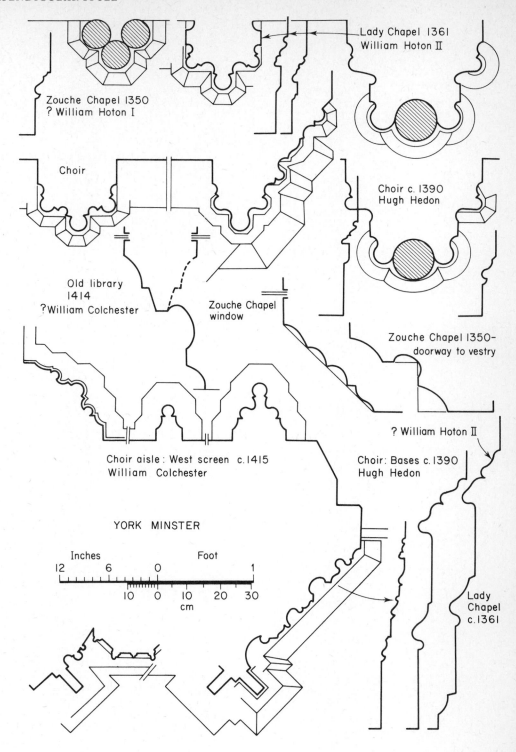

Zouche Chapel 1350
? William Hoton I

Lady Chapel 1361
William Hoton II

Choir

Choir c. 1390
Hugh Hedon

Old library
1414
?William Colchester

Zouche Chapel
window

Zouche Chapel 1350-
doorway to vestry

? William Hoton II

Choir aisle : West screen c.1415
William Colchester

Choir: Bases c.1390
Hugh Hedon

YORK MINSTER

Inches   Foot
12   6   0   1
      10   0   10   20   30
                cm

Lady
Chapel
c.1361

Fig. 27 Moulding profiles at York Minster 1350– *c.* 1415

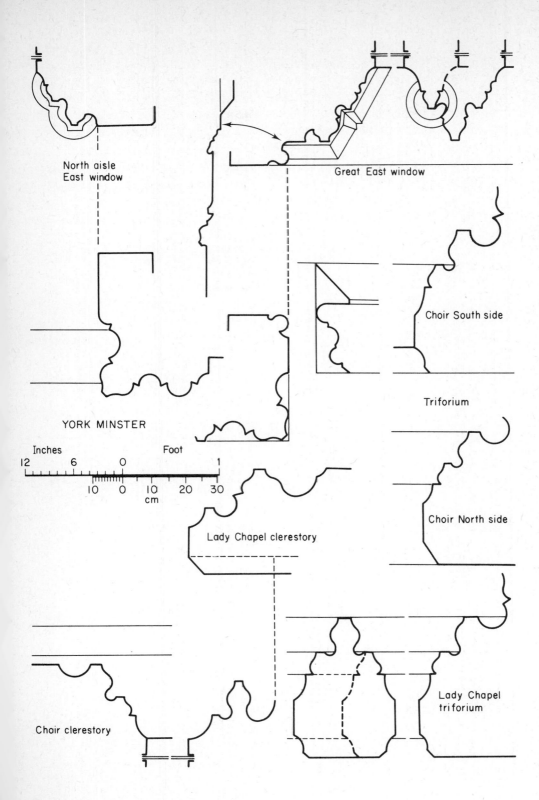

North aisle
East window

Great East window

Choir South side

Triforium

YORK MINSTER

Choir North side

Inches | Foot

12   6   0   1

10   0   10   20   30
cm

Lady Chapel clerestory

Choir clerestory

Lady Chapel
triforium

Fig. 28 Moulding profiles at York Minster 1369–(1400)

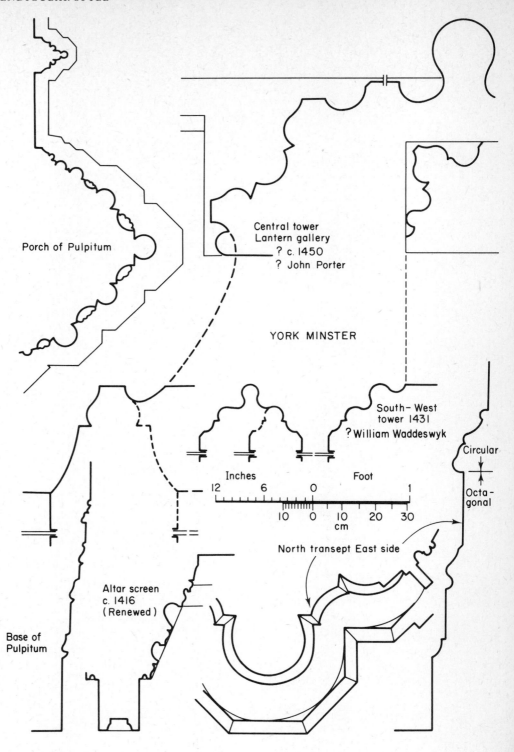

Porch of Pulpitum

Central tower
Lantern gallery
? c. 1450
? John Porter

YORK MINSTER

South-West
tower 1431

?William Waddeswyk

Circular

Octa-
gonal

Inches   Foot
12   6   0   1

10   0   10   20   30
cm

North transept East side

Altar screen
c. 1416
(Renewed)

Base of
Pulpitum

Fig. 29 Moulding profiles at York Minster *c.* 1400– *c.* 1450

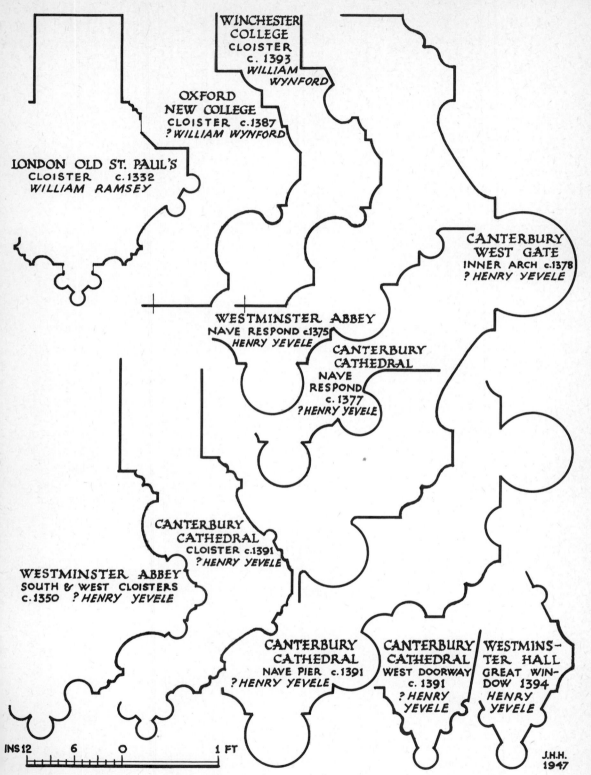

WINCHESTER
COLLEGE
CLOISTER
c. 1393
WILLIAM
WYNFORD

OXFORD
NEW COLLEGE
CLOISTER c.1387
?WILLIAM WYNFORD

LONDON OLD ST. PAUL'S
CLOISTER   c.1332
WILLIAM RAMSEY

CANTERBURY
WEST GATE
INNER ARCH c.1378
?HENRY YEVELE

WESTMINSTER ABBEY
NAVE RESPOND c.1375
HENRY YEVELE

CANTERBURY
CATHEDRAL
NAVE
RESPOND
c. 1377
?HENRY YEVELE

CANTERBURY
CATHEDRAL
CLOISTER c.1391
?HENRY YEVELE

WESTMINSTER ABBEY
SOUTH & WEST CLOISTERS
c.1350   ?HENRY YEVELE

CANTERBURY
CATHEDRAL
NAVE PIER c.1391
?HENRY YEVELE

CANTERBURY
CATHEDRAL
WEST DOORWAY
c. 1391
?HENRY
YEVELE

WESTMINS-
TER HALL
GREAT WIN-
DOW 1394
HENRY
YEVELE

INS 12   6   O   1 FT

J.H.H.
1947

Fig. 30 Moulding profiles by William Ramsey, Henry Yeveley and William Wynford

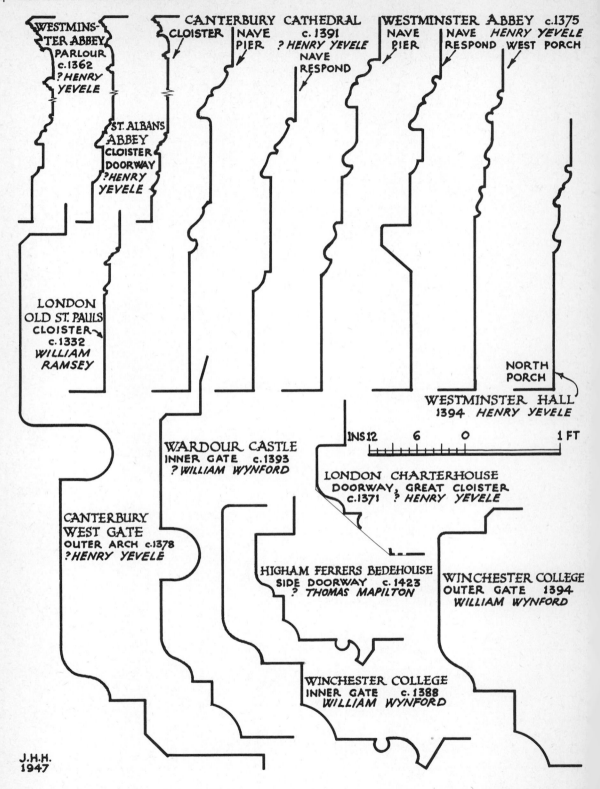

Fig. 31 Moulding profiles by William Ramsey, Henry Yeveley, William Wynford and Thomas Mapilton

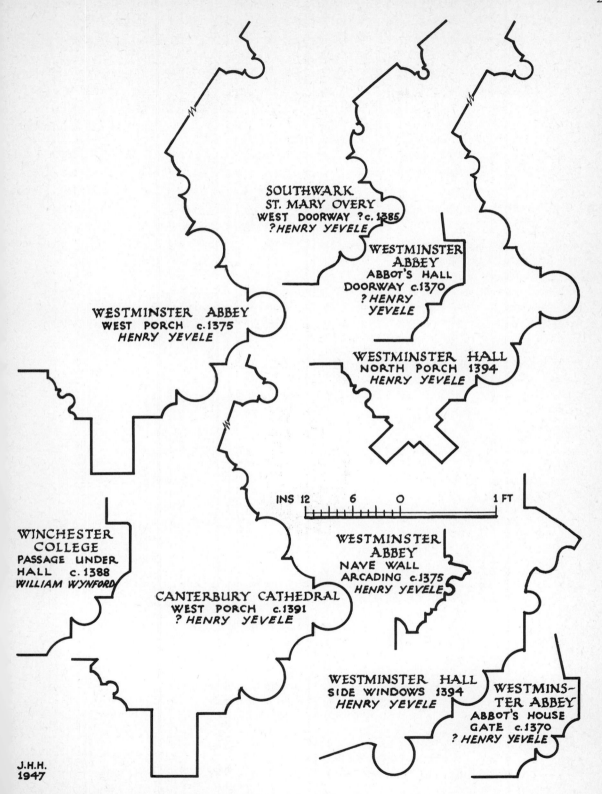

SOUTHWARK
ST. MARY OVERY
WEST DOORWAY ? c. 1385
? HENRY YEVELE

WESTMINSTER
ABBEY
ABBOT'S HALL
DOORWAY c.1370
? HENRY
YEVELE

WESTMINSTER ABBEY
WEST PORCH c.1375
HENRY YEVELE

WESTMINSTER HALL
NORTH PORCH 1394
HENRY YEVELE

INS 12   6   O   1 FT

WINCHESTER
COLLEGE
PASSAGE UNDER
HALL   c. 1388
WILLIAM WYNFORD

CANTERBURY CATHEDRAL
WEST PORCH c.1391
? HENRY YEVELE

WESTMINSTER
ABBEY
NAVE WALL
ARCADING c.1375
HENRY YEVELE

WESTMINSTER HALL
SIDE WINDOWS 1394
HENRY YEVELE

WESTMINS-
TER ABBEY
ABBOT'S HOUSE
GATE c.1370
? HENRY YEVELE

J.H.H.
1947

Fig. 32 Moulding profiles by Henry Yeveley and William Wynford

Notes to the Text

References for dates should be sought in the Table below.

Page **Preface**

13   Curvilinear – Bock 1962
14   Chief Architects – Harvey 1943; careers in EMA
       Kentish style – Harvey 1962A, 161–3
15   French encyclopaedism – Heyman 1966, 250; Heyman 1967
       Langley's embassy – Desimoni 1877
       Pilgrimages – Harvey 1975A, 62
       Travellers – Esposito 1960, 5 n.3; 17; 20 n.2; Golubovich 1919, III, 394; IV, 451; on
       the greatly increased commercial and intellectual intercourse between Muslims and
       Christians in the early fourteenth century, Esposito 1960, 14; for English links with
       Arabic culture see D. Metlitzki, *The Matter of Araby in Medieval England* (Yale U.P.,
       1977)
16   Persian motives – Harvey 1950A, 77; Harvey 1972, 131–2, 153
       Witney – Harvey 1972, 133–6
17   Cairo – Harvey 1962A, 158 n.88; Harvey 1971, 86–7
19   Edward III – Harvey 1976, *passim*
20   Davis – Davis 1939; Davis 1947; Davis 1956
       Gee – Gee 1953; Gee 1954
       Oswald – extensive contributions to EMA; Oswald 1939; Oswald 1947; Oswald
       1949; Oswald 1965
       Roberts – Roberts 1972; Roberts 1973; Roberts 1975
       Freeman – Freeman 1851, 183

Introduction

26   Aubrey – Colvin 1968
       Rickman – Thomas Rickman, *An Attempt to discriminate the Styles of Architecture in
       England from the Conquest to the Reformation*, 1817; and subsequent editions, notably
       those by J. H. Parker, especially the 6th (1862) and 7th (1881).
27   Gloucester – AJ, XVII (1860), 338
       Sharpe – E. Sharpe, *A Treatise on the Rise and Progress of Decorated Window Tracery in
       England*, 2 vols. 1849; *Seven Periods of English Architecture*, 1851
28   Length – Freeman 1849, 394
29   Howard – Howard 1911; Howard 1914; Howard 1936; Howard & Crossley 1917
       Pevsner – For the 50 years 1341–1390 the literature yields over 70 well documented
       builds at churches. Checking these off in Pevsner's plates, only 8 of 17 builds at
       cathedrals, 7 of 21 at monastic and collegiate buildings, and 6 of 34 at parish churches
       are illustrated; even so, some views are woefully inadequate. In the text there is in 12
       cases out of 72 either a major discrepancy between the date given and that in the
       records, or else silence upon the existence of documentation.
30   Continuous – Freeman 1849, 341
32   Perpendicular – Harvey 1962A
33   Four-centred arch – Parker 1836 (1850, I, 42 note)

Stanwick – Bond 1905, 267

34   Fonolly – EMA, 107; J. Vives i Miret, *Reinard des Fonoll* (Barcelona & Madrid, 1969)
Troyes – Harvey 1957A, 271
Mouldings – Harvey 1962A; Harvey 1972, 177–80
Clermont-Ferrand – Harvey 1962A, 151; Harvey 1972, 184
Champagne – Harvey 1950A, 77

37   Ogee quatrefoil – Harvey 1962A, 162, 163 n.13
Building – Harvey 1974A

38   Free courts – Harvey 1972, 137–44, 191–207, 257–61; Harvey 1975A, 24

39   Hereford – Harvey 1972, 142; on the German assemblies, see L. R. Shelby, *Gothic Design Techniques* (Southern Illinois U.P., 1977), introduction.

Chapter One

41   Mediaeval architects – Harvey 1972; cf. Knoop & Jones 1933; Harvey 1974A, 38–64; Harvey 1975A

42   York – Harvey 1975A, 20–9; Harvey 1975B, 118–20

44   Plague mortality – Out of 87 master masons and carpenters whose careers began between 1325 and 1349, 12 died in the plague years 1348–49 and at least 3 in the second pestilence of 1361–62 (EMA).
St. Stephen's – Harvey 1962A, 141–50; HKW, I, 510–27

46   Canterbury mouldings – Harvey 1962A, 143; Harvey 1972, 182

47   Norwich – Fernie & Whittingham 1972; I am obliged to Mr. Whittingham for corrections and additional material in correspondence during 1974, drawing my attention to documents in the *Cartularium Monasterii de Rameseia* (RS, 1884–93), I no. 79; II, p. 375 no. 489; *Chronicon Abbatiae Ramesiensis* (RS, 1886), 272; W. Rye, *Norfolk Pedes Finium* (1881), 102; cf. EMA, 80, 213

50   Thomas of Canterbury – PRO, E.101/468/6(62.)
Tracing-floor – Harvey 1962A, 164–5; Harvey 1969; Colchester & Harvey 1975, 214
False moulds – PRO, E.101/468/6(9.); E.101/469/8 (week of 16 Jan. 1323/4); Norwich Cathedral, obedientiary roll no. 1050
Ramsey – Harvey 1962A, 135–41, 150–2

53   Gloucester glass – J. D. LeCouteur, *English Mediaeval Painted Glass* (1926/1932), 97–8
Redcliffe – Harvey 1961, 55 and n.3

Chapter Two

57   Proportions – Harvey 1972, 52–3, 120–2, 124–6; Harvey 1974A, 52–3, 59–60, 94–5
Witney – above, note to p.16
St. Cross – Freeman 1851, pl. 22.3; VCH, *Hampshire*, V (1912), 63

61   Norwich Carnary – Harvey 1962A, 138 and pl. xii
Sandon – R. Graham in AJ, LXXXVII for 1930 (1931), 21–3; Salzman 1952, 437–8; collated with the original, St. Paul's MS. box A 38, no. 1264

65   Tenurial links – Harvey 1950B; Harvey 1939; Harvey 1974B

66   Constitutions – Harvey 1972, 201

67   Light – Harvey 1944, 5, 7; Harvey 1950A, 66, 74, 85, 88–9

69   Panelled tracery – Freeman 1851, 194–8

70   Squash-tracery – Davis 1947, 82
Top-panelled – Roberts 1973, 123, 126

74   Winchester College – Harvey & Harvey 1936
Carpentry – Harvey 1938; Harvey 1948

Chapter Three

75   Yeveley – Harvey 1944; EMA, 312–20
      Old St. Paul's – Hollar's engravings are reproduced in A. M. Hind, *Wenceslaus Hollar and his Views of London and Windsor in the Seventeenth Century* (1922); G. H. Cook, Old St. Paul's Cathedral (1955), etc.; for Thomas Wyck's drawing of *c.* 1673 see Jane Lang, *Rebuilding St. Paul's after the Great Fire of London* (1956), pl. ix; Wren Society, XIV, pl. lii

79   Tewkesbury, Worcester – Bond 1913, I, 376
80   Gloucester Castle – HKW, I, 211 n.8; II, 655
81   Salisbury, Close Gate – C Papal L 1342–62, 538
82   Lichfield – Harvey 1962A, 151–2
84   Porches – Harvey 1961, 51 and n.3
85   Edington – I owe to Professor R. H. C. Davis full information on the masons' marks from different parts of the church
90   Edington's chantry – N. Pevsner & D. Lloyd, *Hampshire and the Isle of Wight* (1967), 682
91   London Austin Friars – the windows destroyed in 1940 were careful Victorian replicas of the original traceries shown in early drawings and engravings
      Hereford chapter-house – Drinkwater 1956
92   Worcester Cathedral – the dates depend on a chronology contemporary with the works of 1372–86 and giving some retrospective information, in the 'Book of Miscellanies', Worcester Cathedral Library, MS. A xii, f. 77b; and see Harvey 1957B for material from the obedientiary rolls
95   Toledo – F. H. Thompson in ANJ, XLII (1962), 195–7; Harvey 1972, 161, 216
96   Eastminster – C Pat R 1350–54, 465; ibid. 1358–61, 567
      Langley – HKW, I, 259–63
      Dartford – HKW, I, 264

Chapter Four

97   Yeveley – Harvey 1944; EMA, 312–20; HKW, I, 209–13
98   Deviser of masonry – PRO, E.101/472/8. The negative criticism of Yeveley's architectural status by A. D. McLees (JBAA, 3S, XXXVI, 1973, 52–71) is rendered nonsensical by failure to take account of this vital description
99   Continental masters – Harvey 1950A, 28, 52, 100, 112, 116–17
      Fonolly – see above, note to p. 34
      Lethaby – Lethaby 1906, 220
100   Westminster – Lethaby 1925, 136–7
101   North cloister – Howgrave-Graham 1948
      Bristol, Mayor's Chapel – Freeman 1851, pl. 21.95
      Jewel House – Taylor 1956
107   Norwich Great Hospital – Oswald 1947
      Cobham College – C. Hussey in *Country Life*, 4 and 11 Feb. 1944
112   Robert Patrington – C Pat R 1385–9, 13; York Minster Library, L 1 2, p. 56 col. 4
      Screenwork – for the idea of such 'transparencies' or stone grilles see Harvey 1950A, 66–7, 78, 90; N. Pevsner, *North Somerset and Bristol* (1958), 302–3
116   Berwick-upon-Tweed – HKW, II, 569
118   Southampton – HKW, II, 842
130   Canterbury – Oswald 1939
      Yeveley as military engineer – Whitehead 1974
135   Harmondsworth – Winchester College Muniments no. 78
136   Winchester nave – Freeman 1849, 393

Chapter Five

139   Sleford – Stephenson 1926, 55

142   Henley – Roberts 1973, 123–4

145   Wingfield – N. Pevsner, *Suffolk*, 456 and note
Nottingham – C Papal L 1396–1404, 443; I am indebted to the late Dr. Rose Graham
for having pointed out to me this remarkable document

148   Adderbury – Hobson 1926
Values – G. G. Coulton, *The Meaning of Medieval Moneys* (Historical Association
Leaflet, No. 95, 1934)
Fees – see EMA (Appendix ii), 327–32

149   Domestic buildings – though in a minority, the domestic work is of great importance;
for a fully detailed study see Wood 1965

151   Houghton Conquest – Roberts 1975, 72–5

152   Christchurch – Nicolas 1826, 167
London Guildhall – Barron 1974; C. Wilson in JBAA, CXXIX (1976), 1–14

155   Broughton Castle – W. Hayter, *William of Wykeham: Patron of the Arts* (1970)
Skirlaugh – Allen 1932, 20, 115

157   York Minster – Harvey in *History of York Minster*, ed. G. Aylmer & R. C. Cant
(Oxford U.P., 1977)

159   De Bury – Harvey 1976, 38–40, 65

Chapter Six

160   Volume of works – see graph in Harvey 1947, 160

161   Wages – see table of Wages, Prices and Real Earnings in Knoop & Jones 1933, 238
(rev. ed. 1967, 213). The general average of daily real wages, taking 1501–10 = 100
was in 1301–50, 91.4; in 1351–1400, 114.2; in 1401–50, 113.2; in 1451–1500, 115. The
catastrophic drop in the standard of living after the end of the Middle Ages is shown
by the figure for 1551–1602, only 58.
Gang work – H. Poole in *Ars Quatuor Coronatorum*, XLIV for 1931 (1936), 236

162   Beverley – John Bilson in *Architectural Review*, III, 199
Sherborne – Joseph Fowler, *The Stones of Sherborne Abbey* (Sherborne, Sawtells, 1938), 8

163   St. Albans – a photograph of the west window is reproduced in Roberts 1973 as pl.
xxviii B

168   Christ Church nave roof – RCHM, *City of Oxford* (1939), 41

170   Exeter Law Library – AJ, CXIV for 1957 (1959), 138–9
York stalls – J. Britton, *Cathedral Antiquities*, I (1836), York, pl. xxxiv (published 1
Dec. 1818); cf. J. Halfpenny, *Gothic Ornaments in the Cathedral Church of York* (1795),
pl. 54, a less accurate portrayal

172   Walberswick – C. Chitty, 'Kessingland and Walberswick Church Towers', in
Proceedings of the Suffolk Institute of Archaeology, XXV part 2 (1951), 164–71

174   Libraries – see Myres 1967, 166–7; Barron 1974, 33–5

175   Bristol St. Stephen – *William Worcestre: Itineraries* (Oxford Medieval Texts, 1969), 401

183   Cult of simplicity – see the documents in full in Harvey 1972, 252–6
Brickwork – Lloyd 1925; Wight 1972

185   King's College Chapel – G. G. Scott, *An Essay on the History of English Church
Architecture* (1881)
Eton – N. Pevsner, *Buckinghamshire* (1960), 119; A. Oswald in EMA, 62

186   Burwell – see A. Oswald in EMA, 98–9
Chipping Norton – Davis 1939, 12

195   Northleach – D. Verey, *Gloucestershire: the Cotswolds* (1970), 338–9; Verey 1976,
133–4, 142–3; Davis 1956, marks X7, L8, V13, W1

Chapter Seven

197 Yatton – Wickham 1952, 28
202 Lynn – A. Oswald in EMA, 65
204 Durham tower – Snape 1974, 71–4
207 Broxbourne – Roberts 1972
208 Crosby Hall – W.H. Godfrey in Clapham & Godfrey 1913, 119–38
210 St. George's Chapel – Harvey 1962B

Chapter Eight

217 Canterbury family – the main feature which Chipping Campden and Northleach share
with Canterbury is the recession of the clerestory wall-surface behind a moulded wall-
arch
Cambridge, Lavenham, Saffron Walden – A. Oswald in EMA, 281–3
Burwell – see above, note to p. 186
221 Redcliffe – it is here accepted that the vaults of nave and chancel were the final stage of
a major Perpendicular reconstruction after the disastrous storm of 1446; the transepts
were apparently not affected by the catastrophe
222 Fan-vault – Howard 1911
Winchester College – Harvey & Harvey 1936; Harvey 1965
223 Norwich – Bond 1913, I, 352
Lincoln – Bond 1905, 340–1
St. Stephen's crypt – HKW, I, 513
225 Bristol – Evans 1949, 66
Redcliffe – the relevant vaults are those of the transepts and of the north and south
porches
Gloucester – Pevsner 1953
226 Drawings – Harvey 1972, 101–19
Cambridge – Cobb 1942, 73 note; cf. Harvey 1972, pl. 49, 50
229 Salisbury tower – Harvey 1974A, 215–16
230 Lavenham – A. Oswald in EMA, 65
Lambeth – Gardiner 1930, 52–6

Epilogue

235 Orense – Harvey 1957A, 128 and fig. 78
Barbastro – ibid., 179–80 and pl. 104
Cologne – Evans 1949, 79 n.1
236 Nobility – I am grateful to Professor R. H. C. Davis for reminding me of the close
kinship and great wealth of the English mediaeval nobility
237 Local style – Atkinson 1947
Mass-production – Davis 1939, 5; Davis 1947, 82; Harvey 1947, pl. 143, 144; E. A.
Greening Lamborn in *Notes and Queries* (22 Sep. 1945), CLXXXIX, 125–7
False moulds – see above, note to p. 50
238 Aesthetic intention – Harvey 1959; also Harvey 1950B
Ireland – H. G. Leask, *Irish Churches and Monastic Buildings*: III. Medieval Gothic, the
Last Phases (Dundalk, 1960)
239 Reinforcement – Harvey 1950A, 18 and note on p. 139

Bibliography with Abbreviations

This bibliography includes the principal works consulted, and those referred to in the Table of Dated Buildings and the Notes to the text respectively. For a more detailed classified bibliography and additional illustrations, see *Gothic England* (1947, revised ed. 1948), and for careers of architects and designers, *English Mediaeval Architects* (1954).

AASRP	Associated Architectural Societies: *Reports and Papers*
AJ	*Archaeological Journal* (Royal Archaeological Institute)
Aldwell 1926	S. W. H. Aldwell, *Wingfield: its Church, Castle and College* (1926)
Alexander & Finberg	J. J. Alexander & H. P. R. Finberg, *Tavistock Parish Church* (n. d.)
Allen 1932	F. J. Allen, *The Great Church Towers of England* (1932)
ANJ	*Antiquaries Journal* (Society of Antiquaries of London)
APS	Architectural Publication Society, *Dictionary of Architecture*, 7 vols., (1849–92)
Atkinson 1947	T. D. Atkinson, *Local Style in English Architecture* (1947)
Baggallay 1885	F. T. Baggallay, 'The Use of Flint in Building', in TRIBA, NS, I (1885)
Barnes & Simpson 1951	H. D. Barnes & W. D. Simpson, 'The Building Accounts of Caister Castle', in NA, XXX (1951), 178–88
Barnes & Simpson 1952	H. D. Barnes & W. D. Simpson, 'Caister Castle', in ANJ, XXXII (1952), 35–51
Barron 1974	C. M. Barron, *The Medieval Guildhall of London* (1974)
Bates 1891	C. J. Bates, *Border Holds* (1891)
BGT	Bristol & Gloucestershire Archaeological Society: *Transactions*
Bock 1962	H. Bock, *Der Decorated Style* (Heidelberg, 1962)
Bond 1905	F. Bond, *Gothic Architecture in England* (1905)
Bond 1913	F. Bond, *An Introduction to English Church Architecture*, 2 vols. (1913)
Boyle 1895	J. R. Boyle, *History of Hedon* (1895)
Brandon 1849	R. & J. Brandon, *Parish Churches* (ed. 1849)
Cal Inq.p.M	*Calendar of Inquisitions post mortem in the Public Record Office* (1904–)
C ChartR	*Calendar of Charter Rolls*, 6 vols. (1903–27)
Chitty 1926	H. Chitty, 'Fromond's Chantry at Winchester College', in *Archaeologia*, LXXV (1926), 139–58
Clapham & Godfrey 1913	A. W. Clapham & W. H. Godfrey, *Some Famous Buildings and their Story* [1913]
Cobb 1942	G. Cobb, *The Old Churches of London* (1942)
Colchester & Harvey 1975	L. S. Colchester & J. H. Harvey, 'Wells Cathedral', in AJ, CXXXI for 1974 (1975), 200–14
Colvin 1968	H. M. Colvin, 'Aubrey's *Chronologia Architectonica*', in J. Summerson ed., *Concerning Architecture* (1968), 1–12
Coulton 1915	G. G. Coulton, *Medieval Studies* No. 12 (1915) (from Cambridge Antiquarian Society, Publications, XIX, 56)
Cox 1914	J. C. Cox, *Warwickshire* (1914)
C Papal L	*Calendar of ... Papal Letters* (1893–)

C Pat R — *Calendar of Patent Rolls preserved in the Public Record Office* (1891–)

Cranage 1901 — D. H. S. Cranage, *An Architectural Account of the Churches of Shropshire*, 2 vols. (1901–12)

CYS — Canterbury & York Society: Publications

Dallaway 1834 — J. Dallaway, *Antiquities of Bristow* (1834)

Davies 1921 — G. S. Davies, *Charterhouse in London* (1921)

Davis 1939 — R. H. C. Davis, 'Masons' Marks in Oxfordshire and the Cotswolds', in OAS, 84th *Report* for 1938–39 (1939), 1–15

Davis 1947 — R. H. C. Davis, 'The Chronology of Perpendicular Architecture in Oxford', in *Oxoniensia*, XI/XII (1947), 75–89

Davis 1956 — R. H. C. Davis, 'A Catalogue of Masons' Marks as an Aid to Architectural History', in JBAA, 3 S, XVII for 1954 (1956), 43–76

Desimoni 1877 — C. Desimoni (Accounts of Sir Geoffrey de Langley's embassy from Edward I to the Ilkhan Kaikhatu), in *Atti Liguri di Storia Patria* (Genoa), XIII (1877–84)

Dodd 1920 — J. A. Dodd, 'Ewelme', in TES, VIII part v (1920), 194–206

Drinkwater 1956 — N. Drinkwater, 'Hereford Cathedral: the Chapter House', in AJ, CXII (1956), 61–74

Duncan 1908 — L. L. Duncan, *History of the Borough of Lewisham* (1908)

EMA — J. H. Harvey, *English Mediaeval Architects*: a Biographical Dictionary down to 1550 (1954)

Emery 1970 — A. Emery, *Dartington Hall* (1970)

Esposito 1960 — M. Esposito, *Itinerarium Symonis Semeonis ab Hybernia ad Terram Sanctam* (SLH, IV, 1960)

Evans 1949 — Joan Evans, *English Art 1307–1461* (1949)

Fernie & Whittingham 1972 — E. C. Fernie & A. B. Whittingham, *The Early Communar and Pitancer Rolls of Norwich Cathedral Priory* (NRS, XLI, 1972)

Fowler 1898 — J. T. Fowler ed., *Durham Account Rolls* (SS, XCIX, C, CIII, 1898–1900)

Freeman 1849 — E. A. Freeman, *A History of Architecture* (1849)

Freeman 1851 — E. A. Freeman, *An Essay on the Origin and Development of Window Tracery in England* (1851)

Gardiner 1930 — Dorothy Gardiner, *The Story of Lambeth Palace* (1930)

Gee 1953 — E. A. Gee, 'Oxford Masons 1370–1530', in AJ, CIX (1953), 54–131

Gee 1954 — E. A. Gee, 'Oxford Carpenters 1370–1530', in *Oxoniensia*, XVII/XVIII for 1952–53 (1954), 112–84

Godwin 1867 — H. Godwin, *The English Archaeologist's Handbook* (1867)

Golubovich 1919 — G. Golubovich, *Biblioteca Bio-Bibliografica della Terra Santa* (Florence, vols. III, IV, 1919, 1923)

Goulding 1918 — R. W. Goulding, *Annals of Louth* (1918)

Greenwell 1881 — W. Greenwell, *Durham Cathedral* (1881/1932)

Hart 1863 — W. H. Hart ed., *Historia et Cartularium Monasterii Sancti Petri Gloucestriae* (RS 33, 3 vols., 1863–67)

Harvey 1938 — J. H. Harvey, 'The Mediaeval Carpenter and his Work as an Architect', in JRIBA, 3 S, XLV (1938), 733–43

Harvey 1939 — J. H. Harvey, 'The Last Years of Thetford Cluniac Priory', in NA, XXVII (1939), 1–27

Harvey 1943 — J. H. Harvey, 'The Medieval Office of Works', in JBAA, 3 S, VI for 1941 (1943), 20–87

Harvey 1944 — J. H. Harvey, *Henry Yevele, c. 1320 to 1400*: the Life of an English Architect (1944; rev. ed. 1946)

Harvey 1947 — J. H. Harvey, *Gothic England*: A Survey of National Culture 1300–1550 (1947; rev. ed. 1948)

Harvey 1948 — J. H. Harvey, 'The King's Chief Carpenters', in JBAA, 3 S, XI (1948), 13–34

Harvey 1950 A — J. H. Harvey, *The Gothic World 1100–1600*: a Survey of Architecture and Art (1950; paperback 1969)

Harvey 1950 B — J. H. Harvey, 'The Architects of English Parish Churches,' in AJ, CV (1950), 14–26

Harvey 1954 — J. H. Harvey (see EMA above)

Harvey 1957 A — J. H. Harvey, *The Cathedrals of Spain* (1957)

Harvey 1957 B — J. H. Harvey 'Notes on the Architects of Worcester Cathedral', in TWS, XXXIII (1957), 23–7

Harvey 1959 — J. H. Harvey, 'Mediaeval Design', in TAMS, NS, VI for 1958 (1959), 55–72

Harvey 1961 — J. H. Harvey, 'The Architects of St. George's Chapel: I. The Thirteenth and Fourteenth Centuries', in RSG, IV No. 2 (1961), 48–55

Harvey 1962 A   J. H. Harvey, 'The Origin of the Perpendicular Style', in E. M. Jope ed., *Studies in Building History* ('1961'; 1962), 134–65

Harvey 1962 B   J. H. Harvey, 'The Architects of St. George's Chapel: II. The Fifteenth and Sixteenth Centuries', in RSG, IV No. 3 (1962), 85–95

Harvey 1965   J. H. Harvey, 'Winchester College', in JBAA, 3 S, XXVIII (1965), 107–28

Harvey 1969   J. H. Harvey, 'The Tracing Floor in York Minster', in *Report* of the Friends of York Minster, XL for 1968 (1969), 9–13

Harvey 1972   J. H. Harvey, *The Mediaeval Architect* (1972)

Harvey 1974 A   J. H. Harvey, *Cathedrals of England and Wales* (1974)

Harvey 1974 B   J. H. Harvey, 'Building Works by an East Anglian Priory', in NA, XXXV part iv for 1973 (1974), 505–10

Harvey 1975 A   J. H. Harvey, *Mediaeval Craftsmen* (1975)

Harvey 1975 B   J. H. Harvey, *York* (1975)

Harvey 1976   J. H. Harvey, *The Black Prince and his Age* (1976)

Harvey & Harvey 1936   W. Harvey & J. H. Harvey, 'Master Hugh Herland, Chief Carpenter to King Richard II', in *The Connoisseur*, XCVII (1936), 333–36

Heath 1925   F. R. Heath, *Wiltshire* (1925)

Heyman 1966   J. Heyman, 'The Stone Skeleton', in IJSS, II (1966), 249–79

Heyman 1967   J. Heyman, 'Beauvais Cathedral' (preprint 1967), TNS, XL for 1967–8, 15–35

HKW   *The History of the King's Works*, ed. H. M. Colvin, vols. I, II (1963)

HMC   Historical Manuscripts Commission

Hobson 1926   T. F. Hobson, *Adderbury "Rectoria"* (ORS, VIII, 1926)

Hope 1913   W. H. St.J. Hope, *Windsor Castle*: an Architectural History, 2 vols. (1913)

Howard 1911   F. E. Howard, 'Fan Vaults', in AJ, LXVIII (1911)

Howard 1914   F. E. Howard, 'On the Construction of Medieval Roofs', in AJ, LXXI (1914)

Howard 1936   F. E. Howard, *The Mediaeval Styles of the English Parish Church* (1936)

Howard & Crossley 1917 F. E. Howard & F. H. Crossley, *English Church Woodwork 1250–1550* (1917; 2nd ed. 1927)

Howgrave-Graham 1948   R. P. Howgrave-Graham, 'Westminster Abbey: the Sequence and Dates of the Transepts and Nave', in JBAA, 3 S, XI (1948), 60–78

IJSS   *International Journal of Solids Structures*

JBAA   *Journal* of the British Archaeological Association

JRIBA   *Journal* of the Royal Institute of British Architects

Kerry 1883   C. Kerry, *History of St. Lawrence, Reading* (1883)

Knoop & Jones 1933   D. Knoop & G. P. Jones, *The Mediaeval Mason* (1933; rev. ed. 1967)

Lethaby 1906   W. R. Lethaby, *Westminster Abbey and the Kings' Craftsmen*: a Study of Mediaeval Building (1906)

Lethaby 1925   W. R. Lethaby, *Westminster Abbey Re-examined* (1925)

Lloyd 1925   N. Lloyd, *A History of English Brickwork* (1925)

Lysons 1808   D. & S. Lysons, *Magna Britannia: Cambridgeshire* (1808)

Mayor & Gould 1908   C. H. Mayor & A. W. Gould, *The Municipal Records of the Borough of Dorchester, Dorset* (1908)

Miles & Saunders 1975 T. J. Miles & A. D. Saunders, 'The Chantry Priests' House at Farleigh Hungerford Castle', in *Medieval Archaeology*, XIX (1975), 165–94

Morris 1842   W. S. Morris, *The History and Topography of Wye* (1842)

Morris 1910   J. E. Morris, *County Churches: Surrey* (1910)

Myres 1967   J. N. L. Myres, 'Recent Discoveries in the Bodleian Library', in *Archaeologia*, CI (1967), 151–68

NA   *Norfolk Archaeology* (Norfolk & Norwich Archaeological Society)

NCM   New College, Oxford, Muniments

Nicholls & Taylor 1881 J. F. Nicholls & J. Taylor, *Bristol Past and Present* (1881)

Nichols 1780   J. Nichols, *A Collection of all the Wills ... of the Kings and Queens of England, &c.* (1780)

Nichols 1838   J. G. Nichols, *Description of the Church of St. Mary, Warwick, and of the Beauchamp Chapel* [1838]

Nicolas 1826   N. H. Nicolas, *Testamenta Vetusta* (1826)

NRS   Norfolk Record Society

OAS	Oxfordshire Archaeological Society
ORS	Oxfordshire Record Society
Oswald 1939	A. Oswald, 'Canterbury Cathedral: the Nave and its Designer', in *Burlington Magazine*, LXXV (1939), 221–28
Oswald 1947	A. Oswald, 'The Great Hospital, Norwich', in *Country Life*, 12, 19 Dec. 1947
Oswald 1949	A. Oswald, 'Andrew Doket and his Architect', in PCAS, XLII (1949), 8–26
Oswald 1965	A. Oswald, 'The Old Palace, Croydon, Surrey', in *Country Life*, 8, 15 April 1965
Parker 1836	J. H. Parker, *A Glossary of Terms used in Grecian, Roman, Italian and Gothic Architecture* (1836; 5th ed. revised, 3 vols., 1850)
PCAS	*Proceedings* of the Cambridge Antiquarian Society
PDS	*Proceedings* of the Dorset Natural History & Archaeological Society (Field Club)
Pearman 1886	A. J. Pearman, *Ashford* (1886)
Peckham 1921	W. D. Peckham, 'The architectural history of Amberley Castle', in SAC, LXII (1921), 21–63
Pevsner 1953	N. Pevsner, 'Bristol, Troyes, Gloucester', in *Architectural Review*, CXIII (1953), 89–98
PRO	Public Record Office
Raine 1859	J. Raine ed., *The Fabric Rolls of York Minster* (SS, XXXV for 1858, 1859)
Raine 1879	J. Raine ed., *The Historians of the Church of York and its Archbishops* (RS 71, 3 vols., 1879–94)
Raine 1955	A. Raine, *Mediaeval York* (1955)
RCHM	Royal Commission on Historical Monuments
Richards 1947	R. Richards, *Old Cheshire Churches* (1947)
Rickman & Parker 1862	T. Rickman & J. H. Parker, *An Attempt to discriminate the Styles of Architecture in England* (greatly enlarged and revised from Rickman's original of 1817; 1862/1881)
Roberts 1972	Eileen Roberts, 'Robert Stowell', in JBAA, 3 S, XXXV (1972), 24–38
Roberts 1973	Eileen Roberts, 'Thomas Wolvey, mason', in AJ, CXXIX for 1972 (1973), 119–44
Roberts 1975	Eileen Roberts, 'Totternhoe Stone and Flint in Hertfordshire Churches', in *Medieval Archaeology*, XVIII for 1974 (1975), 66–89
RS	Rolls Series
RSG	*Report* of the Society of the Friends of St. George's ... Chapel, Windsor Castle
SAC	*Sussex Archaeological Collections* (Sussex Archaeological Society)
Salmon 1967	J. Salmon, *Rycote Chapel, Oxfordshire* (1967)
Salzman 1952	L. F. Salzman, *Building in England down to 1540* (1952; rev. and enlarged ed., 1967)
Simpson 1960	W. D. Simpson, *The Building Accounts of Tattershall Castle 1434–1472* (Lincoln Record Society, LV, 1960)
SLH	Scriptores Latini Hiberniae
Snape 1974	M. G. Snape, 'Durham Cathedral: an "Unknown" Fire', in *Transactions* of the Architectural and Archaeological Society of Durham and Northumberland, NS, III (1974), 71–4
SRS	Somerset Record Society
SS	Surtees Society
Stephenson 1926	M. Stephenson, *A List of Monumental Brasses in the British Isles* (1926/1964)
Sweeting 1868	W. D. Sweeting, *Historical and Architectural Notes on the Parish Churches in and around Peterborough* (1868)
TAMS	*Transactions* of the Ancient Monuments Society
Taylor 1956	A. J. Taylor, *The Jewel Tower, Westminster* (1956)
TES	*Transactions* of the St. Paul's Ecclesiological Society
Test. Cantiana	Kent Archaeological Society: *Testamenta Cantiana*, ed. L. L. Duncan and A. Hussey, 2 vols. (1906–07)
Thompson 1915	A. H. Thompson, 'Building Accounts of Kirby Muxloe Castle 1480–1484', in Leicester Archaeological Society's *Transactions*, XI (1915–18), 193–345
TNS	*Transactions* of the Newcomen Society
TRIBA	*Transactions* of the Royal Institute of British Architects
Turner & Parker 1851	T. H. Turner & J. H. Parker, *Some Account of Domestic Architecture in England*, 3 vols. in 4 (1851–59)
TWS	*Transactions* of the Worcestershire Archaeological Society
VCH	Victoria County Histories

Verey 1976   D. Verey, 'The Perpendicular Style in the Cotswolds', BGT, 1976

Wadley 1886   T. P. Wadley, *Notes ... of the Wills ... in ... the Great Orphan Book and Book of Wills ... at Bristol* (1886)

WAM   Westminster Abbey Muniments

Watkin 1914   H. R. Watkin, *History of Totnes Priory and Mediaeval Town*, 2 vols. (1914–17)

WCM   Winchester College Muniments

Welch 1894   C. Welch, *History of the Tower Bridge ...* (1894)

Whitehead 1974   J. G. O. Whitehead, 'Henry Yeveley, Military Engineer', in *The Royal Engineers Journal*, (1974), 102–10

Wickham 1952   A. K. Wickham, *Churches of Somerset* (1952)

Wight 1972   Jane A. Wight, *Brick Building in England from the Middle Ages to 1550* (1972)

Willis & Clark 1886   R. Willis & J. W. Clark, *The Architectural History of the University of Cambridge*, 3 vols. (1886)

Wood 1965   M. Wood, *The English Mediaeval House* (1965)

YAJ   *Yorkshire Archaeological Journal* (Yorkshire Archaeological Society)

Table of Dated Buildings of the Perpendicular Style

1331–1485

The following table is a summary only. Space does not permit of fully detailed references when the dates shown result from consideration of several sources of information. Where no reference is given the primary source will be found in the table in Bond 1905 (638–657) or, in the case of castles and fortifications, a licence to crenellate printed chronologically in Turner & Parker 1851 (III.ii, 401–22) and alphabetically in Godwin 1867 (233–51). In a substantial number of cases, buildings dated in Rickman & Parker 1862 or Bond 1905 have been rejected, usually because no work of the appropriate period can be identified in the surviving structure. Dating by bequests *alone* has been excluded except when there is supporting evidence that the works were actually built. Works vaguely dated (e.g. by an episcopate) have been included only where the term is of ten years or less. Destroyed works are in *italics*.

1331 – 1336	Gloucester Cathedral, S. transept	Hart 1863, I, 45–7
1332 – (1349)	*London, St. Paul's, Cloister etc.*	Harvey 1962A, 139
1337 – (1349)	Lichfield Cathedral, Presbytery	Harvey 1962A, 140 & n.22
(1345 – 1348)	*Westminster, St. Stephen's, W. Porch*	Harvey 1962A, 145–6, 149
– 1348	Buckland, Herts., Parish Church	
1349 – 1362	Westminster Abbey, S. Cloister	WAM 23454–459

1350 – 1351	Windsor, St. George's, Vestry	Hope 1913
1350 – 1353	Windsor, St. George's, Chapter-house	Hope 1913
–1351–	Donington, Lincs., Parish Church	
1352 – 1361	Edington, Wilts., Chancel etc.	
1353 – 1354	Windsor Castle, Aerary Porch	Hope 1913
1353 – 1356	Windsor Castle, Dean's Cloister	Hope 1913
– 1354	Salisbury, St. Anne's Chapel	C Papal L 1342–62, 538
1354 – (1360)	*London, Austin Friars' Church*	Nichols 1780, 44
1357 – 1360	Kelvedon, Essex, Chancel	WAM 19853–854
1357 – 1374	Worcester Cathedral, Tower	Cath. MS. A xii, f.77b
1358 –	Welwick, Yorks. E.R., Church E. window	YAJ, XX, 139
1358 – (1375)	*Vale Royal, Cheshire, Abbey, E. chapels*	Salzman 1952, 439
1359 –	Little Dewchurch, Herefs., Tower	Cal Inq. p.M, XV, 447
1360 –	Ingham, Norf., Church	C Pat R 1358–61, 163, 435
1361 – 1362	London, Tower, Bloody Tower vault &c	EMA, 320
1361 – 1373	York Minster, Lady Chapel	Raine 1879, ii, 420
1362 – 1363	Canterbury Cathedral, Black Prince's Chantry	C Pat R 1361–4, 254
1362 – 1365	Westminster Abbey, W. Cloister &c	WAM 23457–459
1363 – 1368	Etchingham, Sussex, Church	EMA, 101
1364 – (1370)	*Hereford Cathedral, Chapter-house*	Drinkwater 1956
1365 –	Great Grimsby, Crossing and Tower	Inscription
1366 – 1371	Durham Cathedral, Priory Kitchen	Fowler 1898, ii, 571
1367 –	Maxey, Northants., N. Chapel	C Pat R 1364–7, 415
1368 – 1369	Castle Bytham, Lincs., Chancel	Lincoln D & C, Bj 2/6
–1368 – (1369)	Poynings, Sussex, Church	
1368 – 1373	Gloucester Cathedral, N. transept	Hart 1863, i, 50
1369 – 1372	Ely Cathedral, W. Tower lantern	Cambridge Univ Lib, Add. 2956, f. 158ff.; Add. 6388, p. 61
1371 –	*London, Charterhouse*	Davis 1921, 9, 15
1371 – 1379	Oxford, Merton College, Library	EMA, 141
1372 – (1375)	Arlingham, Glos., Church, Tower	Salzman 1952, 445
1372 – 1375	Westminster Abbey, Abbot's Hall	WAM 18857–859
1372 – 1380	Durham Cathedral, Neville Screen	Greenwell 1881, 61–2
1373 –	Nunney, Somerset, Castle	
1373 – (1378)	*Boxley, Kent, Abbey, Cloister*	Salzman 1952, 448
1373 – 1395	Coventry, St. Michael's, Tower	VCH, *Warwicks*, VIII, 353
–1374 – (1383)	Cottingham, Yorks. E.R., Choir	Stephenson 1926, 546
1375 – 1378–	Bolton, Yorks. N.R., Castle	Salzman 1952, 454
1377 –	Shirburn, Oxon., Castle	
1377 – (1383)	Amberley, Sussex, Castle	Peckham 1921
–1378–	Swanton Morley, Norf., Church	Blomefield, *Norfolk*, X (1809), 57
1378 – 1390	Canterbury, Walls and Westgate	EMA, 315
1379 –	Southampton, Gates and Towers	EMA, 308
1379 – 1405	Canterbury Cathedral, Nave	Oswald 1939
1380 –	Ropsley, Lincs., Nave pier	Inscription
1380 –	Arundel, Sussex, Church and College	
1380 –	Canterbury, Holy Cross Church	
1380 – 1384	Cowling, Kent, Castle	
(1380 – 1384)	Norwich, Great Hospital	Oswald 1947
1380 – 1386	Oxford, New College	
(1380) – 1390	Balsham, Cambs., Church	
1380 – (1400)	Howden, Yorks. E.R., Chapter-house	
– 1381	Ashwell, Herts., Church Tower (top)	Coulton 1915
1381 –	Cavendish, Suff., Church	*St. Mary's Church, Cavendish* (from notes by W. St. J. Hope)

1381 – 1382	Cowling Castle, Great Gatehouse	Salzman 1952, 461
–1382–	Yeovil, Som., Church	Wickham 1952, 25
–1382–	Cheddar, Som., St. Mary's Chapel	Wadley 1886, 9
1382 –	Sheriff Hutton, Yorks. N.R., Castle	
(1382) – 1386	Worcester Cathedral, N. Porch	Cath. MS. A xii, f.77b
1382 – 1389	Thornton, Lincs., Abbey Gatehouse	
1384 –	Wingfield, Suff., Castle	
1384 – 1386	South Benfleet, Essex, Chancel	WAM 23332–33
1384 – 1397	*London, Bridge Chapel*	Welch 1894, 71
1385 –	Bodiam, Sussex, Castle	
(1385) – 1395	Wells Cathedral, S.W. Tower	Colchester & Harvey 1975, 209
1385 – 1415	Norwich Cathedral, N. Cloister	Fernie & Whittingham 1972
1386 –	Donnington, Berks., Castle Gatehouse	
1386 – 1387	*Morden, Surrey, Church*	WAM 23334
1386 – 1392	Worcester Cathedral, Chapter-house	Harvey 1957B, 24
1387 – 1394	Winchester College	Harvey 1965
1388 –	Effingham, Surrey, Chancel	VCH, *Surrey*, III, 325
1389 – 1399	Dartington Hall, Devon	Emery 1970
1389 – 1418	Hull, Holy Trinity, Nave	
1390 – 1392	Exeter Cathedral, E. window	EMA, 166
1390 – 1403	Oxford, New College, Cloisters	Davis 1947, 84
1390 – 1409	Wymondham Abbey, Central Tower	
1391 –	Coventry, Holy Trinity	
1391 –	Sutton-in-Ashfield, Notts., Tower	
1391 – 1392	St. Asaph Cathedral, Tower	Salzman 1952, 470
1392 –	Wardour Castle, Wilts.	
1392 – 1393	Worcester, Edgar Tower (upper stage)	Harvey 1957B, 24
1392 – (1395)	Houghton Conquest, Beds., Tower	EMA, 104
1393 –	*Pleshey, Essex, Collegiate Church*	PRO, Anc. Deeds L.756
1394 – 1400	Westminster Palace, Hall	HKW, I, 527–33
1394 – (1450)	Winchester Cathedral, Nave	
(1395)	Combe, Oxon., Church	C. S. Emden, *Combe Church*
1395 – 1398	Maidstone Church and College	VCH, *Kent*, II, 232
(1395 – 1425)	York, All Saints Pavement, Tower	Raine 1955, 182
– 1396	Colmworth, Beds., Church	
1396 – 1398	Harmondsworth, Middx., Chancel	WCM, 78
1396 – (1399)	Ely Priory, Great Gatehouse	EMA, 185
1396 – 1399	Portchester Castle, Palace	EMA, 277
1396 – 1400	Oxford, New College, Tower	
1396 – 1402	Knowle, Warwicks., Church	Cox 1914, 99–101
(1396) – 1411	Great Shelford, Cambs., Church	Lysons 1808, 250
1397 –	Penrith, Cumbd., Castle	
1397 – 1398	Hedon, Yorks. E.R., E. window	Boyle 1895, 119
(1397) – 1399	Bridport, Dorset, St. Mary's	PDS, XI, 104
1397 – 1400	Henley, Oxon., Church, S. Chapel	Roberts 1973, 123
1397 – 1414	Canterbury Cathedral, Cloisters	
1398 – 1399	Norwich City Walls, Cow Tower	Hudson & Tingey, II, 52
1399 –	Church Hanborough, Nave and Tower	C Papal L 1396–1404, 278
1399 –	Watford, Herts., Church, Nave	C Pat R 1396–99, 515
1400 – 1403	Addington, Kent, Church Tower	Hasted, *Kent*
1401 –	Nottingham, St. Mary's	C Papal L 1396–1404, 443
1401 – 1405	Skirlaugh, Yorks. E.R., Chapel	*Churches of Yorkshire* (1844), II, 39–47
–1402 – 1403–	Cirencester Church, Tower	BGT, XVII, 37
1402 – 1407	Peterborough, St. John Baptist	Sweeting 1868, 30

– (1403)	Sleaford, Lincs., Chancel	
1403 – 1406	Swalcliffe, Oxon., Tithe Barn	NCM, account roll 'B'
1403 – 1415	Bridgwater Church, Trinity Chapel	SRS, LVIII, no. 576
1404 – 1408	Worcester Cathedral, N. & S. Cloisters	Harvey 1957B, 25
(1404 – 1411)	St. Albans, Town Clock Tower	Roberts 1973, 129
–1406–	Crayford, Kent, Church Tower	Test. Cantiana, I, 16
1406 –	Broughton, Oxon., Castle Gatehouse	
(1406 – 1409)	Battlefield, Salop., Church	Cranage 1901, II, 840
1407 – (1411)	Norwich, Guildhall	NA, XV, 164
1408 – 1418	Adderbury, Oxon., Chancel	Hobson 1926
1409 – 1410	Beverley, Yorks. E.R., North Bar	EMA, 229
1409 –	Rotherham, Yorks. W.R., Tower	Raine 1859, 237
1410 – 1411	Hornby, Yorks. N.R., S. aisle	Salzman 1952, 482
1410 –	Tong, Salop., Collegiate Church	
(1410) – 1415	Stratford-on-Avon, Clopton Chapel	EMA, 156
(1411) – 1423	Bolton Percy, Yorks. W.R., Chancel	*Churches of Yorkshire*, I
1411 – (1430)	London, Guildhall	Barron 1974
– 1412	Dorchester, Dorset, St. Peter, Tower	Mayor & Gould 1908, 201
1412 – 1415	Catterick, Chancel and E. Nave	Salzman 1952, 487
(1412 – 1418)	Hereford Cathedral, S. Cloister	Salzman 486
–1413–	Halstead, Essex, Chancel	Salzman 490
1414 – 1419	Lynn, St. Nicholas's Chapel	E.M. Beloe, *Lynn St. Nicholas*, 151
(1414) – 1419	York Minster, Old Library	Raine 1859, 36–9
–1415–	Wingfield, Suff., De la Pole Chapel	Aldwell 1926, 39
(1415) – 1423	North Cadbury, Som., Church	Wickham 1952, 32
1416 – (1420)	Beverley Minster, E. window	AASRP, XLI.i, 75
(1416) – 1424	Oxford, Merton College, N. transept	
1416 – 1425	Norwich Cathedral, Erpingham Gate	EMA, 300
1416 – 1430	Norwich Cathedral, N. & W. Cloister vaults	EMA, 299
(1417 – 1427)	Croyland, Lincs., Abbey Nave	APS, s.v. Croyland
1418 – 1421	Surfleet, Lincs., Chancel	Salzman 1952, 496
(1418 – 1448)	Cheshunt, Herts., Church	Stephenson 1926, 183
1419 – (1421)	Wyberton, Lincs., Tower etc.	Salzman 1952, 495
1420 – 1422	Lincoln Cathedral, Old Library	Dean & Chapter, A.2/30, f.104; A.2/32, f.14
(1420) – 1424	Wells Cathedral, E. Cloister	Colchester & Harvey 1975, 209
1420 – (1431)	Ipswich, St. Laurence's, Tower	
1421 – 1423	Lynn, Norfolk, Guildhall	EMA, 268, 229
1421 – 1425	Catterick, Yorks. N.R., Bridge	Salzman 1952, 497
1422 – 1447	Ludlow, Salop., Chancel	Cranage 1901, I, 105
1422 – 1450	Westminster Abbey, Henry V's Chantry	EMA, 262
1423 – 1434	Canterbury Cathedral, S.W. Tower	*Arch. Cant.*, XLV, 37
1424 – 1433	Bury St. Edmunds, St. Mary's	
1424 – (1439)	Oxford, Divinity School (I)	Myres 1967
(1425) –	Higham Ferrers, College & Bedehouse	
(1425) – 1437	Winchester College, Fromond's Chantry	Chitty 1926, 143
1426 – (1441)	Walberswick, Suff., Church Tower	Salzman 1952, 499
1427 – 1428	Stratford-on-Avon, Grammar School	EMA, 123
1427 – 1437	Cambridge, (King's Hall), King Edward's Gate	Willis & Clark 1886, II, 444
1427 – 1437	Hedon, Yorks. E.R., Church Tower	Boyle 1895, 121
(1428) – 1437	York, St. Martin-le-Grand, Tower	
(1429) –	Battlefield, Salop., Church Tower	Cranage 1901, II, 840
(1430) –	Louth, Lincs., Chancel	Lincoln D & C, A.2/32, f.57v
(1430 – 1440)	Luton, Beds., Chancel	
(1430) – 1440	Tavistock, Devon, Chancel	Alexander & Finberg, 13

(1431 – 1439)   Buckden, Hunts., Nave   (Heraldry etc.)
1431 – 1445   Lingfield, Surrey, Church   Morris 1910, 115; Nicolas 1826, 246
(1431 – 1460)   Thirsk, Yorks. N.R., Church   VCH, *Yorkshire N.R.*, II, 66; AJ, IV, 362
(1431) – 1461   Southwold, Suff., Church
1432 – (1440)   Ewelme, Oxon., Church   Dodd 1920
1432 – 1445   Wymondham Abbey, Nave clerestory and north aisle
(1432) – 1445   Raglan, Mon., Castle   A. J. Taylor, *Raglan Castle*, 1957
1432 – 1446   Caister, Norf., Castle   Barnes & Simpson 1951, 1952
1432 – 1456   York Minster, S.W. Tower   EMA, 204
1433 –   St. Columb Major, Corn., Tower   CYS, cxxxvii, 20
1433 – 1434   Exeter Cathedral, Chapel Screens EMA, 110
1433 – 1435   Chester, St. Mary-on-the-Hill, S. Chapel   Salzman 1952, 503
–1433–   Mawgan-in-Pyder, Corn., Tower   CYS, cxxxvii, 20
(1433) – 1455   Tattershall, Lincs., Castle   Simpson 1960
1434 –   Fotheringhay, Nave & Tower   Salzman 1952, 505
1434 –   Lambeth Palace, Lollards' Tower   Gardiner 1930, 52
1434   Pershore Abbey, S. aisle   Rickman & Parker 1862
1435 –   Wanborough, Wilts., Tower
1435 – 1438   Worcester Cathedral, W. Cloister   Harvey 1957B, 26
      – (1436) Devizes, Wilts., St. Mary's   Inscription
1437 – 1439   Canterbury Cathedral, St. Michael's Chapel   F. Woodman in *Cant. Cath. Chronicle* (1976), 26
1437 – 1440   Bradninch, Devon, Church Tower   CYS, cxxxii, 72
1437 – (1443)   Ewelme, Almshouse & School   AJ, LXVII, 337
1438 – 1439   *Canterbury, Guildhall*   Salzman 1952, 510
1438 – 1444   Oxford, All Souls College
1439 –   Huntshaw, Devon, Nave   CYS, cxxxii, 156
1439 –   Little Torrington, Devon, Tower   CYS, cxxxii, 131
1439 – (1455)   Oxford, Divinity School (II)   Salzman 1952, 513; Myres 1967
1440 – 1442   Sherborne, St. John's Hospital   EMA, 141
(1440 – 1450)   Chipping Barnet, Herts., Nave   Inscription
(1440) – 1450   Bristol, All Saints, Lady Chapel   Nicholls & Taylor 1881, 96
1440 – 1458   Reading, St. Lawrence, Tower   Kerry 1883, 13, 17
(1440) – 1460   Great Malvern Priory Church
1441 –   Fulham, Middx., Church Tower   EMA, 110
1441 – (1448)   Herstmonceux, Sussex, Castle   VCH, *Sussex*, IX, 131
1441 – 1449   Eton College, Hall etc.   Willis & Clark 1886, I, 380
1441 – 1452   Warwick, Beauchamp Chapel   Nichols 1838
      – 1442   Burton Pidsea, Yorks. E.R., Nave   Raine 1859, 238
1442 –   Chippenham, Wilts., Hungerford Chapel   C Pat R 1441–6, 151
1442 – 1445   Dunster Priory, Church Tower   Salzman 1952, 514
1442 –   Thame, Oxon., N. Transept   *Gents. Mag.* 1865. i, 176
1442 – 1446   Lydd, Kent, Church Tower   EMA, 250
(1442 – 1473)   Blythburgh, Suff., Chancel etc.   M. J. Becker, *Blythburgh* (1935), 31
1443   Farleigh Hungerford, St. Leonard's   Miles & Saunders 1975, 167, 177
(1443)   Rye House, Herts., Gatehouse   C ChartR 1427–1516, 38
(1443) –   South Wingfield, Derbys., Manor   EMA, 156
1443 – 1450   Alnwick, Northd., Bondgate Tower   Bates 1891, 21
1443 – 1461   Cambridge, King's College Chapel (I)   Willis & Clark 1886, I, 465
      – 1445   Tavistock Church, Outer S. aisle   CYS, cxxxii, 347
1445 – 1478   Wymondham Abbey, W. tower
      – 1447   Wye, Kent, College   Morris 1842
1447 –   Plympton, St. Maurice, Tower   CYS, cxxxii, 374
1447 –   Probus, Corn., St. George's Chapel   CYS, cxxxii, 389

−1447 − 1448−   Chipping Norton, Oxon., Nave   Worcester Cathedral, Prior's account, C. 398
  −1448−   Leicester, St. Margaret's, Tower   SRS, XIX, 348
 1448 − 1449   Cambridge, Queens' College   Willis & Clark 1886, II, 1
 1448 − 1452   Oxford, Merton College, Tower   EMA, 147
 1448 − 1455   Canterbury Cathedral, N. Transept
 1448 − 1457   Norwich, Great Hospital, Cloister   EMA, 260
 1448 − 1460   Eton College, Chapel   Willis & Clark 1886, I, 396
 1448 − 1460   York, Guildhall   EMA, 75−6
 1448 − 1464   Wimborne Minster, W. Tower
 1449 −   Rycote, Oxon., Chapel   Salmon 1967
 1449 − (1452)   Totnes, Devon, Church Tower   Watkin 1914, I, 396, 407; II, 956
  −1450−   Stamford, Lincs., St. George's   Nicolas 1826, 266
 1450 −   Hull, St. Mary's, Tower   VCH, *Yorkshire E.R.*, I, 83
(1450) − 1452   York, St. Cuthbert's Church   Raine 1859, 239
(1450 − 1460)   Gloucester Cathedral, Tower
(1450) − 1460   Laxfield, Suff., Church Tower   Ipswich Wills, I, 165; heraldry
 1451 −   Ryarsh, Kent, Church Tower
 1453 −   Lynn, St. Margaret, N.W. Tower
 1453 − 1471   Ludlow, Salop., Church Tower   Cranage 1901, I, 105
 1453 − (1480)   Bristol, St. Stephen's, Tower   Nicholls & Taylor 1881, 96
(1454) − 1464   Burwell, Cambs., Nave   EMA, 98
  −1455−   Tattershall, Collegiate Church   Nicolas 1826, 276
 1455 − (1461)   Winchcombe, Glos., Church
  −1458−   Northleach, Glos., Nave
(1458) −   Woodchurch, Kent, Lady Chapel   Nicolas 1826, 289
 1458 − 1486   *Tattershall, Lincs., College*   Simpson 1960
  −1459−   *Norwich, Blackfriars, Tower*   NA, XXII, 86
 1459 − 1460   Wells Cathedral, Chain Gate   Vicars' Register 1360−1500, 26; SRS, XLIX, 338
 1459 − 1465   Oxford, St. Mary the Virgin, Choir   EMA, 56
(1460)   Thirsk, Yorks. N.R., E. window   (heraldry)
 1460 − 1464   Bristol, All Saints, Library   EMA, 227
(1460) − 1465   Louth, Lincs., Trinity Chapel   Goulding 1918, 22
(1460 − 1469)   Croyland Abbey, Tower   Rickman & Parker 1862
(1460 − 1470)   Wells Cathedral, W. Cloister   Colchester & Harvey 1975, 211
(1460 − 1473)   Westwick, Norf., Church Tower   Brandon 1849, 27
(1460) − 1483   Trowbridge, Wilts., Church   Heath 1925, 304
  −1461−   Tenterden, Kent, Church Tower   Nicolas 1826, 292
(1461 − 1475)   Ashford, Kent, Tower & Nave   Pearman 1886, 8
(1462 − 1467)   Ash, Kent, Chapel of St. Thomas   Nicolas 1826, 292
 1464 −   Folkestone Church, S. Chapel   Nicolas 1826, 306
 1464 − 1472   Norwich Cathedral, Nave vault
 1465 − 1475   Durham Cathedral, Central Tower (I)   Snape 1974
(1466 − 1490)   Stratford-on-Avon, Chancel   VCH, *Warwickshire*, III, 271
 1466 − 1471   Cambridge, Schools, S. Room etc.   Willis & Clark 1886, III, 12
 1468 − (1472)   London, Crosby Hall   C Pat R 1467−76, 52
 1468 − (1491)   Charing, Kent, Church W. window   Test. Cantiana, II, 387
 1469 − 1472   Bodmin, Corn., Church   EMA, 225, 239
(1470) − 1485   Eye, Suff., Church Tower   HMC, 10th Report, iv, 529
(1470 − 1486)   Lavenham, Suff., Church Vestry
(1471)   Cavendish, Suff., Church, S. aisle   EMA, 99
 1471 − 1498   Lewisham, Kent, Church Tower   Duncan 1908, 119
 1472 − 1483   Lynn, St. Margaret, Aisles
(1472 − 1494)   Buckden, Hunts., Palace   RCHM, *Huntingdonshire*, 34
 1472 − 1499   Norwich Cathedral, Presbytery vault

(1473) – 1483	Wells, Deanery	EMA, 246
1474 –	Ashby-de-la-Zouch, Castle	C ChartR 1427–1516, 242
1474 – 1480	Oxford, Magdalen College	
1474 – 1481	Winchester College, Thurbern's Chantry & Tower	ANJ, XLII, 208
1474 – 1484	Windsor Castle, St. George's Chapel	Harvey 1962B
–1475–	London, St. Helen Bishopsgate	*Survey of London*, IX, 31, 44
1475 – 1480	Eltham Palace, Hall	HKW, II, 936
1476	High Ham, Somerset, Church	Wickham 1952, 33
1476 –	Broxbourne, Herts., S. aisle	Salzman 1952, 537
1476 – 1482	Little Malvern Priory, Chancel	
1476 – 1483	*Deptford, Kent, Church Tower*	Test. Cantiana, I, 21
1476 – 1485	Cambridge, King's College Chapel (II)	Willis & Clark 1886, I, 472
1477 – 1488	Wells Cathedral, Cloister Lady Chapel	Colchester & Harvey 1975, 212
1479	Salisbury Cathedral, Crossing Vault	EMA, 252
1479 –	Silkstone, Yorks. W.R., Tower	Raine 1859, 240
1479 – 1483	Oxford, Divinity School, vault	Myres 1967
1480 –	*Bristol, St. Augustine the Less, Nave*	Dallaway 1834, 116
(1480)	Esher Palace, Waynflete's Tower	
–1480–	Prestbury, Cheshire, Tower	Richards 1947, 280, 282
1480 – 1484	Kirby Muxloe, Leics., Castle	Thompson 1915
(1480 – 1486)	Hatfield, Herts., Old Palace	VCH, *Herts.*, III, 94
(1480) – 1501	Steeple Ashton, Wilts., Nave etc.	AJ, LXXVII, 351
(1481 – 1482)	Plymouth, St. Andrew, S. aisle	HMC, IX, 262
–1482–	Ripon Minster, Crossing	CYS, LXIX, 197
–1482–	Tattershall, Lincs., Church Tower	EMA, 77
1482	*Wolvercote, Oxon., Chancel*	Gee 1953, 82
(1482) – 1491	Hawton, Notts., Church Tower	AASRP, XXIII. ii, 331
1483	Ropsley, Lincs., S. porch	Inscription
(1483)	Wetherden, Suff., S. aisle & Porch	Baggallay 1885, 110
1483 – 1485	Lynn, Red Mount Chapel	
(1483) – 1488	Durham Cathedral, Central Tower (II)	Snape 1974
– 1484	Wainfleet, Lincs., School	Salzman 1952, 542
1484 – 1485	Worstead, Norf., Chancel	EMA, 21

Glossary

Affronted   (tracery) set face to face, here used of two asymmetrical lights 'leaning' towards each other.

Alternate   one of the main divisions of Perpendicular tracery, in which no mullion is carried up to the arch in a direct line – opposed to Supermullioned.

Arch   Acute   a two-centred arch higher than equilateral. **Four-centred**   struck from two pairs of centres, one pair on the springing line, and a more distant pair below it.
Ogee   struck from two or more pairs of centres to produce a 'bracket' or pair of S-curves.
Pointed   struck from two or more centres so as to have intersecting arcs at the apex.
Segmental   forming a segment only of a round arch. **Segmental-pointed**   a segment only of a pointed arch. **Three-centred**   struck from three centres to produce an approximation to a half-ellipse. **Tudor**   a relatively low four-centred arch in which the two distant centres are at infinity – i.e. the upper arcs are straight lines. **Two-centred**   struck from two centres on the springing line.

Archlet   a small arch such as that forming the head of a single light. See also Subarcuation.

Ashlaring (woodwork)   vertical timbers, often ornamental, from wall-plate to rafters along the wall line, or between the members of trusses.

Averted   set back to back, leaning away from each other.

Ballflower   a characteristic enrichment of the early fourteenth century, consisting of a globular ball carved with the appearance of an outer skin pierced and folded back in petals.

Bay   the vertical compartment between two columns, roof-trusses, buttresses, etc.

Bowtell   a round moulding; in Perpendicular work usually slender and treated as a shaft with base and capital.

Bracket see **Double-ogee**

Brattishing   ornamental cresting or battlementing on a beam, transom, etc.

Buttress   a mass of masonry built against a wall to resist thrust. **Flying-buttress**   an abutment formed by a slanting member usually carried on a half-arch and transmitting thrust to a pier or buttress loaded with a pinnacle.

Casement   a wide and shallow hollow moulding, much used in the Perpendicular style.

Chantry   an endowment to sing masses on behalf of the souls of the dead; a Chantry Chapel used for that purpose.

Chapter-house   a room for the meetings of the chapter of canons or monks governing a greater church.

Continuous   used of tracery formed by continuing the lines of the mullions, either in curves (Curvilinear and Flamboyant) or straight lines (Perpendicular); the late Gothic styles so characterised, in contrast with the discontinuity of earlier (Geometrical) tracery patterns.

Cresting   enrichment above a horizontal or sloping member, including battlementing. See also **Brattishing**.

Crocket   a projection, usually of hooked form, from the edges of spires, pinnacles, canopies, etc. In Perpendicular work commonly a leaf of square outline.

Cross-bar (tracery) a short length of supertransom, not extending across the whole window.

Curvilinear the name generally applied to Flowing tracery and the style of architecture in which it is used.

Cusp a pointed projection from the inner surface of an arch, formed by two arcs of small radius; or sometimes four-centred curves.

Dagger a form of tracery-light cusped, and pointed at both ends, resembling in outline a dagger; when the longer blade is directed upwards the light is an Inverted Dagger, a form commonly used in Perpendicular. (French *soufflet*).

Decorated in Rickman's terminology, the style of architecture intermediate between Early English and Perpendicular Gothic, used in the later thirteenth and much of the fourteenth centuries. The name has subsequently been wrongly applied to the later (Flowing or Curvilinear) division of the style alone.

Divergent see **Y-tracery**

Double-ogee a moulding of two ogees placed opposite to each other to produce a 'bracket' shape.

Drop-arch a two-centred arch lower than equilateral.

Drop-tracery tracery carried below the springing line of the arch; tracery filling a stilted arch.

Early English (Lancet) the first Gothic style in England, characterised by simple pointed arches without tracery, or with Plate-tracery. The acute arch (Lancet) is typical of the style.

Eyelet a small aperture; here used for one of the smaller openings in tracery; in Perpendicular work usually set lozenge-wise.

Falchion a form of tracery-light of asymmetrical curved shape, distinguished from the symmetrical Dagger; its use is characteristic of Flowing and Flamboyant work.

Flamboyant Flame-shaped tracery, invented in England early in the fourteenth century, but mainly used on the Continent.

Flamenco the Spanish adjective 'Flemish'; here used of the decorative style current in Greater Flanders in the fifteenth century and thence introduced into Spain and into most other western countries.

Flowing see **Curvilinear**.

Flying-buttress see **Buttress**.

Four-centred see **Arch**.

Geometrical the first English style to use bar-tracery: of simple forms such as circles and two-centred arches in contact, without continuously flowing lines.

Gridiron used of tracery consisting of mullions and supermullions only, commonly a form of Drop-tracery beneath a four-centred arch.

Hall-church a church whose aisles are all of the same height and which consequently has neither triforium nor clerestory.

Hammer-beam a horizontal cantilever projecting as a bracket in certain roof-trusses.

Hammer-post a vertical post supported on the free end of a hammer-beam.

Head the top of a window-light, usually formed by an archlet.

Intersecting here used of tracery in which subarcuations cross one another, including the simplest form in windows of three or more lights filled with Y-tracery.

Inverted dagger see **Dagger**.

I-split tracery in which supermullions as well as main mullions are carried up to the arch without deflection or division.

Label a hoodmould surrounding an arch, particularly one of square form containing the arch of a door or window opening.

Latticed see **Transom**.

Lierne a vault-rib which does not start from the springing and is not a ridge-rib.

Mudéjar a Spanish style in the regions reconquered from the Moors, employing geometrical forms in plan and details.

Mullion a vertical member dividing a window or panelling.

Mullioned here used of windows of panelled tracery in which the mullions are carried up to the arch without intermediate supermullions; and of windows divided into vertical sections by main or strong mullions.

Oculus here used of a central opening at the head of a traceried window or subarcuation, larger than an eyelet and distinguished from split tracery (see **I-tracery**, **Y-tracery**).

Ogee a curve of S-form. See also **Double-ogee**.

Panelled used strictly of tracery of mullions only carried up as undivided lights above the archlets, with or without supertransoms; commonly used of Gridiron tracery and for Supermullioned tracery generally in opposition to Alternate.

Perpendicular the English style of late Gothic mainly distinguished by tracery with vertical members carried up to the arch without deflection; and by mouldings such as the **Double-ogee** and **Casement**.

Pulpitum a screen at the west end of the choir, often with a gallery or loft above it, on which the organ was commonly placed.

Quatrefoil a four-leaved opening in tracery. **Quarter-ogee quatrefoil** a quatrefoil with the lowest leaf of ogee shape, commonly used as the oculus of a Perpendicular window.

Rectilinear sometimes used as an alternative name for the Perpendicular style.

Reticulated net-like, used of tracery formed by continuously repeated ogee curves.

Straight-reticulation Alternate Perpendicular tracery in which the ogee curves are replaced by straight lines.

Rib an arch beneath the surface of a vault. **Cross-rib** a transverse arch between the bays of a vault. **Diagonal rib** a rib running obliquely across a bay of vaulting and normally crossing an opposite diagonal at the centre of the bay. This pair of diagonal ribs (French: *croisée d'ogives*) is one of the principal marks of the Gothic style in its original purity. **Lierne-rib** see **Lierne**. **Ridge-rib** a horizontal or sometimes sloping rib running along the crown of a vault. **Tierceron-rib** see **Tierceron Wall-rib** a rib, usually a half-rib, on the surface of the walls at each side of a bay of vaulting.

Segmental, Segmental-pointed see **Arch**.

Sondergotik a German term now used for the particular kinds of late Gothic which developed after 1300 in the different parts of Europe. Perpendicular, peculiar to England, is the earliest to appear of all these types.

Spherical triangle (tracery) a triangular eyelet whose sides are arcs of circles.

Springing the level bed from which an arch begins.

Squash-tracery tracery beneath the arch of a four-centred or other flattened window, entirely above the springing; opposed to **Drop-tracery**.

Stilted used of an arch whose impost mouldings or capitals are below the level of the springing; and for the apparent arch containing Drop-tracery.

Strong mullion a mullion of greater size than the rest, carried up to form a main division of a window.

Subarcuation having subordinate arches as in a traceried window.

Subreticulated (tracery)   used of tracery in which a main reticulation is filled with a smaller reticulation.

Supermullion   a mullion standing upon the apex of an archlet; also extended to include the upward extension of mullions between the main lights.

Supermullioned   one of the main divisions of Perpendicular tracery, in which supermullions continue up to the arch – opposed to Alternate.

Supertransom   a horizontal member in tracery, a transom above the springing. See also **Cross-bar**.

Through-reticulation   reticulations of tracery intersecting subarcuations.

Tierceron   an intermediate vault-rib starting from the springing.

Top-panelled   Gridiron tracery in which there are no strong mullions carried from the sill up to the arch.

Tracery   ornamental patternwork pierced through the head of a window or used as decorative panelling. **Bar-tracery**   tracery formed of stone bars forming the pattern, a French invention of *c.* 1210. **Plate-tracery**   early Gothic tracery formed by the grouping of separate lancets and an oculus beneath an arch, as if pierced through a solid plate of masonry.

Transom   a horizontal masonry crossbar in a window below springing level. See also **Supertransom**. **Latticed transom**   a horizontal connection between mullions formed by intersecting oblique or ogee-curved bars at the same level in adjacent lights.

Transparency   here used of masonry screenwork on a separate plane from that of the glazed windows, commonly internal but occasionally on the outer face of the wall.

Vault   Fan   a vault of conoidal form in which the curvature of all the main ribs (occasionally alternate ribs only) is the same. **Lierne**   a vault patterned by the use of Liernes. **Pendant**   a vault divided laterally in each bay by two pendants, from which the central span of the vault appears to spring. **Tierceron**   a vault with intermediate ribs (Tiercerons) between the Cross-ribs and the Diagonals.

Y-tracery   divergent tracery where a single mullion or supermullion is divided into two beneath the main arch or a subarcuation.

Index

Architects and artists of the Middle Ages are listed separately after the main index. Numerals in *italics* are principal references; those in **heavy type** refer to the figure numbers of illustrations. The usual abbreviations are used for the ancient counties; abp, archbishop; bp, bishop.

Index of Mediaeval Architects and Artists

Topographical Index
of Places in Great Britain

ENGLAND

Bedfordshire
Colmworth
Dunstable
Houghton Conquest
Luton
Totternhoe
Wymington

Berkshire
Abingdon
Donnington
Reading
Windsor

Buckinghamshire
Eton

Cambridgeshire
Balsham
Burwell
Cambridge
Coton
Ely
Shelford, Great
Well

Cheshire
Bunbury
Chester
Prestbury
Vale Royal

Cornwall
Bodmin
Callington
Mawgan-in-Pyder
Probus
St. Columb Major

Cumberland
Carlisle
Penrith
Raughton

Derbyshire
Wingfield, South
Yeaveley

Devonshire
Ashburton
Bradninch
Buckland (? Monachorum)
Dartington
Exeter
Huntshaw
Ottery St. Mary
Plymouth
Plympton
Tavistock
Torrington, Little
Totnes

Dorset
Bridport
Corfe
Dorchester
Milton
Purbeck
Sherborne
Wimborne

Durham
Brancepeth
Durham
Finchale
Raby

Essex
Benfleet, South
Dedham
Halstead
Kelvedon
Pleshey
Saffron Walden

Gloucestershire
Arlingham
Bristol

Cambridge
Chipping Campden
Cirencester
Gloucester
Kingswood
Northleach
Spoonley
Sudeley
Tewkesbury
Thornbury
Winchcombe

Hampshire
Christchurch
Portchester
St. Cross
Southampton
Sparkford
Winchester

Herefordshire
Dewchurch, Little
Hereford

Hertfordshire
Ashwell
Barkway
Broxbourne
Buckland
Cheshunt
Chipping Barnet
Hatfield
King's Langley
Rye House
St. Albans
Sandon
Watford

Huntingdonshire
Buckden
Connington
Elton
Ramsey

Kent
Addington
Ash-by-Wrotham
Ashford
Boxley
Canterbury
Charing
Cobham
Cowling
Crayford

Dartford
Deptford
Dover
Eltham
Folkestone
Lewisham
Lydd
Maidstone
Meopham
Queenborough
Reculver
Rochester
Ryarsh
Saltwood
Tenterden
West Wickham
Woodchurch
Wye

Lancashire
Manchester

Leicestershire
Ashby-de-la-Zouch
Kirby Muxloe
Leicester

Lincolnshire
Boston
Castle Bytham
Croyland
Donington
Grimsby, Great
Lincoln
Louth
Ropsley
Sleaford
Stamford
Surfleet
Tattershall
Thornton
Wainfleet
Wyberton

London and Middlesex
Chelsea
Fulham
Harmondsworth
London
Westminster

Monmouthshire
Raglan

Croydon
Effingham
Esher
Farnham
Kennington
Lambeth
Lingfield
Merton
Morden
Reigate
Southwark

Sussex
Amberley
Arundel
Battle
Bodiam
Chichester
Etchingham
Herstmonceux
Poynings
Westbourne

Warwickshire
Coventry
Kenilworth
Knowle
Sheldon
Stratford-on-Avon
Warwick

Wiltshire
Chippenham
Devizes
Edington
Lacock
Malmesbury
Marlborough
Mere
Norrington
Salisbury
Steeple Ashton
Trowbridge
Wanborough
Wardour

Worcestershire
Cleeve Prior
Evesham
Malvern, Great

Malvern, Little
Pershore
Worcester

Yorkshire
Beverley
Bolton
Bolton Percy
Bubwith
Burton Pidsea
Catterick
Cottingham
Doncaster
Fountains
Halifax
Hedon
Hornby
Howden
Hull
Patrington
Ripon
Rotherham
Selby
Sheriff Hutton
Silkstone
Skirlaugh
Thirsk
Tickhill
Wakefield
Welwick
York

Berwick-upon-Tweed

WALES
Brecon
Caernarvon
Cardiff
Gresford
Haverfordwest
Llandaff
St. Asaph
Tenby
Wrexham

SCOTLAND
Melrose
Roxburgh

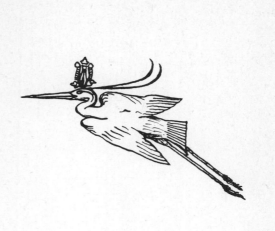